Golden Land Chronicles

TRUE SHORT STORIES OF MISSIONS IN MYANMAR

BY DR. BOB DEWITT

GOLDEN LAND CHRONICLES: *True Short Stories of Missions in Myanmar*

First Published 2021

ISBN 978-0-9984827-7-4

Cover Design: Bibiann Avelar

Editing: Devin Ogdie & John Mark Seay

For Additional Copies of Golden Land Chronicles:

YPLife

3000 Clays Mill Road

Lexington, KY 40503

(859) 321-2536

www.yplife.org

Printed in the United States of America

TABLE OF CONTENTS

Endorsements
Poem: Obedience by George McDonald
Preface
Foreword by Dr. David Gibbs
Dedication

KEY VERSE

"There is gold, and a multitude of rubies: but the lips
of knowledge are a preciousjewel."
Proverbs 20:15

ENDORSEMENTS

"It is refreshing to read these missionary stories – captivating narratives of real people and their struggles in a developing country that has been steeped in idolatry for centuries. Bro. Bob is an ardent student of Burmese history, their culture, and their language, and as his pastor, I saw the Lord begin to burden his heart with the task of getting the Gospel to the Burmese people. Over time, it became obvious to me that God had called him to this mission, and it is now very clear that the consuming passion of his life is to help these precious people find salvation through Jesus Christ. I have traveled to Burma with him, and I have seen evidence of his sincere love for the Burmese. His commitment to reach them for the Savior continues to grow year by year."

Pastor Richard Hack
Lighthouse Baptist Church
Horseheads, New York

"I had the opportunity and privilege to visit Burma with Bro. Bob in early 2020. To say the trip was life changing is an understatement. As I read these stories, I am reminded – in vivid detail – of my time there. It is as if I am there again. The descriptions of the sights, sounds, and smells transport you to this country and give you a first-hand perspective of many aspects of life within its borders. The interjections of historical information further add context and substance to the reading. The pinnacle is the spiritual encouragement and challenge that is found as one reads about God's workings in the Golden Land. There's something for everyone in this book."

John Early, Assistant Pastor
Lighthouse Baptist Church
Horseheads, New York

"In the GOLDEN LAND CHRONICLES BaGyi Bob paints vivid word pictures with a romantic literary style that is captivating reading. These missionary stories from Myanmar are filled with adventure, danger, compassion and sometimes comedy in an "Indiana Jones" type way. They are most importantly stories of FAITH! Faith that saves the lost no matter who they are or where they live. Faith that sends preachers of the gospel to the most remote parts of the world and finds people there that God loves and wants to save. These are stories that must be told, and this book does just that in a most wonderful way. My heart was warmed, blessed and stirred and I believe yours will be too."

Pastor Joe Grimaldi
First Baptist Church of Kenmore
Akron, Ohio

OBEDIENCE

by George MacDonald
(Scotland, 1824-1905)

I said: "Let me walk in the fields."
He said: "No, walk in the town.
"I said: "There are no flowers there."
He said: "No flowers, but a crown."

I said: "But the skies are black;
There is nothing but noise and din.
"And He wept as He sent me back –
"There is more,"
He said: "there is sin."

I said: "But the air is thick,
And fogs are veiling the sun."
He answered: "Yet souls are sick,
And souls in the dark undone!"

I said: "I shall miss the light,
And friends will miss me, they say."
He answered: "Choose tonight
If I am to miss you or they."

I pleaded for time to be given.
He said: "Is it hard to decide?
It will not seem so hard in heaven
To have followed the steps of your Guide."

I cast one look at the fields,
Then set my face to the town;
He said: "My child, do you yield?
Will you leave the flowers for the crown?"

Then into His hand went mine;
And into my heart came He;
And I walk in a light divine,
The path I had feared to see.
(* Public Domain)

PREFACE

WHAT IS GLBM ALL ABOUT?

Golden Land Baptist Missions was born in my heart after God sent me to Myanmar, or Old Burma. Since 2008 I have been consumed with what God showed me there. The Old Testament prophet told us that what we see with our eye affects our heart, and then changes our lives. God has used the Burman peoples to change me. I went there in obedience to Christ. I continue to go there because God put His love for them into me. I can honestly say that I love them, not because I am loving, but because His love for them has changed me. After serving God for thirty years in America, I gave the remainder of my life and ministry to reach the Myanmar peoples for Christ.

Traveling there alone, when the country was still a military dictatorship, I saw people with little hope, who were steeped in religious idolatry but had never heard the Gospel of Christ. Some had never heard the name of Jesus Christ. Some people don't understand that, with all the world's current technology, there remain thousands of people groups who have never yet heard of Christ's death, burial, and resurrection. Dr. Charles Keen of Bearing Precious Seed said there are six thousand such groups who have no self-governing, self-perpetuating, Bible preaching church within their entire society. Many have no Bible translated into their mother tongue, or heart language. Some have no written language in which to translate the Bible. In other words, they have no access to any source of light at all. Most of those people groups are in what has been called the 10-40 Window, and Myanmar, or Old Burma, is in the center of it.

The people of Myanmar are not just the Burmese, but 149 separate people groups with more than 200 dissimilar languages. These languages do not sound alike; they do not look alike or share the same alphabets. Myanmar is the largest geographical country in Southeast Asia, with a population of more than fifty million people. It is bordered by five other countries and surrounded by twelve, making it what I call "The Hub of The Wheel" in Southeast Asia. At GLBM, it is our burden and calling to go there, train national preachers, plant churches, educate and care for orphans, and raise up a new generation of Myanmars who will take the Gospel of Christ, not only across their own land but, out of the "spokes of the wheel" to the surrounding people groups. We believe it can be done, and it is already happening. But we need financial partners and others who will go with us.

Golden Land Baptist Missions is a local church ministry. It is just like our church's bus ministry, or our SundaySchool. When I founded GLBM, I asked my Pastor to be the President, making myself Founder-Director. Our Board of Directors is our local church Deacons. We have other men of God who participate as an Advisory Board, but we, that is me, our staff, and volunteers, are accountable to the Officers of our home church first, then other supporting churches. That is what we

Dedicated to

Carolyn Ruth .

⟋◡⟍

My lifelong love, partner in ministry,
she who shares my burden and vision,
and has worked tirelessly,
sacrificing self, sometimes serenity,
and companionship often.
For this and so much more -
I am grateful.

FOREWARD

Often one listens to missionary stories of old and might wonder if God is still moving the way He has for centuries. These stories told by Brother DeWitt are more than just stories; they are personal experiences from a veteran missionary who, while being in a literal battlefield, listened to the call of the Lord to reach the people of Myanmar and its varying people groups. These stories will undoubtedly lift spirits and confirm what we already know - God is still moving.

Dr. David Gibbs, Jr.
Christian Law Association

spirit, our passion for souls, our heart of compassion for people who are lost in sin, and our willingness to be used by God. We must raise up a new generation of missionaries in American churches.

During one of our Missions Revivals, I sat at a table with Dr. David Gibbs of the Christian Law Association. Others were gathered around, and I told a missionary story. With tearing eyes Dr. Gibbs asked me, "Where's the book?" I played dumb and asked, "What book?" He continued, "You need to put your stories in a book!" I said, "I would not do it for myself. But I would do it for rice." It takes a lot of rice, both literally and figuratively, to do ministry in Myanmar, or in any country.

We have purchased, shipped, and smuggled Burmese Bibles. We have invested hundreds of thousands of dollars in training young people, erecting buildings for churches and schools, purchasing vehicles, eyeglasses, medicine, clothing, shoes, not to mention the ordinary expenses of traveling, both here and there. It takes a lot of "rice." We need partners, like you. Golden Land Baptist Missions seeks faith partners, individuals, churches, or businesses who desire to help us evangelize the Buddhist and Muslim world, starting in the "Hub of The Wheel."

Being honest, I got in the ministry because I loved it, and I loved those who were in it. Certainly, I knew that I was called. But I stay in the ministry because being a preacher is not what I do but what I am. I keep going back to Myanmar because God has put His love for the Myanmar peoples in me. I genuinely love the Myanmar peoples. GLBM is all about love. We all have a passion for what we love. But I submit that you cannot love Jesus and not love the souls of people. You cannot reach people without loving them.

My prayer is that this first volume of true stories from GLBM's ministry in Myanmar, our experiences on the mission field, will be a little spark to ignite a new fire among young people and churches in America and beyond. Now I invite you travel to Myanmar with me in the pages of these true stories.

believe and practice.

Every year, our church hosts what we call a Missions Revival. It is the biggest meeting of the year for our church. We have nationally known speakers and invite other pastors to join us. We furnish their meals and lodging and our families minister to them. It is all about a world-wide vision. I do not like to speak of foreign missions and home missions. I think the commission of the Church, a mandate from God, is missions everywhere and always. My father-in-law, a missionary who spent forty years in Bolivia, South America, said "The foreign mission field is the heart of man where Christ is foreign." If that is true, and I think it is, then none of God's children are ever far from a foreign mission field.

My Pastor said that our church's involvement with the Myanmar peoples has changed him and changed our church. I think that is true. I know it has changed me. God has changed many of us. God has called some young people from our church and other churches to missions through our burden and vision. When I am not traveling to preach and present the needs of GLBM, children gather in my office to look at the many things I have carried back from Old Burma and to hear another missions story. I love the fact that they are interested in missions.

I went to Bible College in the 70's. In every "camp" of Bible-believing Christianity there was much activity and fervor about missions. Young men were either going to the Northeast or the Northwest to plant churches, or they were going to a foreign country to do the same. Max Helton's "Reaching America Report" always listed the "Ten Most Needy Cities in America" for church planting. Those of us in college, preparing for ministry, anxiously waited on that monthly update because we were seeking the Lord's direction. In the New Testament sense, we were ready to go and going! We were like an army, freshly trained and ready, uniformed and equipped, and waiting on orders. We just wanted to know where to go.

Many of today's young people seem listless, not even considering their futures. When you ask them what they will do after high school or college, they stare at you like they do not hear you. Could it be that we are no longer instilling in them a vision of what they can do and what they can be as we used to do? People say that this listlessness is just characteristic of our times. But when I take young people to Myanmar with me, they see what I see, feel what I feel, and talk to me about becoming a missionary. Could it be that we need a revival of pastors and parents willing to send them?

I am not saying that our fire has gone out. There are pockets of revival across America where the flames are burning hot. Some churches still have a wonderful heart for worldwide evangelization. But too many churches have just a token missions' program. They believe it is what they are supposed to do. But church members don't know their missionaries. They don't really pray. They don't think of these missionaries as their ambassadors. They don't think of themselves as their partners. They don't give like they used to. It is time to rekindle our missionary

CHAPTER ONE

Pai Lian Thang

"Brethren, I count not myself to have apprehended: but this one thing I do, forgetting those things whichare behind, and reaching forth unto those things which are before, I press toward the mark for the prizeof the high calling of God in Christ Jesus."
Philippians 3:13-14

The road was not as bad as some, but it still took us half the day to get to the small village. Most secondary roads in Myanmar, especially in the provinces, are constructed by a team of workers, many times women, who are boiling barrels of tar by the roadside and hand-carrying it in buckets, creating a surface that much resembles a patchwork quilt.

Our team was stuffed into a small Toyota taxi from the city and, even with all windows rolled down, the heat and humidity were almost overpowering to us Americans. The streets were narrow with deep ditches of dark, slimy water on either side. The homes were simple, some built of rough-cut lumber, some of bamboo, but most elevated on stilts for rainy season flooding and to discourage nightly visitors of the creeping and crawling kind. Many of these homes looked barely livable to our Western eyes. I thought, as we drove by many, that I had built a better backyard playhouse out of sticks, cardboard, and blankets when I was growing up. Small groups of women and young people were in the streets, some walking or peddling bicycles, some standing at a small corner market or food stand where finger rolls with different fillings were being fried in hot oil. The smoke of cooking curries and burning trash filled the air. Seemingly owned by none but tolerated by all, shorthaired dogs, much resembling the Australian dingo, laid in the streets or scavenged for food.

Women strolled the streets, carrying large and presumably heavy loads, perfectly balanced on their heads. Everyone seemed busy. Carefree and frolicking children played in the streets and parted for our approaching vehicle. I could not help but wave at them. I yelled, "Mingalabah!" (meaning, Hello!) They would smile, wave back, and then point at us, calling everyone's attention to the "foreigners" in their village. In those days, when Myanmar was "closed" and governed by the military junta, foreigners were allowed only in designated tourist areas and most villagers had never seen a Caucasian with round eyes.

As we finally arrived at our destination, each of us peeled ourselves off gate leading to a narrow pathway and a stilted bamboo hut a short distance away. An older white-haired man approached us with outstretched welcoming hands. He had a weathered face and smiling eyes. This was the first time we had ever met. But he hugged me warmly around my neck and shoulders, and I felt an instant connection to him like someone of my own family.

Being introduced to this man, I was told that his name was "Pai Lian Thang." He led us across a thin board that spanned the ditch, then through the gate, and down the pathway to the hut. We took our shoes off and followed him, carefully climbing the single-strand bamboo steps into his abode. I winched with pain as the bottoms of my tender Western feet collapsed like marshmallows on each step. Pai Lian Thang offered his hand to steady me and help me up into the hut. There was one room. The walls and floor were made of flexible bamboo mats that sunk and shifted under my feet but seemed strong enough to hold us all. There was no furniture, no chairs, no stools, or tables. There was only a simple bed sheet hung from roof supports, separating a place where residents slept.

Pai Lian Thang still had me by the hand and led me across the room to an opposite corner where he helped me into a sitting position on the floor and then sat beside me. A young woman appeared and brought us a small bowl of fruit, an aluminum kettle filled with hot Burmese tea, and several small glass cups, still wet from washing. A half-dozen other villagers entered the hut who quietly took their places on the floor along one wall and looked at me with anticipation. I wasn't sure what we would do. It was my understanding that Pai Lian Thang was a preacher and that he had a small congregation in this village. I presumed that this hut was his home. But being a little confused, I sat patiently and waited for further instruction. I thought that I would be polite and compliment his house. I said, "Saya, you have a nice home!" He did not react but simply smiled and changed the subject. One of our GLBM pastors was with me, and he leaned over to me and whispered, "BaGyi, Pai Lian Thang has no home.

I still did not understand who this man was or how he lived. All I had been told was that, on this day, we would visit an older preacher. It was early in my Myanmar experience; I was still learning the customs and culture, and I did not yet realize how many Christians had continued to serve the Lord, even during the difficult years of military dictatorship. I was enjoying Pai Lian Thang's company and he was exceedingly gracious, kind, and honoring to me. We shared some fruit and then I was asked to sing and bring a short message from the Scriptures. It was difficult for me to know what to preach or teach because I did not know these people. If I had known Pai Lian Thang better, I would have felt self-conscious even opening my mouth in his presence.

Twenty-eight years earlier, Pai Lian Thang's wife had died in childbirth. The baby, their first and only child, a son, had survived. It had been their single desire and calling to serve the Lord together. God had put it equally in their hearts. One could easily imagine the emotions that Pai Lian Thang experienced, both immediately and progressively: a broken heart, confusion, perhaps some bitterness, and then nagging loneliness. But with his infant boy in one arm, and a small satchel in the other hand, Pai Lian Thang set out on foot to serve the Lord Jesus, surrounded by both a government and a society that were equally as hostile to him as his circumstances. It is difficult for many with contemporary Western values to grasp his mindset: Above all, he would serve the Lord. He would do it by faith. He would have no salary or benefits, no insurance, no car, and no personal home. He would trust the Lord for food and shelter, for both himself and for his young dependent son.

The Holy Scriptures tell us that Jesus Christ, being the Creator of the universe and the Saviour of all mankind, owned everything but had no place to pillow His head among men. And when Jesus sent His disciples out to do the work of God, He "commanded them that they should take nothing for their journey, save a staff only; no scrip, no bread, no money in their purse: But be shod with sandals; and not put on two coats." (Matt 6:8,9) Jesus said, "...Take no thought for your life, what ye shall eat; neither for the body, what ye shall put on." (Luke 12:22) In his small satchel, Pai Lian Thang had only one change of clothes, his very worn Bible, and an aged spiral-bound notebook with curling and yellowed corners. I quickly learned that my new friend had long lived, and was still living, as Christians did in the earliest days of the Church.

In the winter of 1982, Pai Lian Thang walked into a village where he had never been before. He knew no one. There was no church, no Christians, and no gospel witness. But there was a Buddhist temple and a resident monk. Walking the streets of the village, bowing graciously and greeting each person he met, he had to be careful not to be too aggressive or to offend anyone. Special informers with government-issued cell phones were everywhere. But there was an inherent kindness to Pai Lian Thang that gave people confidence quickly. They did not fear him.

Pai Lian Thang was not Burmese but Zomi Chin, another Myanmar people group. Because of years of civil war, some Chin people hated the country's ruling Burmese. One Chin preacher said, "When I get to Heaven, if I see one Burmese person, I will come back!" But Pai Lian Thang had a burden to preach the Gospel to the Burmese Buddhists and to show them the love of Christ. It was the single truth that had changed his heart and given him the vision that would drive him to village after village.

In each village he would lead a family to Christ and move in with them. He and his young son would occupy a corner of their one-room hut while he was winning other families. He would teach them the Scriptures, hymns, and spiritual songs. He would teach them the Christian life and how to lead a soul to Christ. In each place, eventually a small congregation would be formed. As the converts would grow in faith and in their relationship with the Savior, a leader would become apparent. When he was ready to assume the leadership of that new group of believers, Pai Lian Thang would charter the church, establish him as the pastor, and move on to another village in the true Pauline manner.

As he repeatedly shared the truth of Christ, he realized that some Burmese people had heard of Christianity but knew nothing about it. These precious souls for whom Christ died had no opportunity to hear the true Gospel. There was no church, never had been. No preacher or missionary had ever been to these villages.

As I sat on the floor next to Pai Lian Thang, he looked deeply into my eyes and asked me to pray for him. He opened his spiral bound notebook and handed it to me. I leafed through the yellowed pages and my eyes followed the countless lines of handwritten Burmese text organized into columns. My new preacher friend explained to me, "These are the signatures of those who have turned from sin and idols to Jesus Christ our Saviour in the past 28 years." He said with some obvious regret, "At first I did not keep this record. So, there are some of the early converts who are not here." There were more than I could possibly count. I asked, "Saya, how many are written here?" He modestly admitted, "I believe there are more than 6,700."

I could not keep from weeping. With tears flowing, I placed my wet face on this man's chest and asked him to pray for me. He did so immediately and, as he prayed in his mother tongue, I knew the Holy Ghost was near and I felt that I had stepped back in time to the days of the first Christians and genuine New Testament Christianity.

Jesus Himself gave us the pattern to follow to win souls and to plant and build New Testament churches. There are at least four things to consider in Matthew 6:8,9:

First, we are to GO and not stay. Far too many preachers stay in the place where we were reached for Christ by someone who was already serving there. Why are there so many churches of like faith and practice in the same small towns of America? The Apostle Paul strove to preach where Christ was not named and not to build on another man's foundation (Romans 15:20). I visited a small southern city of 6000 where there were sixty independent Baptist churches and most of them splits of each other. None of their members would speak to each other, but gossip and talebearing had become the norm and the greatest single hindrance to revival and soul winning.

Second, we are to go by faith. I would not say that Americans should shun all their material blessings to serve God. Praise the Lord, I have many. But, if our faith does not make us flexible enough to part with our comforts and safety nets long enough to make a difference in someone's life, how can we be missionaries?

Thirdly, we should never give the impression that materialism has anything to do with our service to Christ. No faithful preacher would do that on purpose. But some do so unintentionally. Paul said that a proof of his faithful ministry was that he made "the gospel of Christ without charge" (1 Corinthians

9:18). I have traveled far and been given much and traveled just as far and been given nothing. But I have never put a price or condition on my coming or service.

Fourthly, Jesus told his disciples not to "put on two coats." In other words, we are to go where we are called without a contingency plan. Otherwise, our ministry is not of faith. And "whatsoever is not of faith is sin" (Romans 14:23). Many well-intentioned family members and friends have asked, "What if it doesn't work out?" They ask this question because they don't really want us to go. But most of all, the Wicked One doesn't want us to go. More than that, he doesn't want us to go in faith, believing. If you have received the call, go in faith. If you have any doubt, stay home.

Might I be so bold as to charge us to the rekindling of Pauline practices and Pai Lian Thang trail?

House in village where we visited Pai Lian Thang

Pai Lian Thang with BaGyi Bob

CHAPTER TWO

Please Help Our Mother

*"For I have no pleasure in the death of him that dieth,
saith the Lord God: wherefore turn yourselves, and live ye."*
Ezekiel 18:32

It was a very warm day in the Tak Province of northwestern Thailand. As my team and I stepped from our vehicle on to the dirt road, sweat immediately began to run down our face and neck and into our shirts. Looking deeper into the village, the streets were filled with people. Several men stood at the corner talking and pointing at us. Our pale white faces and strange clothing drew everyone's attention. But, sending our team by twos and sometimes by threes, we headed in different directions, distributing Scriptures and talking to everyone we met. This was a Burmese village not far from Moei River that forms the border between Thailand and Old Burma. One might be surprised by how much you can communicate with just a few words in somebody else's language. We were doing the best we could. But most people were genuinely glad to see us and interested in what we were doing and what we were giving out.

We had with us some bilingual young people from Myanmar, some from the Karen tribe, and some who were Burmese converts. They translated for us. But learning just a few easy Burmese words and phrases, most of us were able to capture people's attention. As soon as we would say, "Ming-a-la-bah!" (or Hello), their inquisitive expression would turn to a warm smile and we knew everything would be alright. Countless children gathered around us, followed us from door to door, and sometimes held our hands. Most people stood in their doorways, watching us approach. Every person greeted us warmly and invited us in. But we didn't want to pause long at any one place. Our mission was distribution of God's Word in the people's language.

Walking from one bamboo hut to another, suddenly I heard my name being called loudly. "BaGyi! BaGyi Bob!" I looked up and down the street but saw no one. Again, "BaGyi Bob!" This time the call was louder and more frantic. Moorah, one of the young ladies who was with us, appeared from behind a house and was frantic to have me follow her. The house, if you can call it that, was sided with a patchwork quilt of odd and differently colored pieces of material, large and small. The thatch roof was made of dried palm leaves and reeds from a nearby swamp.

As Moorah rounded the corner of the house, she called again, "BaGyi!

Please come! Please come quickly!" She turned on her heels and literally ran around the house and disappeared. I ran after her but lost track of what direction she went. I called, "Moorah! Moorah!" Now she appeared again but down an adjacent street, motioning for me to come. Catching up with her, she led me to a stilted bamboo hut. In front of the home was a large golden spirit-house on a four-foot concrete pedestal that was nicer than the house. She gestured for me to follow her up the bamboo steps and into the hut.

Not taking time to remove my shoes as is customary, I climbed up into the one-room family home. It was small: perhaps eight-foot square. I normally would have greeted everyone by bowing to each and reaching for their hands in the traditional Burmese manner. But the sight that was before me was so awful, I froze in my steps. I was not prepared for what I saw, or what I was about to experience. Sadness, darkness, hopelessness, and sickness filled the air. The stench of soon-coming death filled the room.

An old and frail woman lay on the floor atop a bamboo mat, covered with a thin blanket. Her body was literally just skin and bones with leprous-looking sores around her joints. She laid curled up on her side and was trembling uncontrollably. Her breathing was sporadic and shallow. Undoubtedly blind, her dark eyes lay in deep sockets, covered with a cloudy film. It was unclear whether she could hear anything at all. On one hand, her fingers curled permanently into her palm, the nails piercing her skin but drawing no blood. On the other, her fingers were curled backwards in a crescent shape over the top of her hand, pointing toward her elbow. It was obvious what was going on here: the woman was dying and, maybe, even in her very last minutes or hours of life. Her family, a son, and his wife with two young children, sat on the floor along the wall, weeping.

Moorah instantly knelt on the floor next to the old woman, and took one of her deformed hands in hers. Tears rolled down her cheeks as she looked up and asked me, "BaGyi, what can we do?" I looked over at the son and his wife, and then back to Moorah. I fell to my knees beside the old woman, held her other hand, and asked, "Moorah, what do they want me to do?"

"BaGyi, they want you to pray for their mother!"

"But, Moorah, she is dying!"

"BaGyi, they want you to pray for her soul."

 "But they are Buddhist!"

"Yes, but they know that you are a man of God."

"Yes, Moorah! I will pray. But I don't think we have time to translate. We don't know if this old woman can hear. We do not know if she will understand a thing. I will pray. But I want you to get down close to her ear and explain the plan of salvation. Explain it very slowly and plain, as simple as you can, in her language. I do not know how long you are going to have. But Christ is her only hope. This is her last chance. And you are the only one here who
can tell her about Him."

As the old woman literally slipped away into eternity, we didn't know if she had heard or understood a single word of what Moorah said. It was impossible for her to respond. Her heartbroken family wept. I cannot describe the feeling I had, the anguish in my own soul, as I thought   to myself, "We got here too late!"

I turned and reached out to the woman's son, hoping to console him with my hand or a short compassionate embrace. But, as I turned to him, he smiled through his tears and looked into my eyes.He said, "Saya, Chay zu htin bar de! Chay zu htin bar de!" - which is to say in Burmese, "Teacher, thank you very much! Thank you very much!"

Empathizing with him, my own eyes were wet with tears, and he took his fingers and wiped them from my face. It seemed that the more I tried to console him and his family, the more they wanted to thank me. When I thought they would be overcome with sadness, they seemed to be rejoicing. I was a bit confused.

Our message of the Gospel may very well have been too late for this woman who had suffered so much. Speaking in churches across America, I have often said, "My people suffer every day of their lives, and then die, and drop into a Devil's Hell, having never heard one time that God became a Man to die on a Cross, to pay for their sin with His own precious blood."

Were we too late for this old woman? Perhaps! I think we, as Christians and the body of Christ, have been too late for many, maybe millions or billions who never heard the simple plan of salvation through a Saviour who died for the whole world.

But there was a reason why the old woman's son and his family were rejoicing, even as his mother's body lay dead before them. As Moorah got down on hands and knees, next to the old woman's ear, and told her the sweet and simple truth of the Gospel in terms that anyone could understand, her young family also heard it for the first time. Believing what they heard, they trusted Christ as their Saviour.

Oh! That the world would have ears to hear. Do you know someone for whom it is almost too late?

"How then shall they call on him in whom they have not believed? and how shall they believe in him of whomthey have not heard? and how shall they hear without a preacher? And how shall they preach, except they be sent? as it is written, How beautiful are the feet of them that preachthe gospel of peace, and bring glad tidings of good things."

Romans 10:14,15

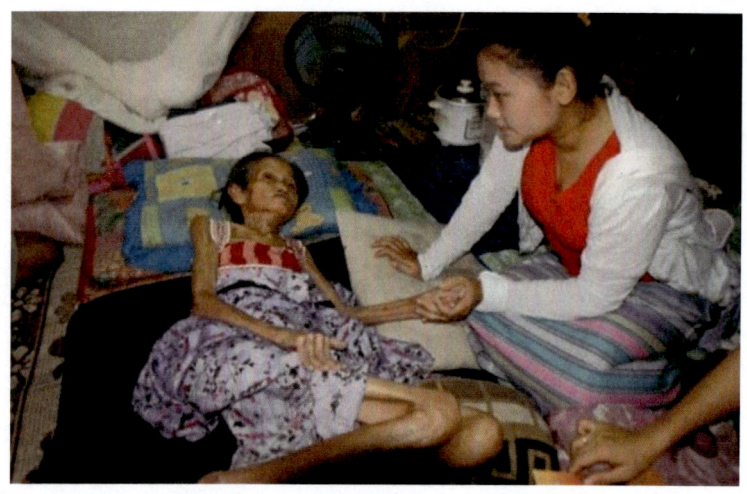

Old, dying Burmese woman with Moora

CHAPTER THREE

The Mru People

"And ye became followers of us, and of the Lord, having received the word in much affliction,with joy of the Holy Ghost."
...the Apostle Paul to the Thessalonians (1 Thess. 1:6)

The sun was just beginning to peak through the tall buildings of downtown Yangon, and we were already stuck in bumper-to-bumper traffic. My pale-skinned arms were shining with sweat and I hung one out the passenger window, trying to find a breeze, only to whip it back inside as another vehicle came disturbingly close to sideswiping us. The air was filled with diesel fumes and the smoke of street vendors cooking by open fires. Our taxi driver did not seem to understand a word of English. But you never know about these things. Sometimes, for whatever reason, they pretend that they don't know what you're saying, especially if you are trying to impress them with what little Burmese vocabulary you possess. But I couldn't seem to make him understand that we would really appreciate him turning on the air conditioning. Perhaps it didn't work. But he wasn't paying attention and I will do just about anything rather than offend one of my beloved Myanmar people. So, we sweat.

I was sitting "shotgun," next to the driver, in a Toyota Probox, which is a small and cheap cross-over vehicle, definitely not designed for hefty Americans. If you are in the front seat, your knees are jammed into the dash. If you are in the back, you get the constant feeling that your Sweet Alabama backside is in danger of sliding off the seat and on to the floor where you might be wedged until reaching your destination. Don't get me wrong! I am always thankful to be in Myanmar and to be traveling the country. I have done so by almost every mode of transportation that there is. But the Probox is only better than an oxcart if the air conditioning works. It gets you from Point A to Point B reliably like all Toyota products but, in my thinking, it is the buckboard of what Japan has to offer.

After almost ninety minutes of being cramped into that Toyota with all our luggage, we finally arrived at the Yangon International Airport. So grateful to open the door and stick a leg out, I unfolded myself slowly, stretched, and grabbed my suitcase which had already been placed on the sidewalk in front of the terminal. I handed the taxi driver 10,000 kyats, which included a tip. It was still early, but people were everywhere. Pastor Thaung Lian, our own Deacon Matt Mayer, and I pushed through the crowd and entered the terminal, dragging our bags behind us.

Myanmar may be behind the United States and other countries in some ways, but I appreciate how they have streamlined both their domestic and international airport procedures. Even though the country was governed by a military dictatorship just a few years ago, they have made amazing progress in many areas and you can now get to your Gate faster than almost anywhere else I have visited. If you travel half as much as I do, you know what a blessing that is.

The ATR-72 twin engine turboprop aircraft taxied down the runway and finally assumed its takeoff position with its finely tuned Pratt & Whitneys singing a sweet song like a racehorse snorting at the starting gate of the Belmont Stakes. I love flying. I wait with anticipation for that moment of exhilarating thrust when the pilot lets off the brakes and pushes the twin throttles forward.

Our flight would take just over two hours. Lifting off through the morning mist, I gazed out the window to watch the city of Adoniram Judson take shape below and soon dissipate in the sunrise behind us. Flying west by northwest, over what I thought might be the Ayeyarwady Division river delta, I kept my eyes fastened on the vast countryside, hoping by chance to see a herd of wild elephants. Small mountain ridges began to appear and, turning due north, we followed the coastline and backwaters of the Bay of Bengal. After two hours, I knew that we were nearing our initial destination: the old Arakan tribal city of Sittwe, on the Bay of Bengal, in what is now called Rakhine State.

After a smooth landing, we disembarked the aircraft, stood on the already hot tarmac, and waited for our bags to be unloaded. Grabbing them as they came off the plane, we walked into the simple, one-room terminal, showed our Passport and Visa to the Security officer, and walked out onto the nearby street. It was really that simple.

I thought we might take another taxi but didn't see one anywhere. Instead, we hailed a horse cart driver who took us and our bags for a short ride, down a back street, to a private marina. We stood in the street and waited while Pastor Thaung Lian negotiated with a boatman. Fifty U.S. bucks was the price for us foreigners, approximately half that for the nationals and, at the time, I really didn't understand what a deal it was. This man and his First Mate would take us on their 60-foot riverboat to the ancient village of Mrauk U, ten hours north, up the Kaladan River and several of its tributaries.

As the Mississippi is to Americans, the Ayeyarwady River is to the Burmese, and the Kaladan River is to the old Arakan people who inhabit Rakhine State. It is symbolic of their culture and history, and it is still a major artery of transportation and trade. It forms far north, defining the border between India and the mountainous Chin State of Myanmar and empties into the Bay of Bengal at the city of Sittwe.

Before shoving off, we purchased the largest bunch of bananas we could find and hung them from a roof support in the boat, over our heads. Not the large Chiquita or Dole bananas you would buy in an American grocery store, but these were small tree ripened, maybe three-inch, deep yellow, and sweet as sugar fruits that any monkey would fight for. We took a few photos of the boat and us with our Captain, and then walked the short plank to come onboard.

There was another man who was also a passenger, a colorfully verbose Brit, who was going as far as our first stop where we would stay overnight. There were three hard-plastic, straight-back chairs, not enough for all of us. We would have to take turns sitting down or prop ourselves up somewhere else onboard. Thaung Lian immediately said that he would sit on the floor. Before too long, I would improvise, sitting on my suitcase and leaning against the curved hull of the boat. I called it my "Burmerican" recliner.

The engine started roughly with several loud pops, a low rhythmless growl, and lots of black smoke. It ran that way at the dock until we got underway, and I wondered if we would make it as far as open water. But soon, clearing the inlet and going to full throttle in the wide-open river, the engine evened out, the smoke ceased, and our faithful water taxi chugged us northward with steady and effortless grace.

We all started the journey standing in the bow of the boat and waving to people who lived along the inlet shore in bamboo huts. They were excited to see us and, without exception, waved back with that famous Myanmar smile that I have come to cherish. In the mouth of the Kaladan we could see a Myanmar Navy warship at anchor in the distance. The vastness of the river delta at that point, as it joins the Lemru River and the Bay of Bengal, was shocking to me. Fishing boats peppered the shining horizon as far as our eyes could see.

Soon the city of Sittwe, and quite literally anything resembling civilization, faded in the distance behind us, and the hot sun drove us under the canopy to enjoy our bananas. But for nearly half the trip I was on my feet with my camera in hand, switching between wide and telephoto lenses, shutter-bugging the countryside filled with herds of water buffalo, tiny river settlements, and playful youngsters with the most delightful smiles. I was amazed to think of where I was and what we were doing. One of my lifelong sayings is, "I just love a good adventure!" This was certainly it.

The river itself provided a great adventure. If I were a nature photographer or a river biologist, this could possibly be one of my dream destinations. To experience the Kaladan river ecosystem, with its amazing varietyof birds, is worth the trip in and of itself: the occasional Spotted-Bill duck leading her ducklings in a perfect column, the cloud-like flocks of Grey-Headed Lapwings, the Long-Legged Asian Openbill fishers, the elegant Painted Storks, or the majestic Black-Headed Ibis standing tall out of the water, yet at time filling the sky - I was captivated by it all.

There were times along the way that I wanted to stop the boat, pause, and meet the people along the river. Fishermen in narrow dugout canoes always smiled and waved. We were all amused at the exuberance of children as they scurried out of their stilted bamboo huts, jumping in the air and waving at us foreigners who were sailing by. A young fisherman was anchored along the side of the river, trying to make his living, while his wife nursed her child under a rounded turtle-shell cover that seemed to be their home, perhaps their only home. Another pair of fishermen in a boat yelled to us as we passed, "Hello! Where you from?"

Our boat captain navigated us through many bends of the river, around small islands, always knowing what turn to make as the Kaladan forked. It is a complicated river system. Using the satellite photography of Google Earth, I can take you right back to the places where we visited. I know where these places are, but the area is very remote. It is one of the three most difficult places to reach that I have visited within Myanmar. The Kaladan River splits into so many tributaries that, using many maps and every asset of the Internet, I have not been able to learn the names of those secondary rivers or creeks, if they have names, where we traveled to get to our final destination: Nabugan village.

As we approached the historic city of Mrauk U from the south, the river divided again with a large Buddhist pagoda positioned like a beacon of either welcome or warning between the forks. The surrounding hills were laden with ancient temples, constructed by the monks and peasants of several historic Arakan dynasties. Mrauk U, pronouncned "Meow Oo," was the capital of 49 Arakanese kings until the last of them was conquered by theBurmese Konbaung Dynasty of King Alaungpaya in 1784. Here we would spend the night and rest for the next day's journey.

Our boat was safely moored to the dock, and we climbed ashore, pulling our luggage behind us to a place where we loaded into another horse-drawn cart. Any visitor to Mrauk U will immediately notice the number of street vendors selling medicines and herbal tonics. The Kaladan River Valley is a breeding ground for disease- carrying mosquitos. We had been warned that, where we were going, everyone had malaria, and many had tuberculosis.

Our cart driver dropped us at the Shwe Thazin, or Golden Flower Hotel. It was a beautiful spot with cabins in a garden setting. But our accommodations, clean as they were, had no western-style beds, just wooden platforms with bamboo mats, a blanket or two, and a pillow for our heads. Our room had a wash basin in the corner, under a small mirror. There was no running water and no electric power. We were given bottles of purified water for drinking and washing.

A handsome longyi-wrapped young man showed us to our cabin and helped carry our luggage. He spoke what Iconsidered good English with a sweet Burman accent. And he was extremely interested to talk to us. So, we sat with him for a while, answered his questions, and witnessed to him about Christ. But we were exhausted. Once we laid down on the hard bamboo mats, even with the chirping lizards clinging to the walls and ceilings as they hunted the flying insects overhead, we fell fast asleep. If you have a fear or distaste for these small, gecko-like lizards, you should know that, because mosquitos are one of their favorite snacks, they are your ally in staying healthy in this environment. King Cobras and Pit Vipers are also an ally in a similar way, but I am not nearly as tolerant of them. Thankfully, there were no such serpents in or near our room that night. At least, I was not aware of them.

By four o'clock the next morning we were awake and gathering in the breakfast room for fried eggs, rice with some stir-fried vegetables, fresh papaya, slices of mango, and hot Burmese tea. We were joined by our Rakhine State missionary who is a national, and another man whom he won to the Lord. By 5:30 am, the five of us plus a driver and his two friends, were loaded into a Willy's-type Chinese "jeep" built for four people. This meant that one man would be up front with the driver, three men would sit melted together on the back seat, and two men would hang on to the sides of the vehicle with one foot and a leg hanging off. And it took several hours to reach the village of Thein Nyo, our first stop.

The sun came up quickly with the wind in our faces. I was wearing khaki pants, a lightweight breathable shirt, and my Tilley's wide brim Harrison Ford- style sunhat. The jeepney had no top; it was open to the sun. I had sunscreen in my suitcase, but that was back at the hotel – in Yangon. My biggest concern, however, was not getting sunburned; it was keeping the dust from the road out of my DSLR. Dust is Enemy Number One of digital cameras. But few Americans, or any Westerners for that matter, have gone and will never go where we were going. I had to have my camera out and ready. So, I spent more time trying to keep my camera from being harmed, than myself. And when we hit a huge bump, I was not ready and was almost jettisoned out of the vehicle. Several times a large truck or an older passenger bus roared past us in a cloud of dust. I tried holding my breath rather than sucking the dust down into my lungs. But whether those vehicles were oncoming or passing by, the dust hung in the air and you had no choice but to take a gulp. I tried tying a bandana around my face; I tried to hold my hat over my nose. Nothing helped. There were dust masks available for purchase back in the village, but I didn't have the foresight to get one. My eyeglasses soon looked like the headlights of a Dodge Ram 4x4 taking last place in a Mojave Desert grand prix.

Finally reaching the village of Thein Nyo, we carefully got out of the small jeep and slowly, painfully unfolded our appendages. It was a good walk into the village from the outer road, perhaps several miles. As we walked the pathway through a very large overgrown field, a loudspeaker could be heard in the distance ahead. I wasn't paying much attention to it. I was watching the grass and brush on both sides of our narrow trail for snakes. It was a great place to encounter King Cobras, Burmese pythons, or a variety of pit vipers, any of which could ruin our day, maybe our lives, and change our plans completely.

Approaching the village, we were met by a group of Buddhists who were carrying what looked like a small parade float with a large banner and a battery-powered loudspeaker blaring Buddhist chants. They all had alms buckets for donations, and they were banging on those buckets to the beat of the recorded chants. I was told thatsomeone tipped them off that foreigners were coming, and they were doing their best to impress us.

We watched and waved politely as they went by and then proceeded through the village on foot to a river boat dock. Waiting for us was two men with a twelve-foot-long motorized canoe-like boat with a lawn mower-type motor on a protracted movable driveshaft. It was designed to raise the driving propeller in shallow and weedy waters. The dock was long, very narrow, and more than six feet high over leech-infested water. The boards were glazed with thick and shining mud that was so slippery it was almost impossible to walk on.

Our nationals carelessly maneuvered it with bare feet. But I must admit, I could not bring myself to do it. And my high-dollar waterproof hiking shoes didn't like the slipperiness of the mud any better. Matt Mayer tried it first, and I was surprised how quickly he made it across and into the boat. Now he was urging me along and razzing me with his usual sarcastic humor. I, with my normally gracious temperament, was having visions of throwing him overboard to the leeches and whatever else lived in the murkiness below. Finally, our nationals grabbed a long bamboo pole, held it like a stair railing for me, and I gingerly walked the plank and hopped in the boat.

This river, a branch of the Kaladan, was not as wide, but it was wild. Deep jungle approached from both sides. Branches with creeping moss draped over the bank, supporting webbings of banana spiders, large as a man's hand. The water was a muddy green color with an eerie stillness. There was no perceivable current at all. Yet, under the surface of the water, it seemed that the muddy bottom breathed and slithered. Close, and yet distant, the sounds of neighborhood guardians were relaying and replying, as if announcing our entrance into their world. This is where tigers roam and snakes, big bad serpents, make their home. We could not determine if the sounds of the jungle came from birds, bats, cats, monkeys, something, or someone. But we could not escape the feeling that we were being watched.

I was sitting in the pointed bow of the boat where the murky water was being parted. Matt was in the stern, just ahead of the pilot. I started whistling a tune that seemed to fit our present situation and surroundings. Matt burstinto his well-known uproarious laughter and asked, "BaGyi, are you whistling the theme song from Raiders of The Lost Ark?" Well, it just seemed appropriate to me. But suddenly there was another series of nature calls from the jungle ahead, as if answering my whistle, and we resumed our restrained alertness.

As we came upon a fork in the river, the pilot navigated to the right, and again the environment seemed to change. The river was becoming ever narrower and meandered through tighter hills. Every bend of the river seemed to be alive and rolling with snakes, sometimes a type of flying snake. As the bow of the boat broke the water before us, they would dodge away violently, skimming the water ahead of our advancing vessel. I wondered what I would do if one of those "flying snakes" jumped into our boat. I quickly devised a plan in my mind. I would not panic, but instantly grab the snake by the tail, or whatever I could get my hands on, and whip it out of the boat before it had a chance to collect itself. My plan seemed viable. But I didn't want to test it. Jumping out of the boat was certainly unthinkable.

As we approached a small village, there was a foot bridge over the river. It was high in the air and consisted of a single strand of thick bamboo to walk, or balance on, and a single rope to hold. There were several people on the bridge: an older woman, a teenage girl, and a younger boy. We waved as we floated underneath. They waved back with that same beautiful smile.

We had already been afloat several hours. Another hour, and the river became not much more than a creek with bamboo huts, some more elaborate than others, adorning the banks. Then came more wilderness and more high foot bridges over the water. They appeared out of nowhere. Obviously, there were tiny villages nearby, but undetectable from our position on the river. Another hour passed. Then unexpectedly in the distance, built into a hillside, we saw the golden glistening of a Buddhist pagoda that appeared like a motion-sensor spotlight that had detected our progress upriver. I did not know it, but below that sidehill lay our destination, Nabugan village, a Mru Tribe community. Would our arrival be considered a blessing or an intrusion?

Beyond two more bends of the river, the jungle opened to yellow fields of grain on either side. Another footbridge stretched high above the river connecting foot trails through dense underbrush that no New Yorker would dare traverse. As we approached a small landing on our port side, a large group of people were gathered along the river's bank, perhaps sixty men, women, and children. No village was visible. But the muffled sound of a rhythmed and incessant drumbeat came from across the field and beyond the tree line.

Whenever a Burmese word is anglicized, an R is pronounced as a Y. Mru, therefore, is pronounced Myoo. The Mru tribe apparently originated as an offshoot of Himalayan peoples, immigrating southward to the headwaters of the Kaladan River in Northeast India. Today they inhabit the borderlands of Bangladesh and Myanmar, with the majority in the latter. The Mru language comes from the Tibeto-Burman group of languages and was not a written language until a teacher named Man Ley Mru alphabetized it in 1980. It is one of the most endangered languages in the world today. In other words, it is disappearing because most Mru people are adapting to more common languages. Many Mru youths can understand the Burmese language but do not read it.

As we cautiously approached the landing and looked for a place to tie on, there was no dock, just a muddy bank with a shining mirror-like glaze. There were no other boats tied up or resting nearby. The only sign of civilization, besides the people standing along the bank, was a small gathering area with a few wooden benches under a thatched roof, apparently used by those who wait at times for some sort of river taxis like our canoe.

To keep our narrow boat from rocking uncontrollably and all of us ending up in the dreaded green murkiness, we stood and climbed out one at a time. The first hurdle was maneuvering up and across the slick, shiny mud bank. We had to step quickly, grab a branch, a seedling, or anything by which to pull ourselves to solid ground where the locals were waiting and laughing.

There, where the sod did not move beneath our feet, stood the village chief and a line of young people, dressed in their very colorful tribal ceremonials. I wondered if I should speak to them in Burmese or just shake hands. Should I bow? Should I give the traditional Myanmar polite greeting, the respectful and peculiar-to-Myanmar handshake, or a Buddhist greeting? I decided that I would do it all.

Very respectfully, and bowing, I gripped my right forearm with my left hand and stuck my right hand out to shake the Chief's hand. I said, "Mingalabar, Saya! Twee yar da wan tha bar de!" If he understood my pronunciation and foreigner-accent, he would know that I was saying, "Greetings, Leader! It is good to meet you!" The Chief smiled, bowed graciously, and exchanged my Burman handshake, and I was relieved.

Then I proceeded down the line of young people and greeted each one in the same way. When I reached the end of the line, I spun around to a whole group of children, jumping up and down, so eager to meet us. Looking into their eyes and putting my hand on their shoulders and my arms around their necks, I instantly made a connection with several boys and girls who latched on to me and never let go. We took a few photographs with them. Then they led us along a narrow trail, across the high-grown field, toward the far tree line and the hidden village where the drum was still beating.

The field was miles wide in either direction, stretching north and south along the river. But it was relatively narrow between the river and where the cliffs of the mountain ridge arose, looking eastward. A herd of water buffalo, with their formidable, curved horns, was grazing in the field to the south. The trail led directly into the center of the village that was organized in lanes of stilted huts. There was no electric or running water. There were no official-looking buildings, like that of government or schools.

We were led to a simple bamboo hut, built on stilts, about five feet off the ground. It was a private home. As I climbed up into the hut with the others, I took a place along the thatched wall, sitting on my legs underneath me. The chief wanted us to rest a bit and then we would meet the rest of the villagers and have a preaching meeting.

The chief sat down next to me in the hut and said, "I want all my people to become Christians." I responded, "Kaung de! Pya Thakin kaunggyi pe ba si." (or, Good! God bless you.) I wondered if he knew what it meant to be a Biblical Christian. But, our GLBM national missionary had contacted him before and explained the Gospel of Christ. The chief was anxious for his people to hear the truth. None of the villagers had ever heard of Jesus, and they had never seen a white man or any foreigner.

By this time, I think that we were all hungry. We had brought snacks along, but I thought it was too hot for me to eat. I wanted only some cold water, and we had brought many bottles with us. A young man with sun-darkened skin, wearing only a longyi, was cooking a chicken on an open fire alongside the hut and the smoke filled our room. I tried not to cough too much, but it was quite irritating to the eyes. Some of the village ladies brought various fruits and laid them out before us. I could smell rice cooking somewhere. The young man brought me a small chicken leg and I put my hands together, bowing graciously, and thanked him much. It smelled like chicken; it looked something like chicken. But it had been cooked to petrification. When I tried to bite into it, it was hard as a rock. I tried sucking on it, thinking that my saliva might re-awaken its texture. I got my pocketknife out and tried cutting it. But it was no use. When everyone was talking, I spied a dog nearby and started asking God to send him my way. Sure enough, he came sniffing around under the hut, and there was a crack in the flooring just big enough for me to feed it through to Fido. Very soon, the young man asked me if I would like another. Years ago, I had a similar experience when eating at someone's home. The woman asked me if I enjoyed her cooking. How would you answer a question like that honestly without being offensive, when it was probably the worst meal of your life? I simply smiled big and said, "Ma'am, that meal was something else!" She replied, "Oh! I'm so glad." But now, how was I supposed to translate that same message into Burmese? I prayed that the dog would show up for seconds!

After we rested for a short time, we were directed to a larger bamboo structure on a rounded knoll, the high point of the village. There was no school there, and no church of any kind. Truthfully, there is no church for a hundred miles in any direction. But this structure served as a community meeting hall and, on occasion, a Burmese volunteer teacher would venture up the river and teach a series of lessons in several area villages. Today, we would use it as our church.

We gathered as many villagers as we could find. One of the men brought a plastic chair which became the only furniture in the room. All the children gathered around us and sat on the floor. A little boy kept smiling at me, touching my legs, and then my hand. I reached out and pulled him to me. He didn't resist at all but jumped up on my lap. I put my arms around him and drew him close. His mother was sitting on the other side of the room and I could see her excited approval.

We started the meeting with singing. There was no guitar or keyboard, no instrument of any kind. Matt and I sang some hymns together a capella. Then the villagers sang a song in Burmese. I knew one song in the Burmese language, and when I started singing it, the smiles on their faces showed their excitement and approval. They sang along with me and clapped the rhythm out with their hands.

When we finished singing, Pastor Thaung looked at me and said, "BaGyi, it is your time! They want you to preach." So, I did. What do you preach to people who have never heard of Jesus, to those who have never seen a Holy Bible, never read it, never heard it, and don't know anyone who believes it? From what point of reference, or by what authority do you proclaim your message as ultimate truth?

Most people in Myanmar practice Buddhism as both religion and culture, with some combining animism, or spirit worship, with it as well. Catholic Jesuits made contact and have done limited work with the Mru people of Bangladesh. However, from what little information we have been able to find, no Christian church group of any denomination has ever evangelized the Mru people of Old Burma – until GLBM.

I simply raised my Bible and said, "The God of all gods, the Creator God, who made the heavens and the earth, and all of us, has revealed Himself to mankind in a Book. He has sent me to you with this book. He wants you to know Him." I carefully established God the Father in their minds, and then introduced to them Jesus Christ, the only mediator between God and men. I explained about sin and our need of a Savior. I helped them to understand why we need to be forgiven. And then I asked them to believe in my Savior and to turn to Him alone for salvation. And they did! That day, nearly the entire village made professions of faith in Christ and prayed with us, turning from their idols and spirits to the Lord Jesus Christ.

When the preaching meeting was over, the children gathered around Matt and me. There were probably thirty children of all ages, thanaka cream on their faces, soiled and mismatched clothes, blackened feet, but all with the most adorable smiles. One of the little girls, perhaps eight or nine years of age, captured Matt's attention and stayed by his side. She had lighter colored hair than most Burmans and it was short, probably from being shaved for lice. She had an impish grin and amusing eyes that gave away the mischief in her heart. But her fun- loving exuberance matched Matt's personality like the perfect piece of fabric to fill the last square on an Amish quilt. He lifted her up, put her on his shoulders and, as we left the First Baptist Mru Tabernacle, she rode her new American Palomino through the remainder of the village. Before leaving the tabernacle, we gathered the children together for a group photograph. I sat in the front of the group with that same young boy on my lap. Matt stood in the back, head and shoulders above everyone, with his new little friend straddling his neck like a monkey on a tree trunk and playing with his ears. With my DSLR in hand, Thaung Lian called for everyone's attention and took several photos.

There was a little girl who caught my attention. She was so tiny! She had a beautiful smile and eyes dark as Mexican onyx. While we were posing for the photos, she stood behind my left shoulder and kept tugging on my sleeve. I turned around to acknowledge her. When I swung around to face Thaung again, the little lad on my lap coughed violently and sprayed my whole face with his saliva. He didn't mean to; it was just perfect timing. I laughed and wiped his kid-juice off my face with my grimy hand. But inevitably, I knew there was a good chance I would test positive for tuberculosis.

According to Mayo Clinic's website on tuberculosis, "The bacteria that cause tuberculosis are spread from one person to another through tiny droplets released into the air via coughs and sneezes." But only approximately 10% of those exposed ever develop an active case of TB. However, after several months, I developed an increasingly severe cough, had the skin test, and was confirmed positive for the disease. My personal physician was a military officer and directed the TB Clinic at Ramstein Air Base in southwest Germany for twelve years. He said that he had never witnessed such a strong reaction to a TB test. So, after some chest x-rays and blood tests, I took the appropriate medicine for ten months. During that time, I was required to report every week to the County Health Department for re-evaluation. Some people asked if I would go back to Myanmar after becoming sick. But I would do the same thing a hundred times over – for my Saviour, for my beloved Myanmars, and those kids.

When we left Nabugan village to return to Mrauk U, our boatman pushed off from the bank and we drifted into the middle of the river. The villagers had followed us and were assembled in a large group, waving goodbye. There was something in me, a feeling, a reservation. Not really a voice in my ear, but a conscious reality that I might never see these people again.

After a short rest on our mats at the Shwe Thazin hotel, we collected our luggage and met our river boat captain again at the docks. We had a whole day's journey ahead of us, and we were anticipating another week of ministry in Yangon before returning to America. Again, we chugged along the Kaladan river, but this time with the current. The trip should have seemed shorter, but the weather had turned cold with high winds. We had minimal clothing and were not prepared for it. I dug my lightweight nylon windbreaker out of my suitcase. Matt disappeared inside his hoodie like a caterpillar inside a cocoon, and we huddled (not cuddled) together. I never thought it would happen in Myanmar, but we were so cold on that river, that we were trembling and in pain most of the way back to Sittwe.

Matt Mayer and I would never be the same after our encounter with the Mru people. We returned home with the faces of those villagers etched indelibly into our minds. When we told the story at home, we would weep. We longed to see them again. But many of them, we never would.

As I crisscrossed America, telling their story, money was given through GLBM to build them a simple church building and to transport Burmese Bibles to their village. Our GLBM national missionary stayed with them to disciple the new believers and the people were growing in the Lord. They had many questions. But they learned much, attending Bible studies, hearing the preaching of the Word of God, and memorizing Scripture. Many of the villagers could not read even their tribal mother tongue, much less Burmese. But some of the young people studied to learn the Burmese language so they could read their Bibles. I was very encouraged!

About six months later, in the middle of our summertime and their rainy Monsoon season, I was traveling, preaching, and raising funds for our Myanmar ministries. I received a message from Saya Thaung Lian in Yangon. It read, "Please call me as soon as possible!" Within minutes I logged into Facebook and called

Thaung on Messenger. What I heard went through me like a sizzling hot sword.

"BaGyi, Rohingya Muslims heard about our preacher in Nabugan village, that he built a church, and that most of the village has converted to Christianity. A large group of them came upriver, invaded homes, burned the church and much of the village. Our people are running for their lives. BaGyi, we have to help them!"

I asked Thaung, "What can we do?" He said, "BaGyi, I want to take some of our men and go find them, bring them back to Yangon, and let them be a part of our church family here." I said, "We will help!"

That was the year 2011. Five years later, as clashes between Buddhists and Muslims became more violent and made headlines, world media groups began to publish stories concerning the plight of the Rohingyas in Myanmar, whom they characterized as a persecuted people without a country. But, what about the natural-born Myanmar citizens whose communities were being molested by an ever-growing threat of hatred? Who are the Rohingya Muslim people, and where do they come from?

The Rohingya Muslims are clearly a Bangla people who have homesteaded in Rakhine State by the grace of the local and federal governments since before World War II. For most of that time, the great majority of Rohingya have peacefully co-existed with the Arakan (or Rakhine) people who are strong Buddhists. Some Myanmar people refer to the Rohingya as Bengalis and, as in Bangladesh where they are considered the "Samaritans" of society, there are those who have deep prejudice against them. This prejudice in Myanmar dates to incidents before World War II. But not all Buddhists in Myanmar have this attitude.

Tensions between the Buddhists and Muslims continued to grow steadily, fueling crazed furor and the indiscriminate killing of innocent men, women, and children on both sides. Entire villages were burned down. Police officers were shot, their bodies dragged through the streets and publicly displayed to bring fear and subjection. Once again, the attention of the whole world was on Myanmar, but not in a good way.

Seeing an opportunity to promote and establish an Islamic State inside Myanmar, radical Muslim groups, willing to scapegoat the innocent, channeled funds into Myanmar and established the Arakan Rohingya Salvation Army (ARSA). The Rohingya people were now organized as never before, but the Myanmar national army was already there and on guard along its western border with India and Bangladesh.

A third player in this complicated conflict is the Arakan Army, or the AA. Desiring independence in the same way as other tribal groups within Myanmar, the less powerful but cunning State forces, always looking for ways to thwart the power of the Burmese within their own "kingdom," have been preparing themselves for years.

Thus, the Myanmar national army now finds itself between ARSA's landmines on one side, the AA's line of resistance on the other, a formula for triangular implosion, with Rakhine's innocent civilians at risk and in harm's way.

Also, in harm's way, are innocent villagers across the Chin State border to the north. There, the AA has invaded communities like Paletwa and Sami, burning their villages, raping women and young girls, and killing anyone brave enough to stand against them. They seek to expand their territory to those areas they believe are historically theirs, and many Chin people have therefore fled northward. As the AA tries to annex this territory for themselves, the Burmese Army has sent fighter jets to bomb their positions, also killing those innocents they are hiding behind. In both States, the daily lives of many have been totally disrupted bringing fear, famine, and homelessness. Tens of thousands have been displaced, some running to makeshift refugee camps in Bangladesh. The Myanmar government has labeled both ARSA and the AA as terrorist organizations, a genuine threat, not only to the health and safety of all Myanmar people, but to Aung San Suu Kyi's young and fragile representative government.

Also, just last year, the Defense Ministers of ASEAN (Association of Southeast Asian Nations) met in Singapore to address the growing threat of Islamic terrorism within their countries. They suggested that Myanmar should ready itself for imminent attacks by radical Muslims who have declared jihad against the Burmese, desiring to capitalize on the Rakhine turmoil.

It seems that many are talking about Myanmar. But few know the truth, and fewer yet want to tell it. While traveling America, seeking missionary support for our works in Myanmar, I have been asked repeatedly about the Rohingya situation there. One afternoon I received a telephone call from an individual financial supporter who wanted to know the truth. But, when my testimony of personal experience began to contradict the story as presented by major networks, such as CNN and ABC, this person became disrespectful and abusive. This person stopped supporting GLBM because they believed the secular news media rather than the people of God on the ground inside Myanmar. That seems to be the current strategy, as these networks, as well as Washington politicians, deny the truth and, for whatever self-serving reason, promote a sympathy and tolerance for Muslims, even radical Islam, worldwide.

The United Nations and the United States Government has deemed the campaign of the Myanmar Army in Rakhine State as genocide against the Rohingya people. But not every Rohingya is innocent, and neither is every soldier in the Myanmar Army. The story of the Rohingyas in Myanmar is complicated, and no one knows the history and the growing problems of their presence in Rakhine State better than the Myanmar government and leaders. While they are trying to protect their own citizens and borders, they are now endeavoring to repatriate Myanmar-born Rohingya Muslims who wish to return. But the political landscape is dangerous. There are many victims. In my estimation, Aung San Suu Kyi and those of her representative government are victims too.

Still yet, a new dimension to the international crisis is taking shape, a movement born in the city of Mandalay, the cultural center of Buddhism in Myanmar. The concern of Burmese Buddhist leaders is so justified in their minds that some monks, who have traditionally and philosophically sought for peace, are rising to organize resistance, even financing a kind of "Burmese terrorism" and supporting the Myanmar Army Generals to push Muslims out altogether or kill them. A very outspoken monk named Ashin Wirathu, following the example of the radical Sri Lankin monk, Galagodaatte Gnanasara (co-founder of the Buddhist Power Force, or BBS, "Bodu Bala Sena"), has made a vow to "protect and defend [Buddhists] the world over" through his own 969 movement – so called for the attributes of the Buddha and his teachings. Because of threats and violence against both Muslims and Christians in Sri Lanka and Myanmar these men were sanctioned by the UN and Gnanasara was briefly jailed. At the same time, the complex and volatile situation in Old Burma continues to intensify on several other fronts: While the Myanmar Army is busy resisting the terrorist groups in Rakhine State, rebel armies from the Kachin, Shan, and Karen States have formed what they call the Northern Alliance and are fighting for their independence from Burmese rule. They believe they are being stripped of their freedoms, resources, and want to govern themselves.

Obviously, Myanmar is a powder keg with a short fuse ready to be lit. I recently sat down in Kentucky with U.S. Senator Mitch McConnell. I learned of his great interest and role in the freeing of political hostage Aung San Suu Kyi and the forming of her NLD movement and government for the past twenty years or more. He wrote about it in his autobiography, "The Long Game." I suggested to him that our window of opportunity to promote democracy and to present the Gospel of Christ in Myanmar is largely dependent upon the strength of that representative government and the resulting liberties we have already enjoyed because of it. If we dare not preach the Gospel in Myanmar now, we may never have another opportunity in this generation.

The cry for help reached Yangon and then to me in Horseheads, New York, a world away. How could this happen? Emotions flooded our souls as we read the words, "Four families have been killed." First, we wept. Then came anger. Then, again, we wept. Then we began to pray. I remember falling to my knees in our office with Matt Mayer, begging God to keep our people from harm. I authorized funds to be immediately wired to Saya Thaung in Yangon. He took some of his men to Rakhine State, traveling as fast as they could, up the same rivers that we traveled. We would pray and do whatever was needed to help our new brothers and sisters in Christ. But would Thaung and his men reach them in time?

The new Mru believers would move in the jungles every day, trying to keep ahead of those who still wanted to take their lives. The question in our minds was, "Who would find them first, the Rohingyas or Thaung Lian? And would Thaung and his men be safe? And what about tigers and snakes, dysentery and malaria? Would they be able to find food and water? Would the young children be alright?

Or would they die? In my mind, I saw the little girl with the beautiful smile. I begged God.

One week passed. I sent a message to Thaung Lian: "Have you found any of the survivors?" No answer came! In my mind, I recalled every bend of the river and the trees that lined the bank, the wide fields and the trail that led to the village just within the jungle border. I tried to block the thoughts of screaming children and wondered how long the men of the village fought for the lives of their families. It was difficult to sleep. But when I did, recurring nightmares would come with the sleep. I could see the lanes of the village and the faces of the inquisitive children. Again, and again, I would check my e-mail or Facebook Messenger. I wondered, "Which families? What children have been killed? Are there more who have died?" Then the thought came to me, "I took the Gospel of peace to them, and it killed them!"

Then one night a message came. "Carolyn! Carolyn! Come quickly!" I yelled. "They found them. They found them! They're alright!"

It took several weeks to find them. When they did, it took some persuading, but they agreed to return to Yangon with Saya Thaung. Again, their questions were many: How would they live? What would they eat? Are there animals to hunt in the city? Is Saya Thaung's church big enough for all to live in? Many of these people had never been outside their river valley, or as far as Mrauk U. They were not accustomed to the conveniences of modern society. Their lives would change completely.

Saya Thaung and his men brought one family out of the jungle at a time to a safe house in Mrauk U. When all were assembled, they rejoiced together and waited for a bus that would carry them to the big city. But none of the Mru knew how far that was. In the dry season, the ride would normally take more than thirty hours. But, during rainy season it would take much longer. Ridges of mountains and impassible rivers were between them and Yangon. More than once their bus would get stuck along a mountain road in mud above the axles. That same bus would become an ATV and ford rivers and streams like a boat.

When they finally arrived in Yangon, the people of Saya Thaung's church welcomed them with open arms, cooking, giving clothes, and providing temporary shelters and bedding. GLBM sent more funds to secure a field and build a long line of bamboo homes on the edge of the city near Thaung's church. They helped them find jobs. Saya Thaung put some of them to work. The children were weaved into the local Burmese school system.

I look back now and wonder if we did right or made many mistakes. We did what we knew to do from the Scriptures. It was an experiment in missions, an act of faith at best. What else could we do? Taking the Gospel to those who have never heard is the work of God. These people were both our children in the faith and our friends in Christ. They followed us as we followed Him.

"And ye became followers of us, and of the Lord, having received the word in much affliction, with joy of theHoly Ghost."

…the Apostle Paul to the Thessalonians (1 Thess. 1:6)

Now, years later, some of those same Mru children are studying in our Bible college and preparing their lives toserve the Lord. They are teaching other children in the surrounding communities. They are singing in the college chorales – not only in Burmese, but also in English – songs like, "Rock of Ages, cleft for me. Let me hide myself in Thee." Some will graduate this coming year, and we will send them out to reach others who have never heard that "Jesus saves; Jesus saves!" But some have already returned to Rakhine State. They have moved back to their own river valley, where the war still rages, to preach the love of God in Christ Jesus to the very ones who persecuted them.

BaGyi Bob and Matt Mayer with Mru Village children

Mru greeting party from the village

Matt Mayer with national missionaries

CHAPTER FOUR

Finding Maitreya at Last
or The 112 Dear Old Man

"With my soul have I desired thee in the night; yea,
with my spirit within me will I seek thee early: for when thy judgments are in the
earth, the inhabitants of the world will learn righteousness."
Isaiah 26:9

Boe Thail stood in the doorway of his home and watched the Japanese soldiers march down the street of his village. Like many others in his community, he had heard of whole villages being massacred and burned to the ground. There was much fear everywhere. Some of his neighbors had already fled their homeland in one of the previous groups of refugees, leaving everything behind and heading for the protection of British-controlled India. Many had died along the way. A Boe Thail decided to stay in Mudon with his family. But the rumors of death and destruction, horror stories, were increasing.

The Japanese had invaded Burma several years earlier to stop the flow of supplies to Chiang Kai-shek's resistance fighters in China, and to create a doorway for spreading their empire into British-occupied India. When Allied supplies could no longer travel to Yunnan along the Burma Road in the south, the Allies built the Ledo Road in the north to keep the Chinese strong. But, as the British retreated from Rangoon, Burma's largest city and capital fell to the Imperial Japanese Army almost immediately. Together with their Thai allies, the Japanese were moving across the Golden Land in a clockwise wave that threatened the stability of all Asia.

Working their way across the Ayeyarwady Delta to the Bay of Bengal, the Japanese entered what is now known as Rakhine State and decided to make an example of the inhabitants there. The Arakan Buddhists and the Rohingya Muslims were fighting among themselves too much to resist the warriors of the Rising Sun. Those who would not submit were slaughtered mercilessly and buried in mass graves.

As the Japanese turned northwest, up the Chindwin River and across the mountains of Chin State, they met the strong resistance of reorganized British forces, reinforced by Indian Gurkhas and African colonials. The Americans and

Australians were coming by sea and the combined Allied armies forced the Japanese Commands southward, back into the hills of the Pegu Yoma or the current Bago province, just north of Mon State. As World War II was being initiated in Europe, Burma's patriot, General Aung San, had just returned from studying warfare in Japanese schools, intent on organizing an independence movement against the British. But, in March of 1945, when it became obvious that the Japanese were to be feared more than the British, he organized the National Burmese Army to fight alongside the Allies, creating a new national thirst for autonomy.

A Boe Thail had been taken from home and forced into slave labor to build the Japanese "Death Railway," a link for transporting prisoners and supplies between Bangkok and Rangoon. Thousands died from the heat, bugs and snakes, various diseases, rockslides in the mountains, and just utter exhaustion. Finally, the railway was destroyed by Allied bombers and A Boe Thail was permitted to go home. Hindered by monsoon rains, famine, disease, Burman guerillas, and Allied paratroopers, the Japanese were increasingly surrounded. The Emperor's finest were losing confidence, and anxiety was mounting, even among the officers.

It was now the first week of July 1945 – just one month prior to the Americans' dropping of the atomic bombs on Hiroshima and Nagasaki. Reports from Japan were horrifying and discouraging. Denying defeat and becoming increasingly angry, Japanese Major General Seiei Yamamoto, Chief of Staff of the 33rd Army, ordered the 215th Regiment of his 3rd Battalian to sweep the villages for guerillas who were said to be assisting Allied paratroopers. When they entered the Mon village of Kalagong, along the Gyaing River and just north of Malawmyine, they herded the inhabitants into a stockade and interrogated everyone. Women and children were beaten and raped. When no information was revealed, orders came from the Malawmyine-based Kempeitai, the secret police of the Imperial Japanese Army, to kill everyone and burn the village down. Kalagong's inhabitants – men, women, and children – were taken in small groups, blindfolded, bayoneted, and their bodies dumped into area wells. More than 600 people were slaughtered in just a few hours. History records it as the horrific Kalagong Massacre.

A Boe Thail had been to the temple early that morning. He enjoyed leaving the house in time to see the sun come over the mountains to the northeast. As the calendar year progressed, the sun rose more and more to the northeast and A Boe Thail quite accurately knew the calendar date by looking to see at what point the sun would rise over the Karen State mountain ridges to the East. After prayers, he sat with his monk friend and talked about better times. He talked about the Maitreya, the Savior-God, or Enlightened One, who would follow Guatama, the Buddha. "He must come soon! No?"

The monk smiled and, with a subdued chuckle, said "Not many people believe that anymore." A Boe Thail asked, "But, why?"

The monk lit a cigar and answered, "So long! It's been so long!"

A Boe Thail stood to his feet and beat his chest. He said, "But Gautama promised! As for me, I will still believe!"

Many Burmese people had lost hope in a coming Savior. Gautama, that Indian Prince who shunned royalty and riches to seek the Great Peace, lay dying and his followers said, "When you pass, we will make a statue and worship it!" But Gautama refused their worship. In the Buddhist scriptures, Guatama wrote, "I cannot help you. But there is one coming after me who will help you. And His name shall be Maitreya," or Savior-Messiah.

A Boe Thail wanted to believe it. But as the beleaguered invaders marched through his village again, rifles in their hands and shining swords on their hips, A Boe Thail watched nervously and wondered if he and his family would be the next to die. And, if he lived, would he live long enough to see the coming of the Maitreya?

I was told that I would never be able to preach the Gospel in Mon State. They said that the Buddhism there was just too strong. Matter of fact, when I first traveled to Myanmar, it was closed to foreigners by the government. Myanmar was still at that time run by a military dictatorship, and there were many provinces that were off-limits to foreigners. There were some locations that were unsafe because local or State militias were still fighting for independence from the Burmese military government.

But from that very first visit to Myanmar, I had an unexplainable craving to go to Mon State. It is not that I had knowledge of the Mon tribal people or of a particular tourist destination there. Bordered by the mountains of Karen State to the East and the beaches of the Andaman Sea on the West, it is known for such sites as the world's largest reclining Buddha, Kyaiktiyo Pagoda, and the Thanbyuzayat WWII Cemetery. It was in the Mon city of Malawmyine that Missionary Adoniram Judson built two churches and buried his first wife, a son, and two grandchildren. I felt compelled to go there. There was a mystery about it for me. Several people had warned me, saying "If they don't kill you, they will beat you and expel you from their State." You see, the Mon have been among the strongest Buddhists in Myanmar and are credited as being the ones who originally introduced Buddhism to Old Burma thousands of years ago.

The Mon are the most Thai-like of the Myanmar people groups. Matter of fact, the King and current royal family in Thailand is of Mon ancestry. With their capital at Pegu, or what is now known as Bago, the Mon people built the Hanthawaddy Kingdom, and they ruled and controlled all of southern, or "Lower Burma," and much of Thailand, or old Siam, for hundreds of years. In the north near Mandalay, King Tabinshwehti inherited the Burmese throne in the year 1530 at 14 years of age. He took the elder sister of his friend, Ye Htut, as one of his Queens, and gave titles and powerful positions to all his confidants. Ye Htut became the King's right-hand man and proved, not only his strong character and loyalty but, his consistently fearless gallantry in every conflict and battle.

Tabinshwehti's kingdom, the Toungoo Dynasty, already had great strength, but it was locked between other rival kingdoms – the strong Shan Confederation farther north, the Prome kingdom to the West – a Shan ally, and the powerful Hanthawaddy (or Mon) kingdom to the south. When suddenly the Shan conquered their Prome allies, Tabinshwehti and Ye Htut became nervous and decided that they needed to act before getting swallowed up by their enemies. Ye Htut was not royalty, but the common son of a Burmese farmer. Even though he and the young King were close, their relationship was severely tested when Ye Htut's secret relationship with Tabinshwehti's sister was discovered. According to Burmese law and custom, it was an act of treason for a commoner to be romantically involved with royalty, punishable only by death. Even though Ye Htut's friends suggested mutiny, he submitted and presented himself to the King and his Court for judgment.

After long deliberations with his cabinet of ministers, King Tabinshwehti gave his sister in marriage to his friend, made him a Prince, and changed his name to Kyawhtin Nawrahta. This decision made the new prince unquestionably loyal and proved to be one of the best things Tabinshwehti ever did for his kingdom. Following the defeat of the Arakanese kingdom along the Bay of Bengal, King Tabinshwehti was so grateful to his brother-in-law that he made him heir-apparent to the Burmese throne.

Kyawhtin Nawrahta went on to lead his King's army to many victories. But even though the Mon King was weak, the Hanthawaddy kingdom to the south was richer and their fortifications were strong. They had superior foreign weapons, several different seaports, and after many attempts to break down their defences, the Toungoo armies retreated in defeat.

Finally, in 1538, Kyawhtin Nawrahta distinguished himself again by leading his light forces to an amazing victory over the vastly larger and better equipped Hanthawaddy army in the Battle of Naungyo in the Ayeyarwady River Delta. Again, the King was so delighted that he changed Kyawhtin Nawrahta's name, this time to Bayinnaung, or "The King's Elder Brother." In 1541 "General Bayinnaung" led his army to another decisive victory and took control of the entire Hanthawaddy Kingdom, their manpower, Portuguese weapons, and maritime wealth. Bayinnaung soon became King, building the largest kingdom that Southeast Asia has ever known, and the Mon people were eventually restricted to their own province.

More than 470 years later, I was preaching in Fort Wayne, Indiana. There are many Myanmar refugees and immigrants in Fort Wayne, and I did not have to search long to find them. I met a family who invited me to their home. When I arrived, I was delighted to meet a man who was introduced to me as the Vice President of Mon State. He said to me, "If you would like to preach the Gospel in Mon State, I will send a car to pick you up in Yangon [an eight-hour drive] that will bring you down to us." I was thrilled, but I never had peace from the Lord about it.

One year later I was preaching in Iowa and I met Kyaw Kyaw Aung and his wife, Say, who were Myanmar refugees. They had been in America five years and had become U.S. citizens, taking the names "Peter and Ruth Judson." They were vibrant Christians, powerful soul winners, and Peter was well-trained in the Word of God. Peter was one of the very first converts from his own people group, the Pa-O tribe. Instantly, the Holy Ghost showed me that meeting them was no accident. I said to Peter, "Myanmar is different now. You should go back, plant a church, and preach the Gospel to your own people." Peter instantly rejected the idea, stating that it was his dream to come to America and needed to continue his theological studies. I argued that he was already trained and an effective man of God. But he would not even consider the idea of returning to Myanmar.

One year later Peter called me "BaGyi Bob"; this is Peter Judson. I love America. It was my dream to come to America. But God will not let me stay here. Will you help me go back to Myanmar and plant a church?" I said, "Where?" He said, "Malawmyine, the capital city of Mon State."

I flew to Des Moines, rented a U-Haul truck, and helped move Peter and his family to New York State. They joined our church, the home-base of GLBM; Peter got a job and saved money. It was a two-year process to get passports and visas for the whole family. It required much patience and tenacity. The process was almost traumatic at times. But after two years, with all the paperwork in hand, our church sent them back to Myanmar to serve the Lord and win their own people to Christ.

After landing in Yangon, the Judsons traveled quickly to Malawmyine. They were back in Myanmar just two days, even before they rented a home, when they started their congregation with a dozen new converts. Almost every week souls were saved and baptized. Our church bought for them a Hyundai diesel truck to use as a personal vehicle and as a Sunday School bus. They now make seven to ten trips every Sunday to transport people who want to know about Jesus Christ.

In January of 2017, with the help of Evangelist Boyd Collins from Summersville, West Virginia and Ken Young from Marion, North Carolina, we held a week-long, open air evangelistic meeting in downtown Malawmyine and saw hundreds of Mon people turn to Christ for Bible salvation. Eight months later, I returned there with a team of four American teenagers. We visited a Mon English School. It was not a church-related school. Run by an NGO to help Myanmar young people learn English to use in business, there was 80 college- aged students and most of them lived on the small campus.

When we arrived at the school, the administrator was excited to have Americans visit and we sat around talking to the students for hours. Each of us gave our testimonies and explained the Gospel and the differences in belief between Christianity and Buddhism. The young people listened carefully to every word and we gave them Bibles and Gospel tracts.

I said to the administrator, "Can I buy ice cream for all your students?" He did not immediately understand, but when I made it clear that I wanted to take everyone to a restaurant and buy ice cream, he answered with a big smile, "Of course!"

We made seven trips in Peter's truck, carrying the entire student body to a restaurant where I bought ice cream and soda for everyone. The entire cost was approximately $28.00, and we had an amazing time of fellowship with the young people, laughing and quizzing each other about our different customs and culture. We went back to the school and taught the young people how to throw a frisbee. They enjoyed it so much that we left two frisbees at the school so that they could practice for our next visit. We formed relationships with those young people, and some still communicate with us, using Facebook Messenger.

Two months after returning to America, I received a message from a young lady who lived in the village of Mudon, approximately 20 miles south of Malawmyine. She had also been a student at the English school but was not there when we visited. One week before we arrived in Malawmyine, her mother had called her home to work for her family who was having financial difficulties.

She contacted me almost every day and we formed a friendship that went beyond Facebook. As I chatted with this Mon-tribe girl who was wonderfully sweet and warm, I introduced her to my wife and our team members. Over the next few months, I explained the Gospel many times, inviting her to believe in my Saviour. She said, "I believe in this Saviour, BaGyi! But my family is Buddhist. It is our culture, and I cannot change."

As I got to know this young lady more and more, I came to realize that I had her confused with someone else whom I had met at the English school. I finally asked her how she came to know about me. She told me that another young lady, a close friend who was also a student at the English school, met us and gave her my prayer card. I was amazed!

For the next year we became close like family. She introduced me to her parents and five other sisters. As I prepared for my next visit to Myanmar, they insisted that I come to their house in Mudon.

On August 1, 2018 GLBM's Timothy Davis and I flew from John F. Kennedy International Airport in New York City to Yangon, Myanmar via Abu Dhabi aboard Etihad Airways. We spent several days in Yangon Division, visiting some of our pastors and orphans, and then got ready for our eight-hour bus ride to Malawmyine.

But the month of August is in the height of the Myanmar rainy season, and the monsoon torrential rains and flooding had made every bridge on the road to Malawmyine impassable. There is one flight from Yangon to Malawmyine each week. When we purchased our tickets for the short 40-minute trip, we learned that they were the last two remaining seats.

Black clouds and sheets of driving rain covered the Yangon Airport and made our departure quite interesting. And as we rose above the clouds and leveled off at a comfortable cruising altitude on a heading of approximately 120 degrees SE, the Holy Ghost reminded me that, not only had my prayers been answered but, God had fulfilled my dream and gone exceedingly above and beyond what I asked or anticipated.

Descending below the clouds and approaching the Malawmyine airport, my excitement reached its fever point. As we disembarked from the aircraft at the Malawmyine Airport, we could see four of the six Mudon sisters jumping up and down with excitement on the other side of a chain link fence. They had come a long way to meet us at the airport and, as we collected our luggage and departed the airport lobby, they were there to greet us with many hugs and tears.

Peter Judson and his family were also there with their truck to take us to our hotel. The sisters had come by taxi. Peter asked, "Where do you want to go first, BaGyi?" I motioned for the girls to hop in with us and then answered, "We need to drop our bags at the hotel, and then I want to go straight to Mudon village."

We had a grand reunion at our hotel in Malawmyine. The staff, who are also our Friends on Facebook, greeted us, calling out "Welcome Home, BaGyi!" I wanted to spend time with all of them, but I was anxious to get to Mudon village and meet the rest of the sister's family.

I had never been south of Malawmyine and, even though it was pouring down rain, the short journey brought all new sights like a seven-story Buddha and vast rubber tree plantations. There was multiple police stations, checkpoints, and tolls, as well as the SE Myanmar Army post that stretched for miles on both sides of the road.

Mudon is a small city of approximately 52,000 people, mostly of the Mon tribe, but also inhabited by ethnic Burmese, a few Chinese, Indians, and Karen-tribe people. It lies between the Karen State mountains to the East and the Gulf of Martaban to the West. People work in small retail shops, the rubber industry, and farming. But their lives are wrapped around Buddhism. The main roads are "paved," but the residential streets are still dirt. Like the rest of Myanmar, most people ride bicycles, motor scooters, and think of cars as luxuries. Of course, there are the usual horse-drawn carriages and carts.

The girls directed us through town, past a parade of curious onlookers, waving and shouting welcomes. We parked in front of their house, and before we could even get out of the truck, the girl's parents, cousins, and neighbors came running to us with umbrellas to help us maneuver through the mud. Their house was built of stucco-covered concrete block with a large front porch and a carport, much like many Western homes and unlike most of Myanmar. Inside was a large front room, connected by a hallway to a large kitchen area in the back, with two small bedrooms and an inside bath. The floors were solid wood and sealed with shiny polyurethane. There was a teakwood furniture set to sit on, and a circular eating table, eighteen inches high, on which to eat. On one wall was a set of cabinets under a line of family photos. On another wall was the family's Buddhist prayer shrine with a formation of small golden idols and candles.

We spent the next three days just sitting around talking, laughing, and getting to know each other. I know that some people might wonder what they wanted from us. That question went through my mind as well, and in those few days I discovered some of their needs. I offered to help financially but they would not take my money.

It was not long before I felt the liberty to talk to them about Christ. The father and I sat together on the front porch, and I said, "I want to tell you the reason I come to Myanmar." He smiled and nodded in agreement.

I said, "The whole world thinks that America is a Christian nation. No?"

Again, he nodded and said, "Yes! America, Christian."

I continued, "A true Christian is someone who believes that Jesus Christ is the eternal God, the Creator of heaven and earth. A true Christian believes that Jesus Christ died to pay for our sin and to set us free from it. A true Christian believes that Jesus Christ is the only true Saviour, that He died, rose from the grave, and is coming again. A true Christian is someone who has acknowledged and confessed their sin and need of a Saviour and turned to Him for salvation and eternal life. I was saved when I was thirteen years old and asked Him to forgive me and to come into my heart." I continued, "In Myanmar, you have many Buddhists, no?"

He said, "Yes, of course."

I said, "But, in Myanmar you have those who are Buddhist by faith – they know and believe what the Buddhist scriptures teach. Then there are those who are only Buddhist because it is their culture. Which, sir, are you?"

The father hung his head for a moment and then acknowledged, "I think, sir, we are more Buddhist by culture."

"Sir, this is the reason I come to Myanmar – to tell people about the Saviour. Sir, I would never disrespect you or your family, but I would like Saya Peter to tell you from the Christian Scriptures how to know Christ. Would that be okay?" With a gracious smile, he agreed.

That afternoon, as they listened carefully, concentrating on every word, the family bowed their heads and prayed with us to receive Jesus Christ as their personal Savior.

Now, again, I can imagine that there would be some reading this who might wonder if they really understood, or were they praying with us just to be respectful or polite? Again, I must admit that the same thought crossed my mind.

But the next day, we returned and presented them with Burmese Bibles. One of the sisters, whom I call "Khinny," asked, "BaGyi, would you like to meet a 112-year-old man?" I paused for a moment because of my astonishment, and finally answered, "Yes, of course!" I asked, "Khinny, why do you want me to meet this old man?" She answered, "He is the most respected man in our village. Does he not need a Saviour also?"

The man lived on the same street and on the same side of the street, just a few blocks away. It was raining hard and the mud was thick, making a suction sound with every step we took. The sisters walked with us to his house, and even though umbrellas did not do much good in keeping us dry, they did their best to hold them over our heads. When we arrived, we were immediately invited inside. Taking our shoes off at the door, we climbed the wooden steps and entered the room where the man's family was helping him into a chair. He looked his age indeed and it appeared that he had trouble even holding his head up. They said, "Our father's name is A Boe Thail."

Peter Judson, Tim Davis, and I sat on the floor in front of him and introduced ourselves. He said that he was pleased to meet us, but I think we were the more impressed. We asked him some simple questions about his life, and I inquired if he had always lived in Mudon. He said that he had.

Then he began talking about World War II and how the Japanese soldiers marched through his village during World War II. It was a 73-year-old memory, but he described their uniforms, their rifles, and the swords on their sides in vivid detail. As a younger man he worked in the nearby rubber tree plantations. He was used to the hot Asian sun and his physical strength and work ethic helped him survive his ordeal with the Death Railway. He witnessed firsthand the ruthlessness of the Japanese as many workers dropped from complete exhaustion and were shot where they fell.

As any faithful Buddhist, A Boe Thail had humbly served the temple and the monks all his life. He was not merely a cultural Buddhist. He had spent his long-life studying and believing. He knew about suffering. He had seen it all around him. But he had not given up hope in the coming of Maitreya.

Peter Judson was sitting directly in front of him. As he spoke of Christ and read some Scriptures from the Burmese Bible, A Boe Thail raised his head and opened his eyes wide. He looked squarely at Peter and asked, "This is the One whom Gautama said would come, no?" Peter said, "Yes!" A Boe Thail said, "I have never heard of Christ or this 'Gospel.' But I have waited my whole life to hear it. This Jesus! This is the One who was promised to come! He is Maitreya! No?" Peter said, "Yes! Yes!" I grabbed A Boe Thail's hand and, looking into his eyes, smiled affirmation. I could not control my emotions, and tears began to drip from my face on to the floor. A sudden silence pervaded the room.

Khinny was sitting on A Boe Thail's right side with her hand on his arm throughout our Gospel presentation. He looked up at her. Her loving smile nodded approval and indicated her deep burden that he would understand and come to faith in this Jesus who was now her Savior.

Out of the silence, A Boe Thail said, "I believe this! I put all my faith in this Savior. Please tell me what I should do."

Peter reached out to take his hand. I placed my hand on his shoulder. With my other hand, I reached out for Khinny whose smile was now glistening with tears like sprinkles of rain out of a sun-sprayed sky.

Sitting there among his own family, between us and the sisters, A Boe Thail bowed his head, confessed his need for a Savior, and asked Jesus Christ to be his personal Maitreya.

Mudon Mon Family praying to receive Christ

Khinny excited to see A Boe Thail believe in Jesus Christ

Death Railway

Japanese soldiers marching through Burma

CHAPTER FIVE

Who Can Be Saved?

"…and everything shall live whither the river cometh."
Ezekiel 47:9

I was in Thailand with Dr. Jim Fish, the founding pastor of the Kingsway Baptist Church in Mickleton, New Jersey, USA. He and I had been there for two weeks already. Doc Fish has a wonderful spirit, an infectious exuberance about him, especially regarding the work of God. A wonderful accompanist on the piano, he and I enjoyed, not only preaching, but singing together as well. He was the first American to travel to Asia with me, and his experience so far had been full of adventure. We had visited several churches and missions in and around the city of Mae Sot, a large city along the Moei River that forms the border with Old Burma. There, on the Thai side, Myanmar people number more than 500,000 from various ethnicities. The King's Siamese are not fond of any of them.

There is a long history of tensions between the people of Old Burma and Siam, or modern-day Thailand. In the years 1765-1767 the Burmese conquered and ruled most of Thailand until forced to return home to thwart a Chinese invasion of their own land. Tensions and mistrust have lived on ever since. While Thailand succeeded in their pursuit of economic and political development, Myanmar's aspirations failed. Today, many Thai consider the Burmese as poor, uneducated and, sometimes, mere merchandise.

Our host pastor transported us to several different villages where we preached the Word of God, distributed Scriptures, and helped the congregations financially with numerous projects. At that time, Myanmar was still governed by a military dictatorship and there were nine refugee camps in Thailand where families fled, living primitively without electricity or running water. Approaching these camps by vehicle, there were always military and police checkpoints designed to keep the Myanmar refugees from infiltrating into the rest of Thailand. One could see hundreds, sometimes thousands, of bamboo or rough-cut wooden huts built of stilts, nestled into the crevices of mountain ridges. I had previously visited most of these camps, but on this trip, Dr. Fish and I preached in the largest camp, called Mae La. Comprised of 538 acres with more than 50,000 people, the inhabitants waited for permission to immigrate to another country. Most wanted to go to America. And some had been waiting for twenty years or more. So, while waiting within these camps, they built schools, stores, churches, and temples. Children played in the lanes outside their houses as in any neighborhood. Some camps had central meeting areas where people would gather to watch TV. There were no Lazy Boy recliners or plush leather sofas, just backless wooden benches. No popcorn, peanuts, or candy – people were just satisfied to watch an old flick or episode of Hogan's Heroes or the Andy Griffith Show. There was little crime. People lived too closely, and they were too busy surviving to have the luxury of misbehaving. But there were small internet cafes where people with some source of income could access e-mail or world news.

We were invited to preach at the Truth Baptist Church inside Mae La camp. I had been there before and met the founder-pastor. He had already been in the camp more than twelve years, and I asked him how long he would stay and when he would go to America. He replied, "I will go after all my people have gone; I will be the last to leave!"

As usual, when we arrived, the people prepared and served us food. I felt badly when I learned that many families had donated food for the occasion, and that we were eating in one sitting what they would consume in a week. Yet, they were overjoyed to provide for us. So, we did our best for them, in eating everything we were served, and we did our best in ministering to them. We were thrilled when dozens responded to our preaching and trusted Christ as their Saviour.

But our plan was to spend the last two weeks of our trip inside Myanmar. We were not allowed to enter the country at the border crossing. The "Friendship Bridge" was closed and military guard posts with machine guns were positioned at the river's edge. So, we traveled by car back to Bangkok, a seven-hour ride over the Dawna mountain range, south along Thailand highways No. 1 and No. 32, through Kamphaeng Phet, Nakhon Sawan, Phra Nakhone Si Ayutthaya, and Pathum Thani. It seemed like a long, painful journey, but not to be compared with traveling most roads in Old Burma.

Bangkok is a sprawling city, similar in population to New York City but, with a far greater land area. Even though the world has formally recognized the city's name as Bangkok by royal decree, no Thai national would call it that unless speaking to foreigners. In their mind it is "Krung Phet," or "City of Angels." Thailand, even with its crime and sex industry, is known for its hospitality and graciousness, a relatively safe country to visit.

Once in Bangkok, we stayed with a Filipino missionary overnight, and the next morning made our way through challenging traffic to Suvarnabhumi, or "Golden Land" International Airport. Going straight to the Air Asia counter, we checked our bags and casually strolled to our Gate. One always needs to be early at Suvarnabhumi, as at New York, Dubai, Tokyo, Seoul, or Beijing. There are long lines, and the walking distance between check- in and boarding Gates can tax any weary traveler.

Unlike my first visit to Myanmar, I knew what to expect. But it was all new to Jim Fish. We were both excited, and he was full of questions. As we boarded our plane, a narrow-body Airbus a320, his first observation was like mine several years earlier: there were many saffron-robed, shaved-headed Buddhist monks on board. I think he may have been even more uncomfortable than I was on my first visit to Myanmar. But at that time, I was alone. Brother Fish would feel more uncomfortable as our trip progressed. It was evening, almost dark, when we landed in Yangon. The airport, unlike now, was adequate but still primitive by international standards. In many ways, for Jim Fish, his true adventure was about to begin.

To most Westerners, Asians look alike. But for those of us who have come to know the people, there are marked differences in the appearance of facial structure and dress. And I am not talking about the difference between Chinese, Thai, and Burmese. But rather, I see the differences between Myanmar people groups, even multiple tribes within a single State. I have come to recognize the characteristic facial features of Karen versus Chin, versus Kachin, versus Lisu, versus Nung Rawang, versus Mon, and so forth. As I pointed out the differences to Pastor Fish, I think he saw them too. Maybe!

As we disembarked the plane and passed through the ramp to the Gate, Pastor Fish encountered faces he had never seen before. His first question was the same as people all over America ask me: "What is the white stuff on their faces?" He was talking about "Thanaka," the cream that comes from the bark of the large Limonia Acidissima, or Wood Apple tree, indigenous to Southeast Asia. The tree grows to 30 feet tall, has a rough bark, and leaves that have a citrus scent when crushed. The tree does not grow apples as Westerners think of, but a hard-shell berry containing considerable amounts of protein, iron, calcium, as well as Vitamins B and C. The cream has amazing antioxidant, antibacterial, anti-inflammatory, and moisturizing properties. The use of it on the skin, however, is peculiar to the Myanmar people, particularly women and children, who use it as makeup and for the wonderful cooling sensation that is gives the skin in the heat and humidity of the Golden Land.

We made our way from the plane, down a long hallway, to the Immigration counters, and waited in line. Back then, the Immigration Officers were all military. Armed guards, bearing automatic rifles, were everywhere, and it was a bit intimidating. In comparison with Thailand, there was a much different spirit in Myanmar, especially among government or military personnel.

I had told Pastor Fish to simply hand the Officer his passport and visa, along with his Visitor's information form, and to smile but say nothing. He asked me, "What is that Burmese word for Hello? Yeah, that Minga...something?" I answered, "Mingalabar! That is Ming...a...la...bah!"

When you are entering Myanmar, an officially Buddhist country, every visitor must fill out an Immigration form and sign a statement, agreeing not to corrupt the morals of Myanmar nationals. You must know Jim Fish to realize that me telling him not to talk to the Officers was an exercise in shear futility. He talks, jokes, and laughs with everyone he meets, a trait that endears him to all. But the more he tried to communicate, the more confused they both became. The officer kept pointing to the small, taped square on the floor where Jim was supposed to stand for the camera taking his photograph. Once we collected our luggage at Baggage Claim, we still had to pass through Customs. And that was another adventure.

One of our Myanmar pastors was waiting with a taxi to take us through the city to our hotel. I had made reservations at the Queen's Park Hotel, on the southeast side of Yangon. The airport is on the extreme north side.

When I first visited Myanmar and the city of Yangon, cars and trucks seemed extremely old. There were many old Russian sedans being used as taxis. They were larger than your average Japanese car, but noisier. I have ridden in many. There were some very tiny, matchbox-like, Mazda cars and trucks that looked like they were older than me. It was doubtful to me if any American would fit in one. On my first journey across the Burmese countryside, I traveled in a 1972 Toyota Corolla with natural air-conditioning between your legs, coming from the floor between your feet. You could see through the holes in the floorboard to the road below, and dust rushed up in your face. So, Pastor Fish's first car ride in Myanmar, although in the city, was another introduction to Old Burma. Once checked into our hotel, as I have described in other stories, he had to get used to the Myanmar beds, the spicy Burmese foods, the bathroom facilities, the lack of toilet paper, the language, and customs, what to do, and what definitely not to do. But he did very well.

Our first church service in Myanmar was with Pastor Thaung Lian and the Bethany Baptist Church, located in Dagon Saikkan, a southeast township of Yangon Division. At that time, the church was meeting in a small rented, two-story, wooden building with a dirt floor, and Thaung and his family lived upstairs. The congregation met on the ground floor and sat on rows of homemade benches. That Sunday morning, the building was packed with people. I had visited them before but was unaware of the extent of persecution they had endured, and how recently it had occurred. They had been stoned many times. And just recently, a mob, led by the Chief of Police, or "Village Chairman," had rained stones on the tin roof of the building while Pastor Thaung was preaching.

Sometimes they would throw stones at the people who were coming and going to services, and the members would hide by the corners of the house. Thaung Lian himself had been arrested several times, and the Chief had beaten him with steel rods. Thaung cried out and begged him to stop. Despite the persecution, they never quit holding services and worshipping the Lord. Instead, they prayed for the Chief and their neighbors.

Thaung Lian came from high in the Chin State mountains. He and his father worked together, collecting and selling precious gems from Mogok, in the Valley of Rubies, located in the Mandalay Region. But, as Thaung saw the hearts of his countrymen, the burden for their souls became stronger than his desire to make money. By faith he traveled to Manila and enrolled in a Philippines Bible college. After four years of school, despite knowing the persecution he would face at home, he journeyed back to Myanmar, found a bride, and started his church in a growing Buddhist community.

The people in Thaung's church were mostly his own converts. He had visited every family in the community and explained the Gospel of Christ clearly. He knew the people who were hurling the stones. They knew him. Thaung and his wife had an infant son, and they were afraid for him. And when the Chief came, leading the mob, Thaung was scared just like the rest of his people. His wife would cry, and he would hold her at night, trying to explain what he could see God doing through it all. Even though the hatred of the Chief was obvious, Thaung had an unquenchable burden for his soul and he led his church to pray and fast for him.

Following some of the most intense persecution, the Chief became ill and was hospitalized. Thaung visited the Chief at his bedside, and the community leader yelled, "Go away! Why do you come here? Do you want to hurt me?" Thaung assured the man of his best intentions and said, "I love you! I want to bless you." The astonished Chief said, "How can you love me? I stone you. I beat you. And you love me? How can this be?"

Thaung returned to his bedside several times and took food to his family. Finally, when the Chief was under much conviction, Thaung visited him again. The Chief said, "How can you love me and my family like this? What is this that you have in you, that I do not have in me?" That day, Pastor Thaung led the Chief to Christ, and he became a member of Thaung Lian's church and one of the strongest witnesses to the grace of God.

As we met that Sunday morning, Pastor Jim Fish played the piano, and I sang. Each of us then preached. I mean, we both preached long messages. You should understand that preaching with an interpreter makes the message twice as long, and Baptist preachers are often long-winded anyway. When we were finished, the people asked us, "Is that all?" You see? Many Americans go to church; but Myanmar believers live for church.

When visitors come to Myanmar with us for the first time, I take them to Shwe Dagon Pagoda. Built in the 6th century A.D., it is one of the wonders of the world. Standing upwards to a height of 326 feet, shaped like a Hershey Kiss, and covered in genuine gold plates, it is the most sacred temple in Myanmar, and a kind of Mecca to Buddhists worldwide. Constructed with multiple levels and an umbrella of jewels at the top containing 5,448 diamonds and 2,317 rubies, it is crowned with a 76-carat diamond. Visitors can only go so far. Only monks and certain privileged males can access the restricted areas closest to the temple's entrance where supposed relics of the four Buddhas are stored and preserved.

Shwe Dagon Zedi Daw, as it is officially named, sits on Singuttara Hill in the center of Yangon, or Old Rangoon, dominating the city skyline. The 19th century missionary, Adoniram Judson, said that in his time it could be seen from anywhere in Rangoon. Located on 536 park-like acres with ten thousand stupas, or small temples, surrounding it, visitors pass the giant guardian leogryphs and walk hundreds of steps barefoot to reverently approach it.

Many times, I have taken American Christians to Shwe Dagon and watched them weep, tears running down their face, as they viewed those who kneel and pray before idols and images of manmade gods. When I first visited Shwe Dagon I thought of the Apostle Paul, in the seventeenth chapter of the book of Acts, as he stood in the Areopagus of Mars Hill and noted a statue with a name tag that read, "TO THE UNKNOWN GOD." He addressed the Greek worshippers there and exclaimed, "Whom therefore ye ignorantly worship, him declare I unto you." Many Burmese people are sincere and faithful in their religion, and they have the best of intentions. But as is the case of many Americans who simply go to church without a genuine faith in the shed blood and sacrifice of Christ, a great number of Myanmar people practice their religion simply because they were born Buddhist. It is their culture and way of life. They pray, meditate, hang flowers, light candles, pour water over the heads of god-like statues, seeking the "Great Peace" and the "Enlightenment" that leads to the cessation of their cycles of life, or reincarnations, and their apparent never-ending suffering. But many have no peace. It has become clear that many today are searching for truth.

Any serious Christian will feel a very oppressive spirit at Shwe Dagon, or any other temple with manmade images of false gods. Pastor Fish did not want to go. I had to talk him into it. But I explained that no one can really understand the predominance of Buddhism in Myanmar culture without visiting Shwe Dagon. He reluctantly agreed to a short visit.

We hailed a taxi from our hotel and the driver dropped us in front of the big guardian lions that keep watch at the entrance to the temple. We entered the covered walkway, left our socks and shoes at a counter for the keeping, and began to climb the hundreds of marble steps barefoot. Pastor Fish was increasingly uncomfortable, and the closer we got to the top where the main temple is located, the more he wanted to leave. A young man approached and asked for 10,000 Burmese kyats as an admission price, like you would pay to enter some American State parks. Pastor Fish refused to pay it. We took a good look through the upper entrance way and descended to the street level again. He had had enough. So, we hailed another taxi and, this time, the driver was a Burmese Muslim.

There is a growing Muslim population in Myanmar, mostly in the city of Yangon and in Rakhine State, which is on the Bangladesh border to the West. There are many large Islamic temples in Yangon, and Muslim neighborhoods have developed around them. In recent years, the Rohingya conflict in Rakhine State has gained world attention and become highly politicized. For decades the Rohingyas, a Bangla people, have homesteaded in Rakhine State, largely ignored by the Burmese government. Rakhine State is home to the old Andaman people who are strong Buddhists. In recent years, I have personally witnessed the unrest of the Muslims there.

A GLBM church planter in northern Rakhine State established a new church among the indigenous Mru, a tribal people who are farmers and herdsmen. The chief of the village was the first to become a believer in Christ and we built a church, transported Scriptures, and taught the people Bible doctrine. When the Rohingyas heard that the village had turned to Christ, they came upriver, burned the church, killed four of our families, and were hunting the rest of our congregation who were hiding in the jungle. I sent funds to bring these people back to the city of Yangon, where we built housing for them so that they could become part of Thaung Lian's church and ministry.

Media groups want the world to believe that the Myanmar government and military is committing genocide against the Rohingya people. I am not witness to any lawlessness by the military there, but I know that big money is being channeled through Yangon mosques for the purpose of establishing an Islamic state within Myanmar and the Rohingya people are being used as scapegoats to gain global sympathies. I am not justifying violence, but as Americans would protect their own people and repel such an attempt in the United States, the Myanmar people should be allowed to do the same.

It is easy to identify a Buddhist taxi driver in Yangon. A small golden image is stuck to the dash, some flowers are hanging from the rear-view mirror, or a photograph of the driver's personal monk is on the windshield or sun visor. But with Muslim drivers, if the man has no traditional beard, a taqiyah (cap), or turban wrap, it might be more difficult. Our driver on this day was obviously Muslim.

As usual, there was much traffic and we jumped into the car quickly as the cars rushed by, me riding co-pilot in the front and Pastor Fish in the back. I said to the driver, "Salaam!" He smiled and returned the Arabic-Muslim greeting. I said, "Queens Park Hotel, please." He said, "Yes, sir! Queen's Park Hotel, no?" I said, "Yes! Please! Queen's Park Hotel." I have learned that, when good communication and understanding is in doubt, repetition is helpful in conversation.

The driver sped off and headed for the Queen's Park Hotel. I asked, "English?" He answered, "Yes sir!" I did not yet know enough Burmese language to help myself and I was glad this man could speak my language.

He immediately asked where we were from and, when I told him we were Americans, he asked many questions. He asked me, "Sir! What are you doing here in Myanmar?" I answered him by telling him that we were Christians, that I had many friends in Myanmar, and that we were trying to tell Myanmar people about Jesus Christ, the Savior of the whole world.

Remember, I was talking to a Muslim, not a Buddhist. I wondered what his response would be. So, I continued and asked, "Sir, do you know who Jesus is?" "Oh, yes sir," he said.

I should be honest and admit that, just as many other Americans, I have preconceived ideas about Muslims because of Islamic terrorism. Many Bible-believing Christians will give gospel tracts to almost anyone, but fear to witness to Muslims. Soon after recognizing God's call upon my life to preach the Gospel to

Myanmar people, I realized that when God put His love for them in me, it did not only include Buddhists, but Muslims, Hindus, Jews, and Animists alike.

During another trip, as I was traveling through the city of Yangon with a group of men, I had the chance to talk to another Muslim taxi driver. As we arrived at our hotel, the men quickly exited the car and went into the hotel lobby to get cool. I stayed behind for a minute to pay the driver. As I handed him 6,000 kyats, I looked in his eyes and asked him, "How long have you been a Muslim?" He looked puzzled, but answered my question: "All my life, sir. I was born a Muslim." He asked me, "How long have you been a Christian?" I answered, "Ever since God convicted me about my sin and my need of a Savior." He looked puzzled again. I said, "I was the first person in my family to become a born-again Christian. I learned through the Holy Bible that I could not save myself. I asked Christ to forgive me and to be my Savior. I put all my faith in Him that day.

I asked, "What is it like being a Muslim in the city of Yangon?" Obviously, he was not prepared for my question. He looked startled. I asked the question again. The driver looked at me and asked, "What do you mean, sir? Why do you ask me this question?" I said, "I think it may be difficult for you." The taxi driver looked at me with amazement. He said, "Sir! It is very difficult for us. We are afraid every day." I replied, "Sir, I would like to pray for you!"

And then his whole countenance changed, and he asked me, "Sir, why do you care about us?" I answered, "I am a Christian and I am commanded in the Holy Bible to love all people. But also, Almighty God has put His love for the Myanmar people in me. You are Myanmar, no?" He nodded, "Yes!" A huge smile came on his face.

The taxi driver asked me, "Sir, why do you come to Myanmar?" I answered, "Because I am obeying the Word of God. And I come because I love the Myanmar people and I want them to know the wonderful love of my Savior. I would like you to know my Savior!"

The taxi driver asked me, "Sir, please pray for my family! Would you do it?" Perhaps by the look on my face he thought that I was confused or did not understand. He said, "Sir, I am asking you plainly. Please help my family!"

I said, "Of course! Let's pray right now!" I asked him to tell me something about his family and, when I prayed, I prayed in Jesus' name. The man wept. I prayed that he and his family would come to the knowledge of the truth and that the Holy Ghost would draw them to Christ.

Just as I reached out for his hand, as if to pray with him, his phone rang with someone requesting taxi service. I thought to myself that this is just like the work of the Devil in hindering the work of soul-winners in America. But I believed then, and I believe now, that God will use my witness to bring that man to Christ. I gave the driver a gospel tract in the Burmese language, quickly discussed how we might see each other again, and he drove away.

Now, we were still on our way to the Queen's Park Hotel and, standing still at a traffic light, I looked around and didn't recognize the surroundings. I thought that perhaps the driver was taking another route unknown to me or a shortcut to our hotel, but I was really concentrating on our conversation. Again, the driver asked, "Queen's Park Hotel, sir?" I said, "Yes, Queen's Park Hotel."

The driver sped off and whizzed through traffic with relative ease. As he drove, making turn after turn, down back streets and sometimes alleyways, I continued to talk to him about Christ. He seemed interested and asked me many questions. But I could sense that he was thinking more about our conversation than his driving. When he pulled up in front of what he thought was the Queen's Park Hotel, it was the wrong hotel and the opposite side of town from where we were supposed to be. I thought to myself, "This gives me more time to witness to the man!"

The driver was embarrassed and promised that he would have us at the right location shortly. What would have been a thirty-minute journey became two hours. And when we arrived at our hotel, the driver parked the car along the curb and turned the engine off. I took my Bible from my bag and showed him Scripture verses that proved Jesus Christ to be God and the Creator of the World.

Throughout our conversation and trip across the city, it was obvious that the Spirit of God had arranged our meeting and given me the opportunity to lead this man to Christ. With tears in his eyes, he bowed his head, confessed his sin and need of a Savior, then asked Jesus Christ to come into his heart. Some would question if he understood enough Scripture or Bible doctrine, whether he was praying just to be polite, or if he simply had an emotional experience. But the next morning, the man was waiting to carry us in his taxi again. The following day he came to my room with his wife and asked me to explain to her what I had told him. There in the hotel, his wife became a believer as well.

The following year, in our annual pastor's conference, hundreds of men filled the room from across the country. I was aware of a few who had converted from Islam. But a certain man named Yazeem, who immediately stood out of the crowd, captured everyone's attention. When I heard his story, I immediately asked him to give his testimony from the platform.

Yazeem had been a high school Math teacher in another province. He had somehow heard the Gospel and was given a Bible. When he learned the truth about Christ, he believed. After being saved, he began to witness to his family and relatives. Those whom he loved, whom he thought loved him, were enraged at his disloyalty to both Islam and to their family. Trying to turn him from what they thought was either folly or dementia, they went to their Imam for help. Yazeem was ordered to appear before a counsel one night at the mosque. When he would not recant, he was ordered to be killed.

Yazeem himself had taken part in such killings before. Some Muslim communities would decapitate the offending infidel. Others would stone the person. Still others, depending on the severity of the offense, would simply banish that person from their community for life. Yazeem was to be stoned. The community would gather in a central location, and the men would dig a pit deep enough that Yazeem would stand in it up to his shoulders. He was then to be buried in that pit where only his shoulders, neck, and head would be above ground. Then the community would take turns throwing stones at his face and head until he was dead. But somehow Yazeem escaped that night and ran for his life. Now he was being hunted across the country by those he had formerly called "brothers."

Somehow Yazeem heard about our Christian conference in Yangon and realized that he must get there. He could not take public transportation because the word was out, and someone would surely recognize him. He walked for three days, through fields and jungles, trying to stay out of congested areas. An unforeseen challenge for him was the fact that our meeting hall was a block from a Yangon city mosque and many Muslims were in the street day and night. When Yazeem arrived, he knew no one. He stood just inside the door until one of our preachers introduced himself and inquired where he was from. Our men not only received and accepted him but loved him immediately.

When Yazeem rose to speak, he did so with authority and power. As they say, he "brought the house down," and so ignited our meeting that the altar filled with people, asking God for fresh power to win souls to Christ. We helped that man as best we could and hid him for a time in one of our churches outside the city. But he was not content to sit or hide. He left us to go preach the Gospel among those of his own people who have never heard the truth of Christ.

Another year, we had rented a large hall in downtown Yangon for the same annual conference and nearly 600 people were in attendance. Christian preachers from all over Myanmar came. Some came hoping for a financial partnership, some for teaching or fellowship. There were a couple American preachers who came to Myanmar with me. As one of them was speaking, I went to the lobby to pray and God spoke to my heart. As I stood looking into the street from a window, Pastor Htein Win Ei came through the lobby and I called to him, saying "Saya! Can you help me, please?"

I asked him to find me a large basin, some soap, and a towel or two. I gave him some money, and he sent a couple boys to the street to buy the things I had requested. When the preacher was finished speaking, I had the boys bring the basin filled with water to the platform. I went out into the crowd of people, sitting in rows of chairs. I looked them over and asked some of the men, those whom I chose, to come to the front. I chose one man from each of sixteen different Myanmar people groups represented in the crowd. There were men from Kachin State, or the Jingpo, the Karen, Tiddim, Hakha, Falam, Zomi, Asho, Maru, Lahu, Manaw, Yaw, Bamar, Rakhine, Yao, Shan, and Naga. We placed sixteen chairs in a line across the platform and the men sat down. I told the people, "Please stay in your seats. Let there be no talking. Please just observe and pray."

God had given me specific instructions, and I was to carry them out perfectly with no deviation: Each man wore a traditional Burmese longyi and sandals or flipflops. As they sat before me, their feet were blackened with the dust and dirt of the street. They wondered what I would do. God told me that I was to give no introduction or explanation, but to simply obey. I went to the platform, got on my knees in front of the first man, took his sandals off his feet, washed his feet with soap and water, then kissed his feet with my mouth, and went to the next man. I had only performed foot washing once before in thirty-some years of ministry, and I have not done so again since that time. As I washed the feet of the second man, he wept and begged me, "Please, sir! I should wash your feet!" I said, "No, Saya! I am obeying the Lord." I washed the feet of all sixteen men in like manner. It took some time. And the people remained seated, still, and quiet.

When I was finished, I stood to my feet, then sat down on the front row, bowed my head, and prayed. The Holy Ghost told me that I was to say nothing. And so, I was quiet. But, in my silence, I was weeping. And so were they. For the next two hours, waves of people filled the altar, kneeling at the front and down the aisles, praying with each other, praying for Myanmar, surrendering to God, accepting Christ. That day, there was not Americans and Myanmars; there was not Burmese and Chin, or Karen and Shan. There was just people and God, and He did the preaching.

I have been told that I have changed since going to Myanmar. I think that God has used Myanmar to change me. I think that I needed to change. We all have prejudices and preconceived ideas. Sometimes our prejudices are passed down to us by those we dare not question. Sometimes our prejudices are founded in fear, sometimes in history. After experiencing the fierce persecution of the former military dictatorship, one Chin preacher said to me, "When I get to heaven, if I see one Burmese person, I will come back!" Too often our prejudices are really masked hatred. But is it ever righteous to hate? King David said that he hated those who opposed God. But I do not think God ever told him to do that.

Could it be that there are people in Hell today whom Christians did not want to go to Heaven? If so, that by no means makes God unrighteous. God desires no one, from any nation, to go to Hell. And when the gospel waters proceed from the house of God, the farther they go, the deeper they get. The prophet Ezekiel said, "...every thing shall live wither the river cometh" (Ezekiel 47:9). Praise the Lord! Everyone can be saved.

"For the love of Christ constraineth us; because we thus judge, that if one died for all, then were all dead: And that he died for all, that they which live should not henceforth live unto themselves, but unto him which died for them, and rose again. Wherefore henceforth know we no man after the flesh: yea, though we have known Christ after the flesh, yet now henceforth know we him no more. Therefore, if any man be in Christ, he is a new creature: old things are passed away; behold, all things are become new." **2 Corinthians 5:14-17**

Nyi Nyaih Shwe

Yazeem giving testimony

Dr. Jim Fish

Yazeem, Pastor Richard Hack, myself, and Thaung Lian

Yangon Mosque

CHAPTER SIX

Nyi Nyaih Shwe

"Behold, for peace I had great bitterness; but thou hast in love to my soul delivered from the pit of corruption: for thou hast cast all my sins behind thy back."
Isaiah 38:17

"Daddy died last week. Maybe it is a good thing. He was in awful pain that never stopped. I don't think I can cry any more. But mom does. And my little sisters? I'm not sure they fully understand yet. He is never coming back. I think I am going to die just like him." Fifteen-year-old Nyi Nyaih Shwe had wandered away from her house and family to her secret place in the jungle. She sat leaning against a tree and staring straight ahead at nothing at all. She had been there many times all alone. Daydreaming had become her escape. But this time she didn't check the surrounding area for snakes or scorpions. She didn't care if there was a danger nearby. She was already contemplating a quick end to her life.

Bitterness and depression, like a creeping black fungus, was growing in her heart and taking over her spirit. All of life looked dark. Nyi Nyaih Shwe sat on the floor, in a corner of their simple one room house, and stared into emptiness. She could not remember a time when life was easy. Happiness was not for her. She was 14 years old. If she had a friend anywhere, she didn't know about them.

Nyi Nyaih Shwe's father, Than Shwe, was a good man. He loved his wife and worked hard for her every day. And, he had a skill. He was a brick mason. He built many houses for the richer families in the community. That is, until he became sick. Like so many others in the village, Than Shwe had malaria. He had battled it for years. But the quinine that would reduce his symptoms was not easy to get for a poor family, and, even if it was available, there was no sanitary needles, intravenous feeding tubes, or antiseptic. As he felt able, he would go work, if not on a house, then in the rice fields. But exhaustion from being under the hot sun would bring his symptoms rushing back. At times he couldn't breathe. Dehydration from vomiting, and severely low blood sugar was making him so weak that he had a difficult time just getting out of bed. His jaundiced skin was an indication that his liver was failing.

There was a "kind of doctor" who started coming to help those suffering with malaria. So, as several times before, on the day when the doctor would be there, having saved enough money for a treatment, Than Shwe made sure that he reserved all his strength to go to the makeshift clinic that was set up in the village. Well before dawn he started getting ready and made sure he would have a good place in the line of those waiting to be treated.

But, as he reached the clinic, a line had already formed, and Than Shwe would have to wait his turn like everyone else. He would be the eighth patient to be seen that day. But could he endure the heat of the sun? He would do his best. It wasn't just for himself. Getting well, or at least stronger, would help him provide food for his wife, Nyi Nyi, and maybe even their future family. For him, it meant the difference between self-respect and utter despair.

Months earlier, lying next to Than Shwe, she caressed his forehead and kissed his face. Nyi Nyi said, "I'm going to have a baby!" Than Shwe sat straight up in bed with his tired eyes now wide open. "What? ...Really? ...Are you sure? ...How will we ..."

Nyi Nyi put her hand gently across her husband's mouth and said, "Shhh! Everything will be okay. You will see! Somehow it will all work out."

"But...but, we have so much to do! ...Oh, my! Oh, my! Will it be a girl or a boy? What will we name our baby?"

"Well, silly, we must wait and see! If it will be a girl, I want to call her Nyi Nyaih Shwe." "And, if it will be a boy?"

Nyi Nyi sighed and answered, "Well, we have to wait and see."

At last, Then Shwe heard his name called. But he was so weak that it took all his energy and a longer time to get to the steps and climb into the building where the clinic was set up. He almost lost his place as the doctor's helper thought he wasn't coming. But, once inside, he was guided to a bench where a woman helped him lay down. She asked him no questions. She did not take his temperature or blood pressure. There was no equipment in the room, only a rusty metal stand from which hung a plastic bag, and a thin rubber hose with a syringe on the end. There was no antiseptic, no gauze, or tourniquet. As before, the woman just stuck the needle in his arm and walked away.

Then Shwe had much hope that the coming of this doctor and clinic would help him and all the others who had malaria. They had wondered if anyone could help them, or if anyone even cared. "But someone is thinking about us!" he said to his wife. "They told me to come back next week, and they will give me more quinine."

Because her husband was sick, Nyi Nyi had been working in the paddy fields to earn some money for their family. Many of the villagers had suffered from dengue fever the year before. It was like a plague and went through the whole village like an arrow of death, and many died. Others had tuberculosis. Somehow, she and her husband stayed strong and escaped it all. But now, Then Shwe was sick. She was working and becoming exhausted. Waking long before daybreak, walking miles to the fields, then working all day under the hot sun, she barely had enough energy to come home, much less to make supper and clean house.

With the quinine treatments, Then Shwe seemed to get better for a while. He went back to work, building houses in their village and, sometimes, traveling to other places. But his malaria always came back. Or so it seemed. More than that, it seemed like he caught everybody's colds. Every time there was influenza in the community, he was one of the first to get sick. Then he began to develop strange bumps on his skin, and sores inside his mouth. Even when he wasn't working, he was lethargic and short of breath.

Suddenly, with the birth of Nyi Nyaih Shwe, none of those things mattered. Everyone was excited. Families from all over the community came to the house and brought gifts. Every woman in the village wanted to hold her. What a happy time it was! "Certainly," they thought, "all will be well!"

Things did seem to get better. Matter of fact, Nyi Nyi gave birth to two more daughters and Then Shwe was as proud a man as any in the whole village. Even though they all had Burmese names, Then Shwe and his family had enough Chin blood to make them welcome in the church on the other side of town. However, Nyi Nyaih Shwe's Dad was always a bit self-conscious about his daughters' clothing. He didn't care about his own attire. But he wanted his wife and girls to look good. The ladies of the church realized there was a problem and sent some second-hand dresses, a couple pairs of girly flipflops, and some hair pretties.

It wasn't long before the girls fit right in and enjoyed the church activities with all the rest of the non-Buddhist religious families in town, and Nyi Nyi Shwe, being the oldest, was happy.

But, just like her father, she and her mother went through many times of sickness. Her younger sisters seemed to be healthier than the rest of the family. They did not know why.

One night late, Then Shwe developed a severe cough. It wasn't like before, his cough came from deep inside his lungs, and there was blood.

Nyi Nyi said, "You must go to the clinic tomorrow."

Then Shwe could barely get the words out without coughing. With difficulty, he managed to say, "We don't have the money!" Later that night he had a seizure. It was severe. And, when his body finally stopped shaking, he laid as a dead man until morning. Frantic and sobbing, Nyi Nyi didn't know what to do. Even though she was not feeling well either, she laid by her husband's side and wrapped herself around his limp body all night. Nyi Nyaih Shwe tried to comfort her frightened little sisters. But they screamed and cried until, out of sheer exhaustion, they all fell sound asleep.

The doctor at the clinic suspected that Than Shwe had contracted tuberculosis. Then Shwe, like many others with TB, would have to go to Kalay, a large city located two hours to the south. There, in the old Tahan community, was a hospital where x-rays could be taken. But, again, money was a problem. This time, however, there was no choice; it had to be done.

As sick as he was, Then Shwe had to find someone who would loan him the money to go to Kalay, do the tests, and buy the medicine needed to treat his sickness. Nyi Nyi would go with him. They would be gone at least two days. The girls would stay with neighbors.

They didn't know it yet, but Than Shwe and his whole family were fighting a battle they could not win. The x-rays proved that what was in his lungs was not tuberculosis. From the dirty used needles, passed from person to person at the village malaria clinic, Then Shwe had become infected with the HIV virus and it had already progressed into full-blown AIDS.

He had sought treatment for his malaria. He had taken the injection of quinine like so many others and did not question anything. At that time, the whole country was suffering miserable poverty. Certainly, the people in the village were grateful for any help they could get. The doctor and his assistant had tried their best to help. But with limited supplies and no extras for anyone, they used the same injection needle once, twice, more times than they could count. After each patient, they tried to clean their only syringe. But it wasn't enough.

Then Shwe was dying, and there wasn't anything that anyone in all of Myanmar could do to reverse the disease. Nyi Nyi also tested positive for HIV. But equally heartbreaking, Nyi Nyaih Shwe was tested, and she had the virus too. She had been born with AIDS.

What did it all mean? How could they explain to their oldest child that her whole life would be defined by something that is not her fault? Back in their bungalow, Then Shwe and Nyi Nyi wept all night. Sleep would not come. In their minds, the flurry of thoughts and fears spun out of control like a runaway horse on a dark stormy night. Would this dreaded virus kill Than Shwe? If so, when? How long would he suffer? Would it also kill the whole family?

There were many times when Nyi Nyaih Shwe felt poorly. Being a vivacious young person, she usually just pushed through it. Of course, sometimes her sickness and weakness were overpowering to her. She didn't like to talk about it. Her life was about going to school and helping her parents.

But rumors were circulating through the community, and the children at school, some who were Nyi Nyaih Shwe's best friends, had started to avoid her.

One day as she walked home from school, she called to a friend: "Khaing Zar Myo! Khaing Zar! Stop, I want to walk to you." But her friend kept walking. Nyi Nyaih Shwe ran to catch up and, dropping a book in the dirt, she said, "Wait!" But Khaing Zar Myo would not wait.

Running to her friend's side, Nyi Nyaih Shwe reached out, grabbed her arm, and said, "Khaing Zar, are you going straight home? Can we talk?"

Khaing Zar Myo pulled her arm away and answered, "Don't touch me! My mother said I cannot talk to you anymore."

Indeed, Nyi Nyaih Shwe had felt the snubs of her classmates, and even the teachers were treating her differently than before they discovered her sickness.

"Momma, it's not our fault. How can they be this way to us? We have done nothing wrong?"

Nyi Nyaih Shwe's mother pulled her daughter into her arms, held her tightly, and they both wept until morning.

Living in the village was becoming increasingly difficult. Nyi Nyi didn't tell her daughter that she had been asked to leave the little corner store near their house. Word of their family's illness had obviously spread to the farmer's open-air market. Several of the vendors said that she should not touch the fruit or vegetables, the meat or fish unless she was sure she would buy it. When she tried to enter a conversation among the ladies, they would ignore her and walk away.

Then Shwe had been fired from his job because he could not work like the other employees. Some weeks he missed more days than he worked. He would have good days and bad days. But increasingly, his bad days were beginning to outnumber his good days. It seemed that with every bout of sickness, his strength was decreasing. Eating was a problem too. After almost every meal he would violently vomit. He was losing weight rapidly.

Nights seemed endless and sleep was not easy for him. Many nights he was restless, thrashing around with pain until morning. There were times when the family thought he had fallen off in sleep and their little house was at last peacefully quiet. But then, suddenly with seemingly no provocation, he would scream out in pain, waking the children and sending Nyi Nyi hurrying to his side. She would search for a way to help her husband, but there was none. There was no medicine to give him. He would be cold, and she would cover him. But even a thin sheet was irritating against the open sores on his skin. She would try to sooth him with her gentle caress, but it only caused him more anxiety. Weeks seemed like months, and months like years. Slowly Than Shwe's breathing became more labored.

A message was sent that there was a center for treating AIDS patients in the city of Tamu. It was on the border with India, a 90-minute ride north on the small commuter bus. Then Shwe and Nyi Nyi decided that they would try to go together, and they borrowed money from a family relative so that they could make the journey for treatment. At the appropriate time, they waited along the main road for the bus to arrive. But, for some reason, it never came. Again, the following day, they waited for the bus, and as it stopped by the side of the road, they boarded, paid the fare to the purser, and took their seats in the far back.

The temperature and humidity were unusually uncomfortable. Then Shwe had a difficult time breathing and, the more he tried to suppress his cough, the harder it was to disguise his infirmity. It was obvious that the other passengers were becoming uncomfortable themselves. So, the purser approached Than Shwe and asked if he needed assistance. Then Shwe asked for a bottle of water. The purser went up front, took a small bottle of purified water from a cooler, and delivered it to him. But the water was so cold that it made him cough all the more. When the bus finally arrived at the Tamu terminal, the bus driver told Than Shwe that he and his wife should seek another way to return to their village.

The AIDS clinic was far from the bus terminal and the heat of the day made the walk exhausting. There were many bicycles and motor scooter taxis, horse drawn carriages too. But Than Shwe and Nyi Nyi had to conserve their limited funds for the trip home and any possible fees at the clinic. So, they walked.

Finally arriving at the clinic, and waiting their turn to see a doctor, Then Shwe's discomfort became less and less tolerable. When his name was called, he and his wife were directed to a small room where there was a wooden table but no chairs. Then Shwe leaned up against the table and finally just sat on the floor next to his wife. A nurse soon appeared to take his temperature and blood pressure. Another nurse came to draw blood. And, finally, after nearly an hour, a man in a white coat and face mask, presumably a doctor, entered the room and explained the AIDS treatment schedule and costs.

To Than Shwe, it all seemed both too technical and too expensive. But he decided to receive the first treatment while they were there. But he did not expect it to be so debilitating. The treatment itself was relatively painless. He even fell asleep. But, upon waking, he found that he was more nauseous than ever before. Weakness had engulfed him.

They didn't have enough money for Nyi Nyi to receive a treatment. But that was alright. She was not near as sick as Than Shwe. And the money they had left over was so little, it was not enough for the trip home. They exited the clinic, sat on the curb along the road, and tried to wave down trucks that seemed like they were going south.

One truck stopped but, when the driver saw that Than Shwe was sick, he would not so much as allow them to ride in the back. He left them standing on the side of the road, and Nyi Nyi began to weep. Another truck stopped. But the driver said he was only going so far. Thinking that it might be their only way to get home or close to home, Then Shwe and Nyi Nyi climbed into the back with bags of rice, chickens, two goats, and a stack of green bamboo. The truck driver took them as far as he could. But with ten miles yet to go, they flagged down an ox cart driver and rode with him the rest of the way to their village.

Then Shwe would need to go to Tamu once every month. But it was too far. The treatments, much like chemotherapy for cancer, was horribly weakening and the after-effects were painful. Treatment was too costly. Then Shwe feared that the medications were insufficient, an exercise in utter futility, and more hurtful to his family than help for him. He was quickly losing hope. But Nyi Nyi begged him to continue.

All the while Nyi Nyaih Shwe was becoming depressed. She noticed that the disease was manifesting itself in her like her father. She had started getting sores in her mouth and on her legs. She was developing an incessant cough. But worse than that for her, school had become intolerable. She begged her mother for permission to stay home. She did not want to go to school anymore. But, in her mother's eyes, her children must go to school and there was no other school they could attend. Nyi Nyaih Shwe would just have to find a way to be happy in school and study as hard as she could.

Then one night during rainy season, it was especially dark. Thick clouds concealed any light from the moon. Wind howled like wolves at the door. Rain came in waves and pounded heavily like deafening bullets upon the thin metal roof. The street outside had disappeared under overflowing pools of muddy soup filled with leeches. Sleep was impossible for everyone. But then, suddenly with seemingly no warning of symptoms, came a scream that pierced the darkness and exceeded the sounds of the storm. Nyi Nyaih Shwe began to toss about on top of her bed mat. Even though, in the darkness, Nyi Nyi could not see her daughter's body shaking and beating against the bamboo beneath her, she could hear her excruciating struggle. On her hands and knees, she reached out to her and scooted over to hold her thrashing body, screaming for someone to help them. Nyi Nyaih Shwe's young sisters were crying. Then Shwe reached through the darkness for an old oil lamp, struck a match to light it, but realized there was no fuel in it. All he could do was to crawl to his family and hold them until daybreak. Nyi Nyaih Shwe had suffered a seizure in the middle of the night. And all through the next day, she lay motionless in her own urine with her hands wrapped around her head. She could not speak a word but made only a muffled and half-hearted whine every few minutes until the next night when she began to cry. Nyi Nyi ran to the small village clinic, but the doctor was not scheduled to visit their area until the following week. There was no help to be found anywhere from anyone. That day Than Shwe decided that he had taken his last AIDS treatment and that he would send Nyi Nyaih Shwe to Tamu instead.

But Than Shwe continued his descent into the abyss of AIDS. After another two months with no treatments, he would succumb to the disease. He died in his own house surrounded by family. A few friends, keeping their distance, gathered in the street outside.

To the average Westerner, funerals and burials in Myanmar are peculiar. But they are ceremonies that reflect the influence of Burmese Buddhism and the religion of nats, or spirit worship, as well as the people's perception of life and death. Nat worship was practiced in the Golden Land long before the introduction and adoption of Buddhism. But at least one Buddhist monk is always involved in the ceremonies which last seven whole days.

The body is bathed and dressed in their finest apparel and relatives come and put a coin in the mouth of the deceased to pay the "ferry toll," or the gadaw ga, to the underworld. On the first day, a monk is invited to chant prayers to protect the soul in its journey into another consciousness where it will seek a higher level of existence in its cycle of life (or, reincarnation). During the first six days, the soul is thought to be unaware of its death and therefore remains in the corpse. It has not yet come to the place of coping with the loss of its mortal life.

Because of this, Burmese people view the seven-day ceremonies very seriously. Wherever the corpse is kept, usually within the home, all doors and windows are kept open so that the soul can find its way out. Family and friends keep vigil day and night throughout the week-long funeral process while friends and neighbors visit and parade through the streets, encouraging the deceased and pointing the way for the soul to escape. Fans printed with the name of the deceased, appropriate sutras (Buddhist scriptures), and a dinner invitation to friends, are distributed among the visitors. The final day of the funeral is called the Yet Le. The grieving family will make a dinner for the monk(s) to show their appreciation for his blessing, after which the week's activities are concluded when he completes a Buddhist water libation ceremony, throwing water out on the ground, signifying the irretrievable loss of the soul from this world. Somewhere in the process the soul (or, leippya) acknowledges his or her death, finds its way out of this world, and is buried or cremated, according to the ability of the family or availability of a burial plot. The Burmese think their customs are simple, but to the Western mind it is a complex system.

However, when Than Shwe passed away, there was no ceremony or rituals. There was no crowds of visitors or parades. There was not even a monk present. His and Nyi Nyi's families, caught between Burmese Buddhism and Chin Christianity, were neither. Having died of a dreaded disease that most villagers did not understand, his family grieved shamefully and alone.

They had prepared Than Shwe's body as best they could, and he lay wrapped in brightly colored blankets in the middle of their small house. Nyi Nyi sat at his side with her younger daughters alone. A few friends stood outside, detached from the scene, but close enough for the sake of propriety. Nyi Nyaih Shwe ran to her secret place and filled her hands with tears. She was old enough to appropriately grieve but still young enough to be confused and afraid. Her mind swirled with thoughts: "Where has my daddy gone? Are the Burmese people right? Will his leippya return another way? Or are the Christians right? Is there a Heaven? Did my Daddy go there? If so, I may never see him again because I am so bad!"

Nyi Nyaih Shwe walked to school alone. She carried her lunch pail with her books. At break time, she ate alone. She walked home alone. Her mother tried her best to encourage her. But, Nyi Nyi now had to provide for her whole family, and was trying to take up where her husband left off. With gift money from a few relatives, she rented a field and was trying to grow enough vegetables to feed her family and sell for a bit of income. She woke long before the dawn of day and rested long after her children found sleep. She was doing her best. But she could hear the growling of her children's stomachs. She often heard her eldest daughter weeping under her bed covers. She could see the unhappiness in her eyes. And she knew that Nyi Nyaih Shwe was becoming, not only unhappy but, bitter and maybe suicidal. She talked about death too much. She noticed a scratch, more like a slice, on her left wrist. She dared not ask what happened or where it came from!

One night, after Nyi Nyaih Shwe's whimpers had ceased, Nyi Nyi stepped out of the house and into the darkness. She began to walk and finally, when she could no longer contain her deep sorrow, she buried her face in her hands, fell to her knees, and cried out to Heaven:

"God! If you are real, I need you. My children need you. Will we all die like Than Shwe? It isn't fair! Why are we suffering like this? What have we done? God, if you are real, please show me. Please help us!"

The skin on Nyi Nyi's hands was thick and rough, almost scaly like her weather-worn feet. Her sunbaked face was framed by the long black hair that was tied in a ponytail behind her ears. She wore a thin flowered dress, and it was soaking wet from her waist down. She had just come from the creek where she was washing her family's clothes against a large stone. She was hanging the clothes to dry in the hot sun, and she could hear some children coming from school. But they were yelling obscenities, calling bad names, and she knew this could not be good.

As she rounded the corner of her house, she could see several of the children throwing stones at Nyi Nyaih Shwe. Her motherly instinct and rushing adrenalin combined to give her the appearance of a charging bear and the offending children sprinted away as if running for their lives. Nyi Nyaih Shwe ran into her mother's arms, weeping uncontrollably and begging her, "Please don't make me go back to school! Please, mother, please!"

There are times in the experience of parents, regardless of the country or culture in which they live, that they face impossible situations and must make a decision for the welfare of their child. Nyi Nyi didn't know what to do. Her children needed education. In Myanmar, like most other countries, those with at least a high school education have opportunities others do not. But, also in Myanmar, many children from small provincial villages never learn basic reading, writing, and arithmetic. Nyi Nyaih Shwe was a very bright young lady. The thought that she would never have those opportunities crushed the spirit of her mother.

A cruel neighbor said, "What are you torturing yourself for? She's going to die like you all anyway." Nyi Nyi could not accept that. So, she kept praying and seeking information from people in the village, some she did not even know.

It was a Friday evening and Nyi Nyi had just finished work. She was hot, her clothes were soiled and soaked with perspiration, and her feet were black from a day's work in the field. But she needed some things at the big market. So, on the way home, she stopped there to do some shopping, hoping that the villagers would be kind and leave her alone. But, as she expected, some people indeed stared a hole right through her. They kept their distance but, thankfully, they didn't stop her.

Nyi Nyi was putting a few things in her bag when someone spoke to her and tapped her on the shoulder. She had become accustomed to people giving her a wide berth, no one coming close enough to even rub against her in the crowd. When someone tapped her shoulder, she jumped and yelped like a puppy. A woman with a big smile was standing behind her, and she had something in her hand. She held a piece of paper and offered it, saying "I would like to give you this. It tells about God and how you can know Him!"

Nyi Nyi was so shocked, she didn't know how to reply. The woman simply put the piece of paper in her hand and walked away. Nyi Nyi almost forgot where she was and what she was there for. She started to walk away and realized she had laid her bag on a shelf of red chili peppers and almost forgot it. She went to the cashier, paid for her goods, and began the walk home. But she couldn't help but try to read the piece of paper. So, she stopped along the side of the road and sat down in the dirt.

The paper was folded in half. On the front was an invitation to a new church. On the inside was a message from the Christian scriptures. On the back there were words that read,

ခြင်း

ကလေလရဟါတာလုပ်ငန်း

Myanmar Baptist Church
Charity Education Center for Children

Nyi Nyi could barely believe her eyes. Nervously, she read the words over and over, flipping the paper from front to back and back to front again. She read every word. Tucking the paper inside a belly pack strapped around her waist, she ran home with her groceries. She didn't mention it to her Nyi Nyaih Shwe. That night she laid on her bed mat with the piece of paper under her pillow and could hardly sleep. But in the morning, she walked her younger daughters to school and left Nyi Nyaih Shwe, sleeping at the house.

She reached into her bag and frantically fumbled through all her things for the paper she received the day before. She feared that she had lost the paper or misplaced it. But finding it in the very bottom of her bad, she quickly unfolded it and read the address of the church and school. It was located on the far side of the village. Walking, it would take a good hour. She thought about Nyi Nyaih Shwe back at their house. She thought, "She will be fine. I need to go!" So, she began walking. Motor scooter taximen passed by and offered her a ride. But she had no money and kept walking.

It was after 9:00 o'clock in the morning when she arrived at the church and school. She checked the address twice. An aged man sat on a shaded porch, drinking hot Burmese tea at a table. She asked him, "Is there a school here?" He answered, "It is a church school." She wasn't sure what to ask. She simply said, "I want to talk to somebody about my daughter."

The man motioned with his hand and answered, saying "Please wait here!" As he disappeared through a passageway, Nyi Nyi thought about sitting on the bench, but she knew how people thought about her family's sickness. So, she stood until she became fatigued and finally sat down on the porch step.

Nyi Nyi had no wristwatch or phone. So, she didn't know how long it had been. But it seemed like the man was gone a long time. She was becoming apprehensive, and several times she thought about leaving. But it seemed that a little voice was telling her to stay. Nervous energy or anxiety was driving her crazy and, after she used everything in her bag to fidget away the time, she finally began to pray again. Then she stood up and walked back out to the street. Then she wandered back to the porch and stood waiting.

After some time, the man returned with a younger gentleman who introduced himself. He said, "I am Van Siang Lian. People call me Saya Peter. How can I help you?"

Even though she had never met Saya Peter, that morning on the porch, Nyi Nyi emptied her whole heart to him. She told him the whole story of how her husband became sick, and then her whole family. She told him what was happening to Nyi Nyaih Shwe at the school and how she could not return there. She begged him to let her daughter come to school. Saya Peter explained that his church's ministry was a boarding school and that the students lived there. Nyi Nyi began to cry, explaining that she had no money and could not pay for her daughter to go to a school like that. But Saya Peter told her that his school was free, and that Nyi Nyaih Shwe would be welcome there.

A woman appeared in the passageway and Saya Peter motioned to her, saying "Mercy, please come!" He said, "Nyi Nyi, this is my wife. Her name is Mercy." Mercy approached and put her hand on Nyi Nyi's arm in a welcoming gesture. Nyi Nyi recoiled, explaining that she, like her daughters and husband before them, had AIDS. Mercy threw her arms around Nyi Nyi's neck and embraced her warmly, saying "We know that we cannot catch AIDS from touching you. It is alright." Nyi Nyi wept a long time in Mercy's arms. Peter and Mercy comforted her as best they could. They told her about the Saviour, and Nyi Nyi gave her heart to Christ.

Nyi Nyi went home as fast as she could, anxious to tell Nyi Nyaih Shwe about her new school. She wanted to assure her that things would be different there. But, when she climbed the bamboo steps into her house, Nyi Nyaih Shwe was not there. She began to search for her, calling her name. But Nyi Nyaih Shwe had gone to her secret place and did not come home until dark, later that night.

"Nyi Nyaih Shwe! Where have you been? Huh? Where? Where have you been? Answer me, child!" But Nyi Nyaih Shwe just slumped down on her bed mat and rolled to one side away from her mother.

"Nyi Nyaih Shwe, I have good news! I have found a school for you. It is a private school. It is a Christian school! It is free, Nyi Nyaih Shwe! Really!"

"Mother, I'm not going! I'm never going to school again! Never! I'm going to die. Just like Daddy!"

Nyi Nyi shrieked out and answered her daughter, "You are not going to die! You will do as I say, and you will go to school!"

"Mother! Please!" Nyi Nyaih Shwe insisted. "You don't know how it is."

"This is a Christian school!"

Nyi Nyaih Shwe rolled her eyes and answered, "Christians? Like those people who don't want us going to church with them? Like the Christian children that called me bad names and threw stones at me? Really, Mother?"

"These people are different. You will see! It is a chance for you, Nyi Nyaih Shwe."

Nyi Nyaih Shwe slumped back on the floor and cried. "No one is different. They are all the same. And…and, what about my AIDS? I am getting sick more often now. It doesn't matter if the school is free; we cannot afford AIDS treatment. How would I even get there?"

"I don't know. I don't have all the answers," Nyi Nyi cried. "I'm doing the best I can for you and your sisters. We must trust God!"

Nyi Nyaih Shwe screamed at her mother, "Trust God? Which god? The God who would not heal Daddy? Why is He going to help us now?"

They could have argued all night. But they didn't. Both mother and daughter fell fast asleep next to Nyi Nyaih Shwe's sisters. When morning came, Nyi Nyaih Shwe woke, rolled over, and saw several bags sitting on the floor next to her bed, filled with her things. Nyi Nyi said, "My daughter, you are going to the school today."

Saya Peter graduated from the Southeast India Baptist Bible College in Bangalore, India. There he studied for four years and returned to his homeland to start a church. He and Mercy married shortly after his return to the village of Kanan and they lived in the stairwell, in the back of his father's store. His father helped him buy property on which to build a church and together they built the first dormitory for orphans and children who would otherwise have no education. Peter has always had a vision to evangelize Burmese Buddhist people for Christ. He was never part of any denomination or association of churches. Everything he ever built for God, he did so by faith.

Nyi Nyi and her daughters appeared at the school that evening and Saya Peter showed them where Nyi Nyaih Shwe would stay. It was on the second floor of a dormitory which GLBM financed. There was a large open room with bed mats all around the four walls. Clothes hung from simple wooden racks.

When they walked in, all the girls ran to meet Nyi Nyaih Shwe. They shook hands, and took her bags from her, carrying them to her place and the mat where she would sleep. Nyi Nyaih Shwe was a bit overcome by their immediate acceptance of her. But she reserved judgment, thinking "They don't know about me!", and she was right.

Even though the students, especially the girls, were very friendly and seemed to accept Nyi Nyaih Shwe, she always sat by herself. When everyone else was playing in the courtyard, she would stay away from everyone. She never smiled. She never laughed like the other children. One day she became violently sick.

One of the students came running and cried out, "Saya Peter, come quickly!

Nyi Nyaih Shwe is sick." Quickly responding and running alongside the student, he reached Nyi Nyaih Shwe to find her vomiting violently and crying. Many of the children asked, "What's wrong with her, Saya?"

Nyi Nyaih Shwe caught her breath, turned toward the students and said, "You want to know what's wrong with me? I have AIDS! I have AIDS! Wanna see?" And she yanked up on her sleeve to display her sores.

"Oh, my!" "What is that?" "How awful!"

One after another, students gasped and moved away. Saya Peter immediately got everyone's attention and said, "Listen to me! Listen to me! You cannot catch AIDS by simple touch. You should not be afraid of Nyi Nyaih Shwe. You can touch her like anyone else. It is ok. You can hug her." With that, he took Nyi Nyaih Shwe in his arms in front of everyone, and she wept on his shoulder.

The bulk of the students at the school accepted that, and they tried not to treat her differently than others. But Nyi Nyaih Shwe was very self-conscious about her problem, and she was becoming sick more often.

Saya Peter did some research and found out about the AIDS Clinic in Tamu. He also learned that, if he were to enroll Nyi Nyaih Shwe in the treatment program, it would be costly, and they would have to take her there once every month. He and Mercy talked about it. Peter's father would help. They decided to make whatever sacrifice they could for Nyi Nyaih Shwe.

So, they began to go to Tamu every month. As with Than Shwe, the treatment was too expensive; it was too far to go; it was insufficient; it was uncomfortable and made Nyi Nyaih Shwe sick. But, regardless, they went every month, and every month when they returned, Nyi Nyaih Shwe would go to her dorm room, ball up in a fetal position on the floor, cry, and vomit. But the treatments helped her. They were not a cure. But they seemed to help her. Peter, however, feared for her and wondered how long she would live with her AIDS. "BaGyi Bob from America is coming to visit us," Peter told the students.

The students were so excited that they made welcoming wreaths from colored construction paper, like Hawaiian leis. They stood in a long line. And when BaGyi Bob came, he didn't come alone. There was a team of six with him. The students all bowed and greeted BaGyi and his team and then placed the wreaths around their necks. Nyi Nyaih Shwe stood alone, far off from the crowd.

BaGyi Bob and the GLBM team would stay several days and speak in preaching meetings day and night. But they would also play with the students. They set up a volleyball net in the courtyard and the students had so much fun. The team also brought what they called "frisbees" from America. They took the students to the street and threw the flying disks in the air until some of the ladies worried that either the children's arms would fall off or they would end up hitting a neighbor in the head. But the students caught on to the sport quickly and loved it. Nyi Nyaih Shwe hid in her dorm room, all alone.

When it was time for preaching, the students gathered in rows and sang songs, clapping and having fun. BaGyi Bob borrowed one of the school's old guitars and sang a Christian song from America. Then he preached, and the students' eyes were glued to him the whole time. Some had never seen a white man, or a foreigner of any color from any country. He made the students laugh. The students gathered around him and played with members of the GLBM team. The little children climbed right up on BaGyi's lap, some hung around his neck, and he did not object at all. But Nyi Nyaih Shwe sat alone, far away.

After the second night of preaching, Saya Peter sat down with BaGyi Bob and talked. They spoke about many things and Peter shared his vision and what he needed for the work there to continue. They needed another dormitory with a water tank for bathing and a separate room where Saya Peter and his family could sleep. BaGyi Bob asked how much it would cost. Saya Peter answered, kind of fearfully, "3,500." BaGyi Bob smiled and said, "Done!"

Then Saya Peter said, "BaGyi, there is a girl, a young lady here. She has AIDS. I am so afraid for her, BaGyi. Would you show her some extra attention?" BaGyi said, "Please point her out to me!"

The following day, in the middle of the afternoon, BaGyi Bob was playing games with some of the students in the courtyard. Again, Nyi Nyaih Shwe sat alone, away from fun and games. As BaGyi saw her, he walked over to her and held out his hand. He said, "You are Nyi Nyaih Shwe, no?" She nodded affirmatively. BaGyi said, "I am happy to meet you. Please come with me and join our game!" She took his hand and walked with him to where the other children were playing. But, when the games started again, Nyi Nyaih Shwe quietly disappeared.

Later that same night, there was a meeting and BaGyi Bob preached. Again, every eye was on him, and the students listened to every word. When he was finished, he invited students to come to the altar if they wanted to receive Jesus Christ as their personal Lord and Saviour. Six teenagers came to the front and stood in a line.

They prayed with BaGyi Bob, acknowledging their sin and need of a Saviour, asking Jesus to forgive them and to come into their hearts. It was a great night, and everyone was so happy. Saya Peter announced that BaGyi Bob would baptize the new believers the following night after another service.

The following night after the preaching, it was late, and a thick darkness had fallen on the courtyard. Men of the church had built a makeshift baptistry pool from old tires and a large vinyl tarp. They filled it with knee-deep water and the crowd of church members and students gathered around. To one side stood the new converts who would receive believer's baptism. Saya Peter directed BaGyi Bob to enter the pool and begin the baptism. By the light of a small flashlight, BaGyi read from the Scriptures and explained the ordinance of biblical, New Testament baptism. He handed his Bible and flashlight to Saya Peter and held his hand out to the first candidate for baptism. One by one they entered the pool and went down into the water.

But as the fifth candidate stepped into the pool, Saya Peter began to weep and sob audibly. BaGyi looked over at Peter, then gazed into the face of the candidate whom he already held by the hands. It was Nyi Nyaih Shwe. Looking up at BaGyi Bob, she said, "I love you, BaGyi, and I love Jesus. Because of Him I am going to live! Yes?"

Overcome with emotions and tears running down his face, BaGyi Bob said, "Upon your profession of faith, I baptize you, my little sister, in the name of the Father, and of the Son, and of the Holy Ghost. Buried with Him in baptism…" BaGyi slipped Nyi Nyaih Shwe gently under the water and lifted her back up. "…raised to walk in newness of life. Amen!"

Peter Van Siang Lian and wife, Mercy

Nyi Nyaih Shwe's first big smile after making a profession of faith

CHAPTER SEVEN

Soul Saving Sojourn
in Shan State

"For whosoever will save his life shall lose it: and whosoever
will lose his life for my sake shall find it."
Matthew 16:25

I have a saying, "I just love a good adventure!" Many have heard me say that. And I mean it. I love driving a road I have never driven just to find out where it goes and see the sights along the way. I even love to try new and sometimes exotic foods. I tell those who travel with me that they must be flexible. Those who visit a Third World mission field must leave their preconceived ideas at home. We should never compromise our Bible- based convictions, but a missionary must be adaptable. When you go to Myanmar, you cannot bring your favorite pillow and mattress. You might be able to bring your favorite shoes along, but you may end up discovering they are not the best or the most comfortable in the Myanmar climate.

Most of us are creatures of habit and don't like change. We have our routines. We go to bed each night at near the same time. Even if we stay up late, then try to sleep longer the following morning, we still wake as usual because our body clocks are set to a certain schedule. As I travel around the world through many times zones, my nighttime is suddenly morning, and morning becomes night. It takes several days for my body to adjust to an opposite sequence of work and rest. I don't mind the change too much because, in my mind, I am changing for a reason.

The salvation experience brings the single greatest change in any human life. It is revolutionary. It is not reformation but transformation. It is more profound than reordering daily schedules, moving to a new house, getting a new job, or attending a new school. Real biblical salvation is not faddish, fanatical, flimsy, or flippant. It is a change from the mundane to the supernatural, from the worldly to the spiritual, from the temporal to the eternal. It is a change from death to life, from mortality to immortality, from darkness to light, from the filth of sin to the cleansing and pardon of being forgiven. It is a change from the world of death and sorrow to a family of hope and joy. That change is a choice. You must choose Jesus Christ and a new life in Him.

The Apostle Paul put it like this, *"Therefore if any man be in Christ, he is a new creature: old things are passed away; behold, all things are become new."* 2 Corinthians 5:17

When you become a born-again Christian, your immediate change is not one of self-determination, discernment, and discipline. Those things do come into your new life in Christ with growth in Him and are given to you like seeds that germinate in the soul, grow into a tree of life, and produce fruit that glorifies God and brings fulfillment and purpose to living. Vance Havner, that great American pulpiteer of the 20th century, said that God gives us opportunities to bear fruit for Him and He desires fruit, "not mere leaves of profession." (Reflections On the Gospels, p. 166, by Vance Havner, compiled by Michael Catt, CLC Publications, Fort Washington, PA 2006). Those opportunities become ours as we grow spiritually in Christ. But the initial change that comes from salvation is by the Spirit of Christ that moves in and permanently indwells the believer. He alone brings remarkable and effectual change.

I know that some of life's changes can be traumatic. And we fear and resist the changes that come by disease, injury, or financial reversal. But change in the Christian life is a continuous spiritual process, like a child growing up and maturing. God uses the Holy Bible to change us. He uses preaching to change us. God uses people to change us, and us to change people. I have decided that the changes God brings into my life are always good. Therefore, why should I resist?

You only have one life, and if it is to be changed for the good, time is of the essence. The wisemen followed the star that would lead them to the Christ child. Everything in their life would be different from that point forward. Moses traveled far from the land of Pharaoh, searching for one thing. What he found, not only changed him but defined his life. Jonah didn't want to go to Ninevah. But obeying God changed his life and the hearts of all those who have ever read his book of the Bible. Joseph's brethren traveled all the way to Egypt, and what they found was not what they were seeking. But it changed their lives. The Apostle Paul's life was changed, not in a church or a synagogue, not in a conference, but on a road. All of these had to leave their comfort zone to find what God wanted to give them. In like manner, God has called His children to GO into all the world, carrying and preaching the Gospel of Christ. But do you know? Going is life changing.

Boy was his name. He was from the Lahu tribe, and he had been asking me to go with him to his native Shan State for two years. I had not necessarily ignored him. But going that far did not fit into my game plan and I always found a reason why it was inconvenient. I had heard rumors about the Shan people. It seemed that any experience with them would be either extraordinary or life-threatening. I wasn't sure that I wanted to discover which. Nevertheless, I committed to go.

We loaded up early because the journey to the northeastern mountain villages of Shan State would be long and arduous. We would not travel through Myanmar, but Thailand. We would be gone nearly one week. It was hot in the city; it would be cooler in the northern hills. I was looking forward to it – the cool, that is! Yes, I was also anticipating the Lahu villages, and eager to reach out to them with the Gospel. We traveled from the Burmese border at Mae Sot, Thailand eastward, across Tak Province and the Dawna Mountain Range, then northward to the Thai Highlands, through Chiang Mai and Chiang Rai, and finally across the Mekong River and back into Myanmar at the city of Tachileik. Here is the famous "Golden Triangle" where Myanmar, Thailand, and Laos come together at the northernmost reaches of the Mekong River, just south of the Yunnan Province of China.

There, in the green hills and red clay banks where hardly a tourist is ever seen, is unseen peril. The concentration of opium farms, drug trafficking, and feuding overlords brings most people pause to visit there. This is where much of the world's heroine comes from, and when we crossed the river from Chiang Rai, Thailand and finally arrived in the city of Tachileik, my spirit, perhaps God's Spirit within me, was uneasy.

The Lahu tribe's name is pronounced phonetically just as it would seem, with a short A and a long U. The Lahu people are an ethnic group of approximately one million in China and mainland Southeast Asia. Their population is strongest in Myanmar, second only to China. They are spread thinly throughout Myanmar, but there are large concentrations of them in both the Shan and Kachin States. They speak their own Lahu language and several similar dialects originating from it, but many also speak Chinese, Burmese, and Thai, depending on their location of residence. Their principal religions are Animism, or spirit-worship, Buddhism, Catholicism, and various distinctions of Christianity. But there are very few Bible-preaching churches among the Lahu people. As in many Western cultures, they have much religion, but not much Christ.

I crossed the bridge into Tachileik on foot and carefully, yet patiently, went through Immigration as a tourist. Then I waited for our Burmese preacher boys and Lahu translator who were in a long line of cars and trucks, trying to re-enter Myanmar as citizens. They said that it was expedient for me to go through alone. Even when you think you understand policies and politics, restrictions, and requirements, it is best to travel in these places with nationals you trust and do what you are told. They told me to go across alone for a reason. They did not explain it. I did not ask.

I had not been standing on the Myanmar side for more than two minutes when a seedy looking, very dark-skinned man approached me. He was very insistent that I employ him as a guide. I was polite and gracious with the man until he became very agitated, demanding that I let him help me. I surmised that he was either some kind of con man or perhaps a government agent. I finally just walked away from him and, after another twenty minutes, saw our van come through. The man never stopped staring at me, and I can honestly say that I have never been so uncomfortable in any other place in Myanmar or in any part of SE Asia. Tachileik did not make a good first impression upon me.

We made our way through town and then headed north, along Route 4, through the Akha tribal villages of Mong Lin and Monghpyak, to the Lahu city of Keng Tung, not far from the Chinese border. We checked into a simple Burmese Guest House which was just slightly more comfortable than sleeping on the street. It was clean and centrally located but had minimal services. No breakfast was given in the morning, but it was a short walk to a little café where we could get an egg with some rice and a little fruit on the side.

I've been in many Burmese markets, from the famous Bogyoke Zay in Yangon to the city market in Malawmyine, the village market on the Ayeyarwady River at Aung Lan, the city marketplace in Tahan (or Kalay), and the shops of Tedim and Kennedy Peak along the Mizoram border at almost 9,000 feet above sea level. But the city market at Keng Tung was amazingly tribal, a complete delight to me, with rare photo opportunities in every direction. I was completely mesmerized by it all. Here, one can see the various peoples and their brightly colored tribal clothing, handicrafts, and tools that you might never see anywhere else in the world. In vain, I searched the market for a used Akha machete and leather sheath. But it was a treat to eat with an Akha family who was cooking fish and chicken inside green bamboo and to drink their jungle tea from a fresh bamboo cup.

Each Myanmar tribe is known for the colors, patterns, and decorations of clothing that are peculiar to their ethnic group. The Lahu people favor black dresses and jackets with bright red beads, tassels, and pom-poms. The Akha people, another hill-tribe of the area, seem to have a culture that is slowly disappearing and melting into that of others. But many of their women continue to adorn themselves with a lavish headdress that frames their face with large steel ornaments.

On our first full day in Keng Tung we loaded the van to go up the mountain to Loi Mwe, a remote village where a church was being planted. I was traveling with several of our preacher boys, a supply of water, some snacks, my camera bag, and six large boxes of Burmese Scriptures.

Keng Tung is in a large fertile valley, surrounded by vast ridges of mountains that seem to rise slowly in every direction. Gazing from the city, they seem far away. But, as you drive into the hills, you are suddenly swallowed up by them as if leaving a former world behind. As a child growing up in Virginia, I often gazed longingly to the Appalachian Mountains and the Skyline Drive to the West. I yearned to go there. I have never enjoyed the flatland as much. So, here I was in my glory! Once inside the mountains, the curvy dirt road was wide at first but continuously ascended into tighter rocky crevices until the valley below totally disappeared.

When you travel through these mountains, much like in Chin State on the western side of Myanmar, you drive along high ledges over vast breathtaking valleys that are so wide and deep that sometimes the sight is overwhelming and intimidating. There are drop-offs over cliffs that seem to have no bottom. During rainy season, many are impassable. Those who dare to go forward may have no choice but to abandon vehicles stuck deep above their axles or spend many hours or even days digging them out. Then there are the rock and mud slides. There is no turning back. You must navigate around them, sometimes along the narrowest of passages, and wait your turn to do so.

It was an amazing thing to me that we were so close to the Chinese border. And not places like Beijing or Shanghai, but the southwestern reaches, or the back side, of China. This is the same topography described by China Inland Mission's James Fraser who traversed these mountains by horseback and on foot in the late 1800s as he evangelized the Lisu people of Yunnan, China. His vivid descriptions captivated me as I read of his journeys of faith, his ever-maturing prayer life, his pursuit of souls, and the attacks he withstood from tribal warriors, witches, wraiths, and wild animals. (Mountain Rain, Eileen Crossman, Davidson Publishers, 2001) Even now, as I write these words, I study Google Earth and look down by satellite imagery on the very roads and village landmarks that remain in my mind and heart. I thank God but can barely believe that He has allowed me to physically travel to these places and their peoples with the Gospel. On our way up to Loi Mwe we stopped at a tiny mountain village with just a few primitive shelters and a simple market, all built into the side of a hill. We were received instantly and warmly. The children gathered around me with no small interest, as none of them had ever seen a white man. One little girl attached herself to me, holding my hand as we walked through the village. Everywhere I went, she went. When I sat, she sat with me. When I stood to leave, she acted as though she wanted to go along. I was very tempted to scoop her up, put her in the van, and become her Daddy, or to take her to one of our orphanages in the country. I learned, however, that she did have a family in the village. She hugged my neck as we departed and kissed my hand.

We gathered the people together, and I grabbed an old, beat up guitar, sang some hymns, and then preached the Word of God. Many had never heard of Christ. They could not imagine that One had died for them. But some of them quickly received the Word that we preached and believed on Christ. We left a few Bibles with the intention of returning as soon as possible to plant a new church. Again, I was overcome with the thought that it does not take long, and you don't have to go far, to find people who don't know about Christ. Still, the harvest truly is plentiful, and the laborers are few.

Making our way, still upward through the mountains, carefully maneuvering around muddy hairpin turns and narrow ledges, I saw many settlements of homes, down in narrow mountain gorges, some near, some far away in the distance. And with seemingly no road or even a path that led to them, I said out loud, "I want to meet those people!" But our driver said there was not enough time, that it would take another whole day to reach them. Time is always my biggest problem. We must constantly remind ourselves, both on the so-called "mission field" and back in our own country, to redeem the time. We fritter away so much of our time, and it is precious.

Finally reaching Loi Mwe, I realized that my host had neglected to tell me that there was a military base at the village – perhaps a full battalion of men and families. As we arrived at the place where we would preach, I greeted the young church-planter and his family. Then he introduced me to a man whom I will never forget. He had been one of the first converts to Christ in that village and had become a charter member of the new church. He was a three-star Burmese Army officer, a Captain, and the base commander. After years of Buddhism and idol worship, he was now taking a stand for Christ. (Can somebody shout Hallelujah?)

After the service, he took us on a short tour of the village. It was a beautiful place with a central lake and a footbridge across the middle of it. As we drove through the village, I spied a woman and her young child down in a field at a water well. I hollered out, "Stop! Stop!" The driver slammed on the breaks and everyone looked at me for an explanation. I said, "Look! It's the Woman at the Well. We must go talk to her!" And so, we parked our vehicle and walked down, off the road and into the field, to the mother and her child. We gave her a gospel tract and explained to her how she could know the Christ and have her sins forgiven. She did not immediately believe on Christ but received our Scriptures and listened intently to our gospel presentation. As we spoke of the love of Christ and forgiveness, tears filled her eyes and we thought perhaps the Holy Ghost was bringing conviction of sin and giving her the gift of faith. I believe that she wanted to pray with us. But I understood that turning to Christ without her husband and family also believing would mean great turmoil in her home and possibly bring persecution upon her in the village. We spent the rest of the day knocking doors and talking with people in the village.

After a whole day with the dear pastor, his family, and young congregation, we left with them the six boxes of Burmese Scriptures and made our way back down through the mountains to the city of Keng Tung. The road led us in a northwesterly direction most of the way back and the sunset was spectacular. It is one of the reasons why Old Burma is called the Golden Land.

The following day we traveled outside the city again, but this time just a short distance, to an orphanage supported by the area Lahu churches. The Director and his wife were a delight with a wonderful heart for Christ and for the children. Again, we sang and preached the Gospel. I told stories to the young people who sat and listened with amazing attentiveness. After the service, the Director asked us to join him for a meal in his apartment there on the grounds.

I was sitting next to an open window and, as the men were having a discussion, I saw a girl, perhaps fourteen years old, who was standing outside and staring at me with a huge smile. She balanced herself with a single crutch because she had only one leg. But her beautiful smile captured my attention, and I could hardly look away. I waved at her, and she immediately turned and hobbled away as if being shy or ashamed.

There was a break in the discussion, and I asked the Director about the young lady. She had been involved in a motorcycle accident and was in a small area hospital for many months. She had extensive injuries and, at one point, was not expected to live. She lost her leg and, because she had no real family, could not take care of herself. My heart broke instantly. I asked the Director if we could invite her inside with us because I wanted to talk to her. But the Director told me that she was very shy and probably would not come. Regardless, he sent a boy to invite her to come inside.

I was sitting on a wooden bench as she approached and stood in the door. I motioned to her, inviting her to come inside several times. But she stood still, yet smiling, leaning on her crutch. Finally, I stood and walked over to her, speaking gently. I offered my hand, and she took it. She then followed me into the house and sat by my side. It wasn't long before she felt comfortable enough to talk with me and then stayed with me the remainder of the day. I was so impressed with her spirit that I searched my shoulder bag for something to give her. Despite her injury and handicap, she manifested a joyful meekness that was beautiful to behold. I had an elastic jade bracelet that I had purchased in another State. I presented it to her, but she did not understand what I meant to do. So, I took her hand and placed the bracelet around her wrist. I said, "Remember. The greatest gift comes from God." What rapture of joy was mine when I heard that she had given her heart to Christ! I may never see her again in this life, but I will never forget her.

On another day we traveled to several different villages, preaching, singing, and distributing Gospel tracts and Scriptures. It was extremely hot that day and, by the end of the day, I was worn out. My clothes were soaked through with sweat, my head ached, I had become weakened and felt dehydrated. I was ready to return to my air-conditioned hotel room. It was already evening, and our young men said to me, "BaGyi, we go one more village!" That village was two hours away by car, farther from our hotel, and we would have to travel the roughest roads yet to get there. They insisted that we go.

I said, "Gentlemen, I am not feeling well. We will have to do this on another day." I can honestly say that I didn't want to go, and being rare for me, I argued with them and gave all kinds of reasons why we should return to the city. I was told, "BaGyi, many people wait us!" They had been waiting for half the day. So, I got some water, and mustered as much strength from a bag of chips as I could, and we headed for the village.

Where the road was paved, the surface was broken and littered with menacing potholes. The going was slow and painful. And yet I nodded off to a tortured sleep, being consistently roused by every jolting bump and the creaking of the vehicle's aged suspension. The road became narrow and took us over a high mountain, around many sharp curves, through a jungle-covered valley, and up again to a mountain side where a small village was concealed from view. There, along the roadside, was a market and tavern. I was told the meeting would be inside.

As we entered what seemed like a small building, we were directed through a passageway to another space where I was amazed to see more than one hundred people sitting on the floor. They were all waiting for me, and I was late. Yet, they applauded vigorously, and I was asked to sit in the only chair in the room. In their own language, they sang from very worn and soiled songbooks tunes that were immediately familiar to my ears. I opened my Bible, picked out a verse of Scripture, and God gave me a clear line of thought, how to present that singular Gospel truth in a simple and clear way. When it became my time to preach, my fatigue faded into zestful oratory of the love of God and the grace of Christ's purchased redemption for all. I preached as if it was my first message of the day and God gave me new strength. When I invited my listeners to come to Christ, many souls were gloriously saved and my spirit soared like an eagle riding the updrafts of wind to stormless open skies.

I was mingling among the new converts, shaking hands and encouraging the brethren, when one of our preacher boys approached me and said, "BaGyi! Man outside; he cry!" I said, "Say again?" He said, "Man outside...very cry, BaGyi!" I said, "Show me!"

When I walked back out on the street, I saw a dark, red-skinned man sitting in a wheelchair. He, indeed, was weeping. I approached him and asked, "Sir, why you cry?" He answered, "I am too late!"

His wheelchair was a three-wheeler with a pump handle mounted between his legs, used to propel him forward. His legs were dead, nothing but skin and bone, and folded beneath him on the seat. He had on shorts and no shirt. As he wept, he leaned over the handlebars, and I wondered if he might even fall out of the chair to the ground.

I asked, "What did you say?" He answered again, "I am too late?" I responded, "Sir, too late for what?"

This man had heard that a foreigner was coming with The Book that teaches about a Savior. In his wheelchair, he had pumped his way along mountain dirt roads for two days, sleeping in his chair at night, so that he might hear the Gospel message of Christ. When he finally arrived at the service, he was told that we were already finished. There, outside our meeting hall, he sat in his chair and wept. I told him, "Dear sir, you are not too late. It will be my privilege to tell you about Jesus right now."

Any soul winner knows that it is the Holy Ghost who convicts of sin and brings a person to belief in Christ. They also know that there are those who are difficult to persuade and others who, for various reasons and circumstances, are ready to be saved and leading them to Christ is like picking low-branch fruit. This dear gentleman was not only ready to be saved, but he was also anxious to receive Christ. Any one of the Lord's many husbandmen could have harvested his soul quickly for the Saviour.

But, what if I had not gone to that last village? Selfishly and callously, I was thinking of myself and my own needs when many on the mountain were seeking the Saviour. I wonder how many times I have ignored the hints of the Holy Spirit as He was making a soul ready for redemption, but I was occupied and oblivious to that which is spiritually obvious to others. A servant of the Lord must learn to discern the winds and whiffs of God's work among people.

In this chapter, I have written a narrative or sequence of things that occurred on my first journey to Eastern Shan State. I have not told all. There may seemingly be no one character or place that stands out above the rest. But, as I remember the trip and those things that God did, I am persuaded that perhaps He did the most, not in others, but in me. I learned much. I needed to learn. I needed to change. God used what I saw and the people I met to change me for Him and for them. For me, Shan State was Change State. And I am very thankful I went there.

I had never considered the words to the old hymn, God Leads Us Along, in this light before. But as I look back, certainly God has led me along. My desire is that He would keep leading and that I would follow.

In shady, green pastures, so rich and so sweet
God leads His dear children along
Where the water's cool flow bathes the weary one's feet
God leads His dear children along

Chorus:
Some through the waters, some through the flood
Some through the fire, but all through the blood
Some through great sorrow, but God gives a song
In the night season and all the day long

Sometimes on the mount where the sun shines so bright
God leads His dear children along
Sometimes in the valley, in darkest of night
God leads His dear children along

Though sorrows befall us, and evils oppose
God leads His dear children along
Through grace we can conquer, defeat all our foes
God leads His dear children along

Away from the mire, and away from the clay
God leads His dear children along
Away up in glory, eternity's day
God leads His dear children along

CHAPTER EIGHT

Boy With Guitar or How It All Began

"a great door and effectual is opened unto me, and there are many adversaries."
1 Corinthians 16:9

It was a day like any other. I had breakfast and filled a tall travel mug with my favorite coffee, started my car and let it warm up, then headed for my office. I had a list of things to do and several people to contact. I fired up my desktop computer and opened my e-mail browser. As was my morni ng ritual, I looked for important messages first, then began to shuffle through the "junk mail." I usually had so many advertisements that I just kept my finger on the delete button and moved through them quickly, sending them to the Recycle Bin like roaches on extermination day. Like many others, I had received messages from Nigeria and Amsterdam with promises of millions of dollars. All I had to do was send my Social Security number and bank account information. But, as my eyes scanned the day's inbox, one email message stood out and looked different. It had originated in a place where I had never been and never thought too much about. Like most Americans, I had to check the world atlas to confirm where it was. And, despite my experience with scads of dubious dispatches in the past, this one seemed to have a look of authenticity.

Htein Win Ei, a tribal pastor with a church and school in the middle of Myanmar, or Old Burma was asking for my help. He stated, "I found your website for troubled youth. I see that you help troubled children. I have sixty orphans who are getting one spoonful of rice each day. Sometimes we must decide who will eat and who will not eat. Will you help us?"

In 1962, during a time of widespread anarchy, General Ne Win seized control of his government, dealing treacherously with all opposition, and hurling the country into a 50-plus year dictatorship. Because of its reported human rights abuses, the paranoid government became the target of global criticism and economic sanctions. Isolated from the entire world, Old Burma collapsed into abject poverty and decay. And, yet, according to Htein Win Ei's e-mail, the work of God survived and continued.

I read his message several times, still thinking and trying to prove to myself that it was a scam. I thought that if this pastor were so poor, and if he lived in a small village in the middle of a Burma jungle, how would he have access to internet service and e-mail?" I still had my finger on the Delete button, but that "still small voice" would not allow me to push it. Taking my finger off the keyboard, I bowed my head and said, "Ok, Lord. What is this? What do you want me to do?" The answer came into my mind, "Answer the man."

I asked Htein for his testimony of salvation in Christ and for a doctrinal statement from the Scriptures, stating what he believed. I honestly thought that I would never hear from him again. I placed his e-mail into an archive file and went about my business. Within four days, I received Htein Win Ei's reply: a detailed testimony of salvation by grace through faith in the substitutionary sacrifice of the shed blood of Christ and a extraordinary explanation of sound doctrine from the Burmese Scriptures of Adoniram Judson.

I had read of Adoniram Judson while taking a general missions course in Bible college. He was lumped-in with other greats such as William Carey, Hudson Taylor, and David Livingstone. So, I knew of him. But, even after graduation, becoming a pastor and overseeing a local church missions' program, his life and work meant little to me. I was concerned with two things: building a ministry to reach souls and leading my people to pay for it.

I was 52 years old and had been in the ministry for more than thirty years when I received the message from Htein Win Ei. I had a nationwide ministry to trouble youth, a toll-free hotline, gospel tracts and literature in print, and a schedule that kept me traveling most of the year. I had traveled to Mexico, Canada, Ukraine, Great Britain, Amsterdam, and forty US States. But I had never been in Asia.

I knew people who had been duped into sending money to internet preachers. But I was fascinated with Htein's message. And, after praying for him, I told my wife, Carolyn, that we needed to help him. I suggested that we send him two hundred dollars per month as God would give us the extra funds. But I did not know how to get the money to him. We literally sent $200.00 to a man I knew nothing about in Singapore. That man sent our money to a man we didn't know in Bangkok, Thailand. He sent the money to a friend of his Yangon, Myanmar. Then the man in Myanmar sent our money to small general store in Aung Lan, a village along the Ayeyarwaddy River of Old Burma, and Htein Win Ei walked miles to get his money and collected every single penny. How does something like that happen without God? Any one of those men could have kept the money and we could have done nothing about it. My wife and I concluded that God himself was "IN" this thing, and whatever He wanted to do was going to be a "big deal."

There have been times when I have been accused of trying to "bite off more than I can chew" or even grandstanding. I will admit that I am not above the appreciation of accolades as anyone else. But, in trying to serve God, I have not sought the praise of men. Some have said that I march to the beat of a different drummer. Regardless, my philosophy has been that of India missionary, William

Carey who is credited with being the Father of Modern Missions. He is famous for saying, "Expect great things from God; attempt great things for God."

I became a born-again Christian in 1969. I was thirteen years old and I was the first person saved in my family. I believe God called me to preach and full-time ministry in 1971, an old-fashioned missionary filmstrip Sunday night church service. As a fifteen-year-old boy, I did not enjoy reading much. But I liked TV shows like I Love Lucy, McHale's Navy and movies with John Wayne. I liked peanut butter and jelly sandwiches, cottage cheese with pineapple, ice cream, and Baked Alaska. I loved my mother's meatloaf, my grandmother's apple pie and her homemade mayonnaise, but not together.

Born at the old Doctor's Hospital in Washington DC, I was grew up across the Potomac River in northern Virginia and graduated from West Springfield High School. My grandparents on my father's side lived in Arlington, Virginia, near the junction of Glebe Road and Columbia Pike. On more than one occasion, my grandmother and I walked to the Columbia Theater for a good Disney movie or old-fashioned musical. One weekend, as I was staying overnight, my Grandmother mentioned that there was a special movie at the theater for young people. It was called "The Cross and The Switchblade," and she wondered if I would like to go.

We walked to the theater and saw the movie about Evangelist David Wilkerson, a skinny country preacher who gave his life to reach the gangs of Harlem in New York City. Nicky Cruz was the warlord of the Puerto Rican Mau Maus and had a heart of stone. He tried to kill the preacher. But instead, the love of God broke his heart and the preacher led him to Christ. He became an evangelist, reaching young people around the world and his autobiography, called "Run, Baby, Run," records it vivid detail. On our way out of the theater, young people were distributing free copies of the book. I took that book home, read every word overnight, and still have it in my library today.

I had started a Bible Club in my high school and the attendance had outgrown several different classrooms. After reading Nicky's book, I told the club, "We need to organize an evangelistic crusade in our high school." There was information in the back of the book on how to contact Nicky Cruz and I called the number provided. Somehow, I was able to talk to Nicky himself and he agreed to come and preach in our school.

I didn't know how to organize a big meeting. I was only fifteen years old. My own pastor was afraid to get involved. But Nicky's staff sent big color posters and we put them in store windows all over the area. I secured free advertising announcements on radio, television, and in the newspapers. On the first night of the crusade, Nicky Cruz entered the building and peaked through the heavy stage curtains to see more than 6,000 people sitting in 2,800 seats. Every night, a thousand people were turned away that couldn't get inside the building. It was a fire marshal's worst nightmare but, by the end of the five-night meeting, several thousand people had made public professions of faith in Christ, we had paid all the expenses, and gave the evangelist near $20,000.

Very early in my Christian experience, God taught me that He could answer prayer and do, as is described in the third chapter of the book of Ephesians, "abundantly above all that we ask or think." Later, in 1992, I started a ministry called Solid Rock Youth Ministries Inc. and, preaching in youth detention centers and children's homes across America, we recorded more than 40,000 professions of faith among troubled youth in sixteen years.

So, when God began to work in my heart toward winning souls in Myanmar, on the opposite side of the globe, difficulties and challenges didn't even occur to me. I just wanted to obey God.

I began to correspond regularly with Pastor Htein. And, as he sent photos of his students and orphans, as I began to hear their stories, I fell in love.

In the early morning of April 27, 2008, I was shaving in our upstairs bathroom and my wife hollered up the steps, "Honey, you need to get down here right now." A special news report was airing on TV about "Cyclone Nargis," a storm that had formed in the Indian Ocean, cutting a path of destruction across southern Myanmar with 165 mph sustained winds, a direct hit on the city of Yangon (Old Rangoo) and its population of 7.5 million people. 86,000 had been killed overnight. Within the next three weeks nearly a half million people would perish. On the Internet I saw images of dead bodies floating in canals and hanging in trees. As I watched and realized what had happened, I literally fell on the floor of our den and wept. Yet, God was continuing to put the Myanmar people in my heart. Why? I didn't know.

Within a couple months Pastor Htein asked me, "What would hinder you from coming to visit us in our country?" I replied, "Your government!" Myanmar was still closed. But as I traveled to the Burmese Embassy in Washington DC, I was granted a Visa.

In the next few months, almost everyone I knew attempted to discourage me from going to Myanmar. Six other preachers said they would go with me. But, as the date for the trip neared, they all backed out. So, in February of 2009 I boarded a flight in Elmira, New York alone and flew to Detroit. Then I flew on Delta Airlines to Narita International Airport in Tokyo, Japan. I asked a stewardess, "Exactly how long is this flight?" She answered, "It never ends!" The flight was fourteen hours, non-stop.

After a four-hour layover in Japan, I boarded another flight for Bangkok, and I was so ignorant that I thought it would take only a couple hours to get there. Seven hours later we landed in Bangkok, Thailand. There, at the Suvarnabhumi (meaning "Golden Land") International Airport, I had a nine-hour layover, and there wasn't a seat available in the whole place. Every square foot of flooring was occupied with people sleeping in rows like parked Sunday School buses at the First Baptist Church of Hammond, Indiana. But I finally found a sandwich shop and spent the night painfully balancing myself on a counter stool.

In the morning, my next plane's boarding time was announced, and I stood in line among a delegation of saffron-robed, shaved-headed Buddhist monks and tried to prepare myself mentally for Myanmar. I must admit that I was feeling both excitement and anxiety. I really did not know what to expect.

When we landed at Yangon, I stood in line again, waiting to give my passport and Visa to one of the Burmese Army soldiers who were manning the Immigration counters. I prayed a lot, saying, "I'm following you, Lord. Please help me!"

Htein Win Ei was standing just outside the main doors, pressing his nose up against the glass windows like a little boy outside a toy store at Christmas time. We greeted one another and quickly haled a taxi to take us to the Golden Guest Inn, a small hotel on Insein Road known for housing Christians without asking awkward questions. The owner/manager was a very friendly Chinese businessman, a Buddhist, and he welcomed us warmly and, even though he needed to make copies of my passport and visa and report my presence to the government, he tried his best to streamline the process. Pastor Htein and I would room together, and after laying down, I slept through the night.

I had many experiences that first week in Myanmar; some were exciting, and others a bit harrowing. There was a heavy military presence in the city. Soldiers with AK-47 rifles stood at every intersection. Truckloads of soldiers drove up and down the boulevards. Two bombs blew up in the city while I was there, one that rocked my hotel. I took a stroll one night after dark and stood on the street, talking to the Lord: I said, "Okay, Lord! I am here. But why am I here? What do you want from me?" I really didn't know why I had come halfway around the world. I just knew that God wanted me to do it and I was following Him.

Suddenly, a fat rat scurried across the broken sidewalk in front of me, so close that I yelped like a puppy and jumped backwards, scanning the street for any other friendly and vivacious vermin. I spoke out loud, "Okay, Lord. I think it's time for me to go inside." I turned toward the front door of the hotel and came face to face with a large bat stretched out and plastered like wallpaper to a fruit tree. Its body was larger than a fox and had a wingspan of at least five feet, resembling the flying monkeys of the Wizard of Oz movie. I did not loiter any longer. I didn't want to meet the rest of the flock. As casually and nonchalantly as my intimidated spirit would allow, I sprinted back into the hotel like the Cowardly Lion running from the Wizard, where Htein Win Ei was enjoying a good belly laugh. He said, "They are harmless to us; they only eat Methodists."

Pastor Htein led me to preach in several underground churches in Yangon. He was not in a rush to take me northward, to his ministry compound located in another province. I sensed that my first week in Myamar was to be my initiation into their society and culture, and I had much to learn. On the second day, we traveled across the city by taxi. The driver was a friend of Pastor Htein, and his old and frail Toyota would become our transportation throughout most of my month-long stay. I had to watch my feet because much of the floorboard was rotted away and I could see the road under the car. The heavy urban traffic was more chaotic than rush hour in Manhattan or any American city. Our driver seemed to be highly skilled at maneuvering through all the congestion. A half dozen lines of cars, trucks, and buses crammed into two or three lanes, whose drivers were all trying to get through the bottlenecked blockage of vehicles at once was nothing for him. But I was having a small panic attack. Not from his wheeling and weaving through the world's largest bumper car experience but, like Dorothy and Toto, I suddenly realized that I wasn't in Kansas any longer. I never mentioned it to Pastor Htein or anyone else. I never sent a message home like that. But, in my mind, I was thinking, "DeWitt, what in the world are you doing here?" Then I prayed. And, as many times before, my God gave me peace.

A decade earlier, I traveled to Ukraine four times. The political situation there was intense and, as in Myanmar, soldiers were posted in public places and poised to protect, not so much the people but the present regime. I remember being nervous about talking to the wrong person. The country, even as now, was divided by language, as well as political and ethnic loyalties. Some people spoke Ukrainian, some Russian. You could not be sure who was a Ukraine nationalist and who might remain loyal to the former Soviet Union and communist sympathizers.

My companion and I decided to travel by train to a young church in the southern city of Mykolaiv (or, in Russian – Nickolaiv), east of Odessa on the Black Sea. The railroad cars appeared to be older than myself, and a national pastor insisted that I reserve a "Looks" cabin. I had no idea what he meant but learned that it was about ten dollars more expensive. When we boarded the train, we were shown to a small, very cramped berth with a sliding door and two narrow and unpadded wooden benches either side of a tiny broken window. There was a small pull-down shelf between us where we had just enough room for a laptop computer or our Bibles, but not at the same time. Sitting opposite of each other, we struggled to get comfortable and resolved to play footsie all night but not to publish it on Facebook.

I was told that the alternative was not nearly as preferable. So, I had to find out for myself and went exploring. Moving from car to car as the train rolled down the tracks, I came to a door, opened it, and saw a hundred men laying on racks like hens in a chicken coop. The smell was so overpowering that I immediately flung the door closed and ran back to my home on rails. I quickly learned that my tight little space, the "Looks," was not only good enough for me but rather the Lux, or Deluxe. Later, the conductor brought us a steel security bar for our compartment door. He saw our laptop computers, cameras, watches and said, "Use this to secure your door after nine o'clock and do not go outside your compartment alone because of the 'train pirates.'" All night, as the train click-clacked down the track, we envisioned our door being flung open by a Nazi soldier, pointing a submachine gun at us, and demanding our papers.

During another trip in 2004, I stood with others in the middle of Kiev's Independence Square, distributing Gospel tracts and preaching the Word of God during the Orange Revolution. 400,000 people gathered from every province, forming tent cities and warming themselves by trashcan fires in 18-degree weather, to protest fraudulent elections and demand a legitimate democratic process. Thousands of citizens had been held at gunpoint, loaded on busses, taken to different polling stations across the country, and repeatedly forced to vote for the Russian-puppet and socialist candidate. The people of Ukraine knew they had elected Viktor Yushchenko, the "Our Ukraine" center-right candidate, but the ballots were not proving it. I stood alongside the people, wearing a florescent orange band around my arm like them, when the Chief Justice of their Supreme Court announced that there would be another national election. The masses of protesters erupted in a celebration like I have never seen anywhere, at any time, even on television.

However those experiences readied me for Myanmar, I was determined to obey God and follow His leading wherever it took me. Yet I still did not know why I was there.

Htein Win Ei was called away for a short time and I went for a walk with another national pastor. A group of sixty believers had gathered in a garage and they wanted me to preach to them. As I stood before them with my Bible in hand, suddenly several men jumped up and grabbed me by the arms without explanation, took me out the back door and down a flight of stairs into a damp and moldy basement. They buried me under boards and blankets and motioned for me to be quiet. I heard shouting and stomping around upstairs, then a deafening hush followed by slamming doors. Police had swarmed the building, looking for a foreigner who was doing something illegal or was in a forbidden location. Not finding me, they left. Then the same men came downstairs, dug me out, brought me back into the garage, put me again before the people, and simply said, "Please continue." When I did, and having explained the Gospel clearly, several souls prayed with me to receive Jesus Christ as their personal Savior and I returned to my hotel.

At that time, it was unlawful for foreigners to visit in family homes and residential communities. Most provinces in the country were "off-limits" to tourists and travel was extremely restricted. Yet I was repeatedly invited to preach to small groups of believers, or underground churches, within the Yangon Division.

Everywhere I went, it became obvious that I was being followed and people were watching me. The following Monday we traveled to the village of Aung Lan, the place of Htein Win Ei's ministry. I was anxious to see those precious children whom I had prayed for. We loaded our luggage into our driver's 1972 Toyota Corolla, said a prayer, and headed out of town. Before we had gone five miles, the car broke down in a busy intersection and we pushed it to the side of the road where our driver could get "out and under" and try to resuscitate our only means of conveyance. But praise the Lord and our driver/shade tree mechanic, in minutes we were on our way again, and I was more than happy to feel a breeze coming through my open window. Aung Lan was a whole day's journey up the never-ending Pyay Road, which parallels the Ayeyarwady River. We left before lunch and would not arrive until following morning around 4:30 am. Along the way there were tolls and military checkpoints. The road was so rough, like many in New York State, that I wondered why we had to pay to drive on them. At one point, we were stopped at what looked like a kid's lemonade stand. Several men approached each passing car and demanded 200 kyats. Later that night, as we approached a man sleeping in a hammock, he suddenly jumped to his feet, threw down a barrier, and requested another 200 kyats. I wondered if these were government tolls or family businesses.

We stopped at what seemed like a roadside café, a place where cross-country buses would pause to give their passengers a break and an opportunity to eat something. Here, like so many other places in Myanmar, were vendors, selling packaged food, fruits, and soda pop. A long-haired man covered with tattoos had a platter stacked high with a kind of cooked meat. I was told it was "fried sparrow," – translation: Baked Bat. I opted for a can of Pringle-looking chips, a can of Chinese cola, and some small mandarin oranges.

We finally arrived in Aung Lan and the bus dropped us by the side of the road in the dark. Boys from Pastor Htein's school came and, without a word, carried our bags into the jungle along a narrow trail. As we followed them, the path led into a deep ravine with sharp drop-offs and it was difficult to see where to step. I had a small flashlight, but it was packed deep inside my luggage. Finally reaching the ministry compound, I was guided into to a two-story structure with wooden fence-like, see-through walls and a fastidiously swept dirt floor, clean as surgical steel. Children were asleep in an adjacent room and in an upper loft. Ladies gathered around a center table, heated water for hot tea, and set out small packages of sweet snacks.

I knew nothing of the Burmese language and Pastor Htein spoke a very broken English. But somehow, we communicated and, as more and more people arrived and surrounded me, I answered all their questions and rejoiced that we were finally meeting face to face. After a while, they showed me where I could lay down on a bamboo mat. They gave me a hand-woven blanket and a small pillow, and I fell fast asleep for nearly thirty minutes.

With the rising of the sun, I could hear the children playing and running about outside. I looked at my watch and it was just a few minutes past seven o'clock in the morning. Unoffensive smoke hung in the air and breakfast rice with leafy green vegetables mixed with spices was being cooked on an open fire. The children soon assembled in a pavilion to read their Bibles and have morning devotions. A wonderful spirit, something I had never experienced before, seemed to permeate the entire compound. I have often attempted to describe it but never found sufficient words: It felt like peace, like being engulfed in joy and contentment. I knew what it was. The Spirit of God was in that place. His presence was so strong there that I came to describe it as having a Mount of Transfiguration experience.

The students had already done their chores and, after breakfast was finished, they went to their respective places for school classes. I stayed in the pavilion with my Bible and sat on a wooden bench, talking to the Lord. A young man approached with an old guitar and sat down next to me. He spoke just a few words of English and I tried my best to understand him. He strummed the strings lightly and played the song "Amazing Grace."

When he was finished playing, I motioned for him to give the guitar to me. He did so, and I played and sang another Christian hymn. When I was finished, I handed the guitar back to him and said, "Your turn!" He said, "Excuse me, sir?" I said, "Yourrr...turn!" He took the instrument from my hands and, again, played Amazing Grace. When he was finished, he handed the guitar again to me and said, "Your ... tur...turn!" I played and sang another song, then returned the guitar to him, and repeated, "Your turn!"

Again he played Amazing Grace. It was the only song he knew. But he played it beautifully. And there was an instant connection between me and that boy. His name was Chit Myae, he was fifteen years old, and his family was from the Asho Chin tribe of Old Burma. I loved him at first sight.

Pastor Htein gathered the children and staff together inside the pavilion and led them in singing many hymns. I could not control myself; I wept as I heard their hearts. Pastor Htein called on me to speak and I opened my Bible to the book of Colossians and began to read in chapter one. I stopped at verse four and told them, "I have heard of your faith and now I see it with my own eyes." We rejoiced together, singing and making melody in our hearts to the Lord Jesus Christ.

I returned to my shelter to lay down for a few minutes before lunch. I was weary from the trip the night before, and I fell asleep quickly. But within minutes, I was awakened as Pastor Htein nudged me, saying, "Brother Bob (I was not yet BaGyi), I need your passport." I asked, "Why?" He said, "Police are here. They demand your passport."

I stayed in the shelter, and soon Htein returned to tell me that I would have to leave. I did not know what was happening. But when I walked out to talk with the officers, they arrested me. They led me from the compound property and took me to a holding point in the village where I was interrogated as an American spy. When they realized that I was nothing more than a Baptist preacher, that was worse. At that time, Christianity was seen as subversive to the Myanmar government.

I can honestly say, that despite the arrest, I had a great peace. For some reason, even though I probably should have been fearful or at least nervous, I was not. I will not discuss the details of all that happened during multiple interrogations but suffice to say, I was soon released and forced to leave town. The authorities told me that I could go to a local café and eat before leaving. But when I arrived at the café with Pastor Htein, police and military intelligence officers were waiting. Two plain-clothed men, presumably government agents, sat on the other side of the café and stared at me incessantly. The look in their eyes was unsettling.

We ordered a simple rice breakfast and while we were eating, Htein Win Ei's wife and students walked into the café. They sat down at our table and stood around us weeping. I will never forget the look on her face, as tears filled her eyes. They had prayed long for me to come. Now, I was forced to leave, even before getting to know them.

I was aware that Pastor Htein had suffered much persecution for starting his ministry without government permission. He was jailed and beaten four separate times. He never speaks of it. But before we left Aung Lan, I was more concerned about him than myself and I talked to him about it briefly. I asked him, "After I leave, will they trouble you because of me?" He casually replied, "I may experience a short time of unpleasantness." But praise the Lord, he did not.

We fueled our vehicle at what seemed to be someone's residence. Pastor Htein and another man went behind the house, siphoned diesel fuel from a tank into a smaller can and brought it to our car parked along the road. We then left town, driving South through the rest of that day and night, arriving back in Yangon at five o'clock the following morning.

I went straight to the U.S. Embassy where there was no Ambassador. Relations between the two countries was officially broken because of Myanmar's human rights abuses. But when I informed the woman at the glassed-in counter what had occurred in Aung Lan, she said "Please wait. The Consul will definitely want to talk to you."

I was guided down a hallway and into his office for a quick chat. After describing my experience, he said this: "Mr. DeWitt, you need to collect your things as quickly as possible, go straight to the airport, and take the first available flight out of Burma, no matter where it's going. You don't want to see the inside of their political prison." (Note: Still today, the U.S. government does not recognize the name change from Burma to Myanmar.)

The Consul was speaking of Insein Prison, just outside the city of Yangon. At the time, there were 52,000 political prisoners who were incarcerated there for activities against the military regime. According to the Internet, deplorable conditions were well documented and horror stories abounded on many websites.

So I went back to the Golden Guest Inn, packed my bags, and hailed a taxi to the Yangon International Airport. Back then it was not a simple task to enter the airport with luggage. Your taxi would take you to the front doors, and you had to maneuver your way through hundreds of people, including travelers, transportation company agents, security guards, and vendors, all shouting at you simultaneously. Finally making your way through the doors, you would run your suitcases and any other bags through a security-screening process which would be repeated twice again before getting to your gate. Yangon International Airport has since grown much larger and has been updated to provide one of the smoothest terminal experiences I have encountered anywhere.

Finally at the airline counters, the agents tried to find for me a seat on any outbound flight, aboard any carrier. But they were unsuccessful, as there was nothing available for one week. I believe that God shut every door of escape and made it crystal clear to me that I should stay in Myanmar for another fourteen days until my planned departure. During that time, many more souls were saved. Then, one month after my arrival in Myanmar, I departed for America with an uncanny desire to return to the Golden Land as soon as possible.

My pastor asked me to give a testimony and take a few minutes to talk about the trip. When I was finished, he said, "Well, folks, I guess we have a mission board!" Then he asked me, "Brother Bob, what's a mission board do?" I had not yet thought that far ahead. But I answered, "I'll let you know."

I had agreed to host a Myanmar preacher who followed me back to America and I helped him to get a U.S. Visa. We traveled together for six months, seeking financial support for him and his ministry in Myanmar. We drove far into the South and across the Midwest, preaching and telling the story of my trip and his ministry.

Meanwhile, I was studying and learning about missions and Myanmar. But I still didn't know why.My intention was to get him a little monthly support, send him home, and continue my nationwide ministry to troubled youth. But I was praying every day, still asking God what it was that He wanted from me. One day, as we drove along Interstate 90 in Indiana, I braked suddenly and stopped the car along the shoulder of the highway. Staring straight ahead I said, "I need to start Golden Land Baptist Missions." That Myanmar preacher got so excited that he screamed and jumped out of my car, then ran across the field, jumping in the air, crying, and shouting, "Golden Land Baptist Missions, Golden Land Baptist Missions!"

God was working in my heart. Every day I searched the Internet, reading, studying, looking over maps. I wondered what was so important about Myanmar, that it had become America's first foreign mission field? Why did God send Adoniram Judson there as opposed to every other continent and people group in the world? Was there a reason? And now, why did God send me there? Was it merely because the country had been closed for fifty-plus years and was now in the process of opening? Would there be a rush of cults into the country once it opened? I had very little experience in foreign missions. Why me? And what did God want me to do?

Because of my Myanmar visitor, I learned that there was at least one lost tribe of Israel there – people with Asian skin and faces but Jewish culture, dress, and laws. I learned that Jerusalem scholars had been going there for years and were totally convinced that the Kuki tribe of Myanmar was a lost Jewish people group. I thought, "That's the reason! God's people are there!" Or was there more?

Through my study, I saw that Myanmar is geographically bordered by five other countries and surrounded by twelve. God showed me that Myanmar is strategically centered in the Buddhist and Muslim world of Southeast Asia, and that

America's first mission field could be the "Hub of The Wheel" for sending preachers, not only across Old Burma but, out the "Spokes of the Wheel" to the hundreds of surrounding people groups, many who still have no Gospel witness.

In regard to Myanmar, everything I had done so far was in obedience to Christ. But now, with every passing day, it seemed that God was putting His love for the Myanmar people into me. I could not talk about them, or even think about them, without weeping. I dreamed about Myanmar. I literally had the memory of their smell in my nostrils: the food, the smoke of their cooking fires, the smell of a child's hair as I held them on my lap. Then I began to find the Burmese refugees in my travels across America. Sometimes they would find me. I was in North Carolina and a Pastor took me to an Asian Mall. He said, "Perhaps there are Burmese people there!" I took one step inside the mall and began to weep. The pastor looked curiously at me and asked, "Are you okay?" I said, "My people are here." Again, he asked, "How do you know?" I answered, "I can smell them!" Sure enough, in just minutes I came face to face with Burmese people who were running a grocery and café inside the mall.

Have you heard people say something like, "I am in my head?" It means, that because they are in such deep thought, they are unaware of others around them. I got back to my hotel room and, through that night, I was in my head. I kept hearing my own words: "My people." The Apostle Paul said to the Thessalonians that he remembered them "without ceasing" and that he was "affectionately desirous" of them. He told the Philippians that he "longed after" them. I wept all night because I missed "my people." I had traveled around the World to Myanmar for Jesus. But I would return there for both Him and them.

But it had not yet occurred to me, that God wanted me to give the remainder of my life and ministry to reaching Myanmars for Christ. I kept asking the question, "Why me?" I knew that there were many others far more equipped for missions than myself. A Burmese preacher said to me, "Quit asking that question. Just do it!"

Several months passed and, again, I was in my office and received an e-mail from Pastor Htein Win Ei. The e-mail read as follows:

"Boy with guitar will die. Please pray for his family."

As I read those words, I stood and yelled out, "No!" I shot an e-mail back to Pastor Htein and wrote: "I will come!"

Pastor Htein replied:

"There is no time." I sent again:

"I will send money!" Pastor Htein answered:

"Boy with guitar will die very soon!"

They said that Chit Myae literally shook to death. It was as if a member of my own earthly family died. I, myself, was shaken. And the Spirit of God whispered in my ear and said, "...a great door and effectual is opened unto [you], and there are many adversaries...watch ye, stand fast in the faith, quit you like [a man], be strong.

Let all your things be done with charity." (1 Corinthians 16:9, 13-14) When I first traveled to Myanmar, there were no missionaries from any established board or agency. Many people tried to discourage me. People said it was too dangerous. I was told that I was crazy. And many church members stood at my display table, saying things like "We need missionaries right here in America!" Regardless, God had made a way for me to win souls in the Golden Land and had me a people as if they were my own.

Shortly after that, on another trip to Myanmar, I met a man from the family of Aung San Suu Kyi, a Nobel Peace Prize winner and one of the leaders of the country. He said, "You need to have nickname! You will be BaGyi Bob." And so, from that time forward, people in both Myanmar and America began calling me "BaGyi Bob." It means Great Uncle, an older respected person. At the time of this writing, I will soon be 65 years old. I have been traveling to Myanmar for almost thirteen years and hope to continue many more. After more than forty years in the ministry, God has changed my life, my heart, and my identity. Wow! Serving God is great!

Children from Aung Lan Christian School.Chit Myae in the gold jacket.

Pastor Htein Win Ei at his ministry jungle compound in Aung Lan, Magwe Division, Myanmar

CHAPTER NINE

King On My Street

"And he turned him unto his disciples, and said privately, Blessed are the eyes which see the things that ye see:For I tell you, that many prophets and kings have desired to see those things which ye see, and have not seen them; and to hear those things which ye hear, and have not heard them."

Luke 10:23-24

The maze of market aisles was more crowded than usual, and it was only Tuesday. People were everywhere, and some areas were impassable as groups of visitors bottlenecked into the narrow passageways lined with shops. Squeezing through where possible, we could hear individuals speaking Russian, some Dutch or German, others Korean, all trying to make their best deals despite the language barrier. It wasn't necessarily the big tourist season in Myanmar but, for whatever reason, foreigners filled the market like shoppers at a Chicago Walmart on Black Friday. I had with me a small group and, as futile as it always is, I was trying to keep them together. I finally gave them a time and place to meet and let them go to explore the market for themselves.

Our team was visiting the world-famous Bogyoke Aung San Market in the center of Yangon, or Old Rangoon, a city growing soon to nine million people, mostly Buddhist and Muslim. I take all those who travel with me to this place. It is a super-sized indoor/outdoor flea market, named after the General who is one of Old Burma's most beloved heroes. His picture can be seen on the walls of countless homes across Myanmar, in both one room bamboo huts and large, exquisite mansions.

For years the General espoused communism and traveled to study warfare with the Japanese, in hopes of overthrowing the 120-year oppressive rule of the British. But, with the rise of World War II and realizing that the Japanese would be worse to live under than the Brits, he joined himself and his Burmese national army with the Allies and promoted nationalism and a representative government. For this he was soon martyred, passing the baton of freedom to his daughter, Aung San Suu Kyi.

Most people in Yangon simply refer to the large market as Bogyoke Zay. Bogyoke is pronounced Boo Joe and, in the Burmese language, Zay means market. Organized much like the Kentucky Derby at Churchill Downs in Louisville, Kentucky, there is a track, or lane, around the perimeter with much activity in the center, but two floors. It is the largest such market in Myanmar and one of the most popular tourist attractions in the Yangon area. There are some days when the market area is so congested that, for time sake, it is better to get out of your taxi several or more blocks away and walk to the entrance. You will get there faster.

On any given day there are thousands of visitors to Bogyoke Zay, buying, selling, and trading. Here you can find all kinds of jewelry made of gold, silver, jade, the world-famous Burmese ruby, sapphires, pearls, and tribal beads. There is clothing, fabric, furniture, food, produce, livestock, eyeglasses, shoes, artwork, musical instruments, tribal crafts, antiques, and artifacts. There are a few small cafes. Black market money changers move through the crowds and offer a tad better exchange rate than you can get from local banks. Then there are the young children, some who beg, some who are working. They come to you and it is amazing how many speak understandable English. But I have often asked them why they are not in school. I always hear the same answers: "My family has no money for school." Or "I must work for my family." You never know if that is completely true; they might be street orphans, simply trying to survive. Whatever the case, I am usually drawn to them quickly, and them to me. They soon discover that I am a friend and gather around.

The best thing about Bogyoke Zay is that you never need to pay the asking price. You dicker, or haggle, and make your best deal. Unless you are going deeper with me into the Myanmar provinces, this is the best place to purchase souvenirs for family and friends back home. Over the years I have met and talked with many interesting people at Bogyoke and made some friendships. I have some favorite vendors, those who know me and give me and my visitors the best bargain prices. Upon arriving, I usually take my visitors to the center of the market where there is a wide lane, and we venture out from there. Invariably, as I enter that center lane, I am met promptly by one or two young people who know me well. They immediately attach themselves to us and serve as guides. They help us find whatever we are looking for.

One such young lady is named "Aung Say." Over the years, we have come to know each other closely, and to the point that, when I arrive with a group of visitors, she points to me and says with a huge smile on her face, "This is my Uncle!" I remember when she got married. And one year, she spied me coming and rushed to me, jumping up and down exclaiming, "BaGyi, I will have baby!"

Another year, as I entered the market, her sister came to me. And I asked, "Where is Aung Say?" She began to cry and said, "She at hospital, BaGyi! Baby sick!" I could tell by the look on her face that this was serious. My first thought was, "I wonder if she has enough money?" Hospitals are not free in Myanmar, and Aung Say and her family are extremely poor. I understand that many missionaries will not give nationals cash. And I am often leery also. But I honestly love these people; when I see their true need, and I have the ability to help, it is difficult to turn away.

I asked Aung Say's sister, "Which hospital?" And, I said, "I will go!" Can you imagine being admitted to an American hospital, being given medicine intravenously, with around the clock care, and being charged $10.00 to $20.00 per day for everything? We would think that to be, not only cheap but, impossible. But, for many of the poor people of Myanmar, that kind of money is beyond their ability to pay. And many Myanmar hospitals will not allow you to be discharged until you pay your full bill. These families have, therefore, only two options: don't go to the hospital at all or get a loan from someone you know and sell your soul to them. So, I went to the hospital. And for less than fifty U.S. dollars, Aung Say's baby was released a few days later completely well.

I have witnessed to Aung Say and her sister, but like most Myanmar people, they are Buddhist. It is their culture and their life. But they are my friends, and I believe they have good hearts. I have met their mother and some of their cousins. And, to my knowledge, I am the only one who has ever told them about Christ, the true Light of the World.

So, here I was again, strolling through the market aisles filled with shoppers and sellers, helping a new set of visitors to find what they wanted and to make deals. And I began to think back about the first time I myself visited Bogyoke Zay.

It was during my second trip to Myanmar. I had not yet adjusted to the heat and humidity and, even though my hotel room had almost-adequate air-conditioning, my clothes were wet with sweat day and night. There was still the daunting presence of armed soldiers throughout the city and even inside the market. Myanmar was still officially "closed" to most visitors. And I barely knew how to say "Hello" in the Burmese language. I had made it through a day of what I thought was a bit of culture shock, when doubt and fear became my nagging companion. But when I realized that I was focusing on the wrong things and that the voice in my head was not my Saviour, but Satan instead, Christ gave me victory through prayer. I can honestly say that from that time, I have never felt uneasy again but confident and at peace always in Myanmar among those who have become "my people."

I was with a national pastor who was showing me the sites of the city and he said that Bogyoke Zay was a "must experience" attraction. It was certainly a great introduction to Myanmar cultures and part of what would be my ongoing education.

We had some lunch nearby; then our taxi dropped us right in front of the main entrance to the market. I must admit that in all my life and travels I had never seen anything like Bogyoke Zay. And, walking through the market for the first time, I was intrigued with everything and everyone I saw. I greeted each person with whom I made eye contact, using English. Then I quickly learned some traditional Burmese greetings and gestures. But when I tried to speak a Burmese word, the people would laugh hilariously. I wasn't sure if they were laughing at my pronunciation or accent, or if they were amused that a white man was speaking their language. I could tell that most Burmans had seen very few Caucasians. Years ago, a dark-skinned Sicilian-American preacher in Buffalo, New York said to me, "DeWitt, you are painfully white!" So, I guess, to these brown Burmese, I was particularly fair-skinned and stood out among the crowd. They stared, pointed, touched me, and some people even followed behind respectfully.

I was on a strict budget and because I was not yet familiar with the exchange rate between U.S. dollars and Myanmar kyats, I was cautious about spending too much. But I saw many things that I wanted. On my next visit I would see and desire yet more, and I would be more confident to buy.

I am not much of an impulse buyer. Rather, I shop to learn all my options, do my research on quality and prices, and usually wait for sales and discounts. Also, I was aware that whatever I purchased, I would also need to carry back to America within the limited space of my suitcase and carry-on. But I was intrigued by almost everything I saw. And, not so much for myself but, I wished to buy things for my wife and daughters, other things for ministry display, and bags of candy and snacks to give the Burmese children along the way, as I would meet them.

Upon entering Bogyoke's main building, you find yourself amid a virtual vivarium of the many different Myanmar cultures that all blends together into a symphony of sights, sounds, colors, and smells. Many of Myanmar's tribal people groups are represented. One cannot soon forget the experience, but it requires some time to absorb. I was trying my best to take it all in but was quickly overwhelmed and yet overjoyed.

Walking through the market, I became increasingly aware of a strident bellowing shout above the hubbub of it all. A man was calling out repeatedly and his disturbing chant was incessant. It was obvious that whoever was making the noise was increasingly frustrated. And his cry was insistent and progressively louder. It seemed that wherever we went in the market, we were never far from his annoying voice. I looked around several times, but it was difficult, in the mass of people, to distinguish which individual was making the offensive mantra.

As the man came closer to us, he hobbled through the crowd on crutches. He was short of breath, but still trying to relay his insistent message. I tried my best to ignore him. But despite my preoccupation with the colorful goods and tribal wares of each vendor in the market, the loud-mouthed man became overly distracting. And, as we gazed at each other, still at some distance, I got a good look at him and the desperation in his eyes.

Perhaps in his early thirties, he was short with dark skin, and had a childish look about him. His strait black hair was combed to one side and hung down over the left corner of his forehead, almost covering his dark eyes. He hobbled about on crutches because he had only one leg. His soiled clothes hung on him as if they were several sizes too big.

At first, I thought he might be a beggar. But he carried a large flat black satchel by squeezing it under his right arm, and it seemed to indicate business. I wanted to take a photograph of this man, but it was obvious that my host was trying to put some distance between us and him.

We turned another corner and I looked behind me. The man was still coming, more insistent than ever. Waving his hand in my direction while trying to keep his balance on the crutches, he motioned to me, and cried out. The faster we walked to try to get away from him, the more frustrated he became and the louder he cried. My national pastor friend was trying to move me away and protect me. But now I was determined to find out what the man wanted.

Finally, I asked the national pastor with me, "What does the man on crutches want?" He answered, "He call to you, BaGyi!" Astonished, I said, "Me? What is he saying?" The pastor smiled and said, "BaGyi, he says 'King on my street! Please stop! King on my street!"

There are things that happen in the Christian life, in a moment of time when, if you can hear the voice of the Spirit, if you know what it feels like to be led by God, it becomes apparent that He has orchestrated the musical instruments of your life to make beautiful harmony with someone else's life. I am speaking of the will of God for our lives, His plan for how He will use us in the lives of others. And sometimes, God will use others, even strangers, to change our own lives. It becomes more obvious the longer we walk with Him. We walk by faith because we never know when those moments will occur. It may seemingly be a chance meeting at a gas pump or happen while walking down the hallway in a hospital, hearing someone cry out. You might be sitting at your office desk or running a machine in a factory or on a farm. You might be sitting in a high school or college class. You could be on vacation far from home. And suddenly, like Esther, it is obvious that you are in a certain place, at a certain time, "for such a time as this." Or perhaps it is not so obvious to you at that moment. But later, after your faith has become what someone else needed, in reflection, you realize it was God.

The hobbling man's words, "King on my street," kept resounding in my mind. And, of course, I thought, "I'm no King. But I serve The King!" Then I remembered that my Bible tells us that we who belong to Christ are kings and priests; we are members of a royal priesthood. It wasn't until my flight home, more than three weeks later, as that man's haunting repetition replayed in my conscience again and again, that I prayed, "My Lord and my God, do those who live on my street, in my neighborhood, do they know that there is someone nearby who belongs to the King and is part of His royal family?"

Now, don't get me wrong. It is not me, or you, that is important. And no one is going to be permanently, eternally, or even practically helped by your personality, wit, or wisdom. But, if God is willing to use you to convey His truth and reveal Himself to others through you, in a moment of time they and their lives can be changed.

People often say that things happen for a reason. It's amazing, however, how many folks feel that way, who don't know God or His Word. I do not know what they base their assumption on. But after all these years and all the times I've seen God work, knowing it wasn't me who worked, I have learned that it is not only about Him but always by Him.

I turned and greeted that small broken man who was now approaching me like someone who had just run a race. He was out of breath but was still filled with excitement and anticipation.

He said, "Please, sir. I want to show you my work." I think that the smile on my face brought him quick relief. And he began to fumble through his underarm satchel.

I said, "Please sit with me." I sat down on the curb and helped him down next to me. I drew close to his side and said, "Please show me what you have; I also have something I want to show you." He nodded in agreement.

Inside his satchel were some of the most beautiful drawings I have ever seen. He flipped through the drawings quickly – portraits, landscapes, religious, cultural, and historic pieces. He flipped too quickly, and I stopped him. I stared at the portrait of a young Burmese girl and nearly wept. The eyes of the subjects in his portrait drawings were intensely gripping. There was emotion. He was able to capture the mood of a subject and to draw the viewer into that emotion. It was obvious he was a gifted artist. But it was also obvious that he was not so much aware of it. I pulled that certain portrait out of the satchel and was held it in my hand. He was still trying to show me everything he had. But my attention was locked on that single portrait that had so gripped me. I asked him the price of it, and I was shocked. The price was so low that I was embarrassed to pay him such a trivial amount for such fine artwork. I looked for another, similar portrait and bought a set of two. They now hang beautifully framed in my office.

I said to him, "Friend, your drawings are worth much more!" He smiled and said, "Kyay zu htin bar de!" Which is to say, "Thank you very much!" But, of course, any businessman will charge for his wares what he believes he can get. I would have been willing to pay four times what he charged me. And I did give him more than he asked. I don't hardly ever do that. My father's family is of Dutch background. People have asked what it means to be "Dutch." I have answered, "It means you are stubborn and cheap!" They ask, "Cheap?" Then I say, "You have never heard of 'going Dutch?'" That day, I forgot that I was Dutch.

This poor, crippled Burmese artist had tracked me down, begging for my attention: "King on my street! King on my street!" But I wasn't feeling much like a King. By this time in our encounter, I was not thinking of him as a pauper or indigent. I was so impressed with him, his humble spirit, his talent, his intelligence, his initiative. I was feeling humbled. I was addressing him as my equal, and he didn't understand why.

Normally, an American traveling to any Third World country is quickly aware of the national's perception of us as a people. Especially in Southeast Asia, people seem to treat Americans as superior. Southeast Asians especially, and most Burmese, are eager to extend hospitality and serve us. Usually, they will not allow me to carry my own bag. I say to them, "My arm is not broken!" They laugh and grab my bag anyway. They insist that I take the front seat of any vehicle. They want me to eat before they do. And the longer I stay with them, it becomes increasingly obvious that this special attention is not about money. It is their way. And they are openly loving.

While there are those who say they despise America, an overwhelming number of people from other countries want to immigrate to our land. I am asked regularly to help people get to America. Our nation is seen as a land of opportunity. But people also want to come here for freedom and safety. Whatever their reasoning, they view the United States as a special place.

Is America a special country? Are we a special people? Many Americans believe that! Paul the Apostle said that we, as Christians, are a peculiar people, meaning different than those who live by the standards of the world.

But does that make us special? I have said in many pulpits, "We are not special; we are blessed." There is a big difference. I believe that America has been richly blessed by God. But we are clearly losing that blessing because a growing majority seem to think we do not need it anymore.

We say that America is the greatest country in the world. What do we base that on? Most Americans make the statement without any experience elsewhere. Most high school and college students today don't know or understand enough real history to explain why America is a great country. If you went to the average college campus and asked the students what makes America great, I wonder what answers they would give. The rest of the world seems to know the answer to that question.

I would suggest that America is great because the governing principles upon which our nation was founded come straight from the Holy Bible. That foundation and influence has historically determined how we treat each other, as well as other nations around us. Our record of benevolence toward other countries cannot be debated. Despite those who are attempting to change our history for the purpose of re-educating today's youth to suit a political agenda, the record is clear: America was established as a God-fearing, Christian nation, and that has made it great. We have sustained that character because of the liberty we enjoy, purchased for us at high cost.

Our businesses, industry, arts, sciences, schools, sports, military, religion, and families thrive because of that liberty. But, as we take it for granted and neglect God, there being those who want to take it from us, we will lose our liberty. And it may never be restored in our lifetime.

I believe Myanmar, or Old Burma, is a great country, but for different reasons. I love it. I love the Myanmar people. Their country has survived many invasions and wars for thousands of years. When you travel there, you discover that most people deeply love their country and culture, just as we do ours. They are proud of their heritage. Their thinking is not centered around themselves as individuals, but on their people, or people group. It is the difference between "me thinking" and "us thinking." There is no doubt, Myanmar, after thousands of years, is unmistakably Buddhist. It is both their religion and culture. I have tried, not only to learn something about that faith but, to understand it. It is a way of life. It is a mindset. In Myanmar are hundreds of people groups and languages. But, despite their diversity, they have many things in common and, for the most part, I think they are a moral, happy, generous, and kind people. That is my perspective as a foreigner who loves them.

H. Fielding Hall was a high-ranking English military officer who lived in Burma from before the 2nd British- Burman War and long afterwards. He lived most of his life with the Burmese people because of his affection for them. He was an author, and among his many books, he wrote two great works on the Burmese people and their culture. The first, The Soul of a People, he wrote from a foreigner's perspective – his own. The second, "A People at School," he wrote from the Burmese people's perspective, or how they see themselves.

As I travel to Myanmar for extended periods of time, two to four trips each year, I see their Buddhism. The pagodas, or temples, are everywhere. They literally pepper the landscape, glistening from the rays of the sun. It is one of the reasons Burma has been called The Golden Land. But my perspective of their Buddhism goes far deeper than the outward visualization of temples, the many statues of idols, the prayers and chanting, the lighting of candles, the saffron-robed monks, and monasteries. I see a faithful people, committed to their religion and to each other.

I have traveled deep into Burmese provinces and to tiny tribal villages where there was no church of any denomination, no Bible, no preacher, no Jesus. But every family home or hut had a mother, a father, and children who were in submission to their parents. Sure, there were a few vices I found on occasion. But, marriage, family, authority, love, giving, faithfulness are Christian, Bible-based principles. And most Burmese people have them.

If my beloved Burmese people were to travel to America and visit our churches, how would they see us? What would be their initial impression? Would they see us being faithful in church, and obedient in tithing? Would they see respectful children who honor their parents? Would they be able to tell that we are a praying people? Would they believe we are an honest people? Would they think we are happy and satisfied with what we have? Would they get the impression that we are still today as much a giving people as those who financed the great ministries of David Brainerd, Adoniram Judson, George Boardman, Lottie Moon, John Livingston Nevius, William Townsend, Amy Carmichael, and Jim Elliot?

How would the average foreign visitor view American society generally? What would be their initial impression? Knowing that we have been a "Christian nation," would they being shocked to know the current divorce rate, even in our churches? How long would it take them to see the percentage of dysfunctional families in America, the use of illegal and addictive drugs, the number of juvenile offenders in our prisons? When trying to speak our language, how soon would they learn the common expletives, those which used to be spoken only in back alleys and bars, those that would embarrass the ladies, but are now common in movies, TV shows, school hallways, or even around the dinner table when parents have had a bad day? How long would it take them to learn the most popular American excuses for what is considered heathen behavior in their societies.

Frequently, I have been asked about the number of orphans in Myanmar. But what about the number of at-risk children in America. New York State cannot afford to take care of the tens of thousands of troubled youths thatfill detention centers and prisons, much less the adult populations.

We, in America, have had the truth of God's Word for hundreds of years, and churches cover the landscape. We have printed and distributed more Bibles than any society in the history of Christianity. But our society is failing and, whereas Old Burma has followed a works religion for thousands of years, will the Gospel of Grace and our brand of Christianity preserve American society, as we have known and loved it, even into our fourth century?

If we are to continue as a nation, we must have a spiritual revival. It is our one need today. We need a revival of dependence on God, of walking humbly with our God, with men, and the governments of other nations.

There is an old Burmese proverb that states, "Death means to go to the ground; living means being under a golden umbrella." Of course, we Christians have more hope after death than the ground or grave. But the proverb has a greater meaning: Burmese kings would always sit or stand shaded under a golden umbrella, symbolic of their prestige and power. The proverb means that if you are alive, you are blessed. If you draw breath, you are becoming, and you can make a difference in this world. The Burmese people, like many others of the world, seem to think that all Americans are born under a golden umbrella, much like being born with a silver spoon in your mouth. I think that I was like that. Part of the American dilemma today is that we don't know, or have forgotten, how blessed we are. And, we and our children take those blessings for granted, as if they will always be ours. Perhaps not!

So, the challenge for me, and us, when traveling to Myanmar is this: Knowing how they see me, and me knowing how they see themselves beneath me, like in a caste system, how can I demonstrate to them that we all are sinners, and we all need a Savior? How can I demonstrate to them that I see them as I see myself? How can I make them believe that I am their equal? In this context, consider what Paul the Apostle wrote:

"What is my reward then? Verily that, when I preach the gospel, I may make the gospel of Christ without charge, that I abuse not my power in the gospel. For though I be free from all men, yet have I made myself servant unto all, that I might gain the more. And unto the Jews I became as a Jew, that I might gain the Jews; to them that are under the law, as under the law, that I might gain them that are under the law; To them that are without law, as without law, (being not without law to God, but under the law to Christ,) that I might gain them that are without law. To the weak became I as weak, that I might gain the weak: I am made all things to all men, that I might by all means save some. And this I do for the gospel's sake, that I might be partaker thereof with you." 1 Corinthians 9:18-23

Hundreds of Myanmar national preachers were gathered one year at our GLBM Annual Pastor's Conference in Yangon. I had left the platform and was refreshing myself with a drink of water in the hallway, outside our rented hall. A guest preacher from America was speaking and I stood at the double doors, praying for him. I looked over the crowd that was the largest we ever had. There was literally standing room only and not much of it.

Suddenly, as I prayed, the Lord spoke to me. The message was as clear as an audible voice in my ear. I immediately turned and spotted Pastor Htein Win Ei coming from the men's restroom. I said to him, "Saya! I need something." He nodded affirmatively and said, "Yes, BaGyi, how can I help you?" I asked him to find for me a large basin of water, a few towels, and a bar of soap. He said, "BaGyi, I will have to go to the street." I gave him some money, he turned and left the building, and I continued to pray

When the American preacher was finished, I returned to the platform, and several young men carried the things I had requested to the platform. Then I asked them to bring sixteen chairs to the platform and set them in a row from one side to the other. Because every chair in the hall was being used, the occupants of those sixteen chairs gave up their seats and sat on the floor. I walked through the crowd and chose sixteen men, each one from a different area of Myanmar, and each representing a different tribe. They came forward immediately and sat in the seats on the platform.

Then I turned to the crowd and simply said this: "Friends, I have received some instructions from the Lord, and I must do exactly as I have been told. Please be patient with me. And I request that, if possible, no one leave and that we all remain in a spirit of prayer."

Then I turned to the men on the platform, approached the first man on the right, and got down on my knees in front of him. The men were already barefoot, having left their sandals or shoes at the outside door, as is the Burmese custom. Many of the men's feet were black with soot from the dust of traveling there that day. I took the first man's feet in my hands one at a time and washed them both carefully, dried them with a towel, and then kissed each foot, not once but, top and bottom.

As I began washing that first man's feet, he began to weep and said, "No, BaGyi! I wash for you." He began to get up and I pressed his knees down. I smiled and said, "Please, Saya, let it be so. God has told me. I must do it."

I washed their feet, moving down the row of the sixteen preachers, one at a time, on my knees. At one point I began to topple over because the floor was hard, and my knees hurt. The preacher in front of me jumped up to help me. I quickly righted myself and gently pushed him back in his chair.

When I had washed the feet of all sixteen men, again I did exactly what God had put in my heart. The word that had come to me from the Lord was that I should wash their feet and then sit down on the front row of the main floor and say nothing. And so, I did.

There was, at first, an unsettling silence throughout the hall. But then, one by one, every preacher, hundreds of them, and every young man, many of the ladies and young girls, came to the front, and knelt at the platform, making an altar. I will never forget the sobs and tears of those on their knees, as they prayed before the Lord. And I was now among them. That day many were saved. God did His work and His Spirit dwelt among us. What message did those men receive? I did not ask them. God was the One who was talking to them that day. But I wanted them to know that I was not coming to them as someone special, not a king, not a rich man, not a prince of preachers. But a servant with a message from The King of Kings.

The crippled artist with one leg? ...There are images in my mind that play over and over like a video recording, of that moment in time when I came face to face with that dear, broken Burmese artist. In my mind I can see his arms around my waist and his head on my chest, with tears of joy flowing down his face. For, as I spoke to him about my Savior, God gave him the gift of faith. He believed and was saved.

I have seen him many times since then. There is always a wonderful smile on his face. But hast year, just as I was leaving the market, he appeared. He wanted to thank me. I bowed respectfully and put my left hand on his shoulder and my right hand in his. I said in Burmese, "You are welcome, my friend!" He said, "BaGyi, I want to thank you for caring about my cousin and witnessing to her about Christ." I said, "Who? Who is you cousin?" He said, "You know her, BaGyi! Her name is Aung Say."

CHAPTER TEN

Loving the Unloved
Sheri and Senecal

"And as Jesus passed by, he saw a man which was born blind from his birth. And his disciples asked him, saying, Master, who did sin, this man, or his parents, that he was born blind? Jesus answered, Neither hath this man sinned, nor his parents; but that the works of God should be made manifest in him"
John 9:1-3

There had been a mudslide in the camp. It seemed like the whole side of the mountain had fallen around the bamboo huts, trapping some and burying others. It could have been worse, but parents were calling for their children, young men scurried to pull their motor scooters out of harm's way. Just when residence thought that everyone was safe, they heard the faint cries of young children. But it was difficult to tell where those cries were coming from.

"They're over here! Quick! Come quickly!"

Two small children, a boy and a girl, had been located. They were clinging to the support stilts of a hut, half buried in the mud that had come down the side of the mountain. It took some time to get to them, and their cries were becoming faint. When the children were finally rescued, no one knew who they were, or where they came from. But they knew one thing: they were sick and burning up with fever.

The girl was eight years old; her brother was five. It took some persuasion to discover their names, but they finally discovered they were "Sheri" and "Senecal." Sheri was especially sick with oozing infected sores throughout her beautiful long black hair. Both children were wet, dirty, and fearfully emaciated.

Several ladies from the camp took the children, bathed them, gave them some clean and dry clothes, and tried to treat their scrapes, bruises, and Sheri's infected scalp. They gave them hot soup and rice, made a place for them to sleep, and stayed with them until they fell asleep.

In the morning, the ladies agreed, "We have to cut her hair off and treat the sores on her head. The infection will kill her." Sheri's beautiful hair was so matted, and her head hurt so much, she did not protest. The ladies cleaned and dressed the sores. Sheri found an old, dirty towel, and put it over her head in shame.

"Where did they come from? Who are the parents?" someone asked. Nobody knew. And the children were not talking or giving much information. That night, even though Senecal slept without waking at all, Sheri was up and down, vomiting in a bucket set next to her bed mat. The ladies of the camp agreed: "The children must go to a medical clinic soon." Sheri, especially, was becoming critically sick.

The day before, my team and I had been distributing Gospel tracts and Burmese Scriptures in the hot sun. It had been between 96 and 103 degrees and, even as the sun disappeared over the majestic western ridges, the hotel thermometer still read 90. Gritty sweat soaked our clothes and black dirt filled the creases of our skin. Our bottled water had run out and we were all looking forward to a tall cold drink and a long cool shower, in that order. The heat isn't so bad in Southeast Asia once you get used to it. But combined with the high humidity, it wears on most Yankees quickly. So, we were all looking forward to the following day's trip up Thailand's "Death Highway," where it would be cooler at a Refugee Camp high in the mountains along Myanmar's border.

There are several roads I have traveled that, in my mind, could qualify as a "Death Highway." I have enjoyed them all. I'm a bit of an adventurer and I love a good roller coaster. I have problems balancing myself on a rooftop or crossing a narrow plank over water to board a boat, but I don't necessarily mind heights. However, I must admit that riding along narrow mountain ledges in the back of an open truck, when the wheels are right on the edge of a high drop off, looking down hundreds or even thousands of feet, sometimes makes my stomach roll. This "Death Highway" has certainly lived up to its name over the years and claimed the lives of many unfortunate travelers.

In some places the harsh incline is paved with asphalt, but with potholes aplenty. However, most roads are unpaved and, in rainy season, deep with thick and slick mud. Steadily climbing to an altitude where oxygen becomes thinner as you go, the road suddenly disappears, nothing but sky before you and a sheer wall of rock to one side. Cautiously presuming that the road continues around a coming curve, you proceed even though it cannot be seen. So, you honk your horn, hoping that any oncoming motorist, or heavily loaded truck that is barreling down the mountain, will hear and either come slowly or yield to you.

But, despite the hazards, it is beautiful up there. Along the way there are small villages and outposts, high slopes and deep gorges blanketed with thick clumps of banana trees and fields of white sugar cane or orchards. There may be free-roaming cattle or buffalo in the middle of the road. There are no guarantees. Drivers and passengers must constantly be ready for what lies just around the bend. Half the road may have broken off and slid down the side of the mountain, or the side of the mountain above may have slid downward, covering half or more of the road ahead. I am told there are more than 120 "hairpin" turns, or what West

Virginians call "switchbacks," where you literally meet yourself coming and going. But the native drivers know the road well, and it is evident because of how fast they drive it. Of course, most of those who have been killed along the "Death Highway" thought they were altogether familiar with it too.

Some may ask why we go up there? The answer is because there are people, lots of souls, up there. There are small villages and outposts. And there are refugee camps in those hills, along the Burmese border, some with populations of 10,000 to 50,000 people. The people live in rows of bamboo huts, some with electricity, some without, none with running water. We were headed to one of those camps to preach the Gospel and support one of our preachers there.

That morning we loaded the truck with boxes of Burmese Bibles and big bags of Thai egg noodles – I mean, 600 pounds of noodles. Two men sat in the front cab with the driver. I sat in the back of the truck with Pastor Steven, GLBM's Jim Reedy, and my adopted Burmese son, Kaung Htet Kyaw. Jim Reedy sat, balancing himself on a bench near the tailgate, using one hand to steady himself through every bump and curve, keeping himself from falling out, and using the other hand to hold on to his DSLR camera, trying not to miss any of the breathtaking views. Pastor Steven sat on the opposite bench, leaning over the tailgate, and looking greener with every curve. Kaung Htet Kyaw was severely motion sick also. I sat on top of the noodles with several of our preacher boys on either side and enjoyed the ride immensely.

It took more than half the day to get to the refugee camp, even when our speedy driver was well-acquainted with the curves and undaunted by them. Finally arriving, everyone was glad to get out of the truck, stretch our legs, relieve our backsides, and insides. Young men came immediately to unload the Bibles and noodles, and we were led to a small church enclosure where we would have a preaching service. Children came running from every direction to greet us. As usual, I immediately latched on to several of them and they stayed by my side through the remainder of the day.

There is nothing I love more than walking through a Burmese community, greeting, and getting to know people. Those who go with me find that there is not a more hospitable group anywhere than the Myanmar peoples. They will smile and wave as you go by. And, if you stop, they will invite you into their homes and immediately put drinks and fruit on the table for you. I have found, especially in these camps, that even the Muslims are as eager to have visitors as anyone else.

As we strolled through the camp, we found some young ladies who were practicing their bamboo pole dance, something that is performed by Karen tribe groups as a cultural exhibition. They move together in perfect synchronization, stepping and jumping quickly between the heavy moving poles that are being struck together and pounded on the ground alternately and rhythmically. If you don't jump fast enough or lose your cadenced step, your feet can be crushed. These teens seemed to have mastered it very well. And it was obvious that it is as much fun to do as it was for us to watch. Our preacher boys thought so. They jumped right into the middle of it all, joined the fun and, of course, broke the rhythm of the whole dance. But, just like any red-blooded American boys, they never miss a chance to flirt with the young ladies. And those girls responded with the average giggles, blushing, and batting of the eyes, giving our preacher boys encouragement to the point we had to call them away.

These people had fled the military conflict in Myanmar and were living with bare necessities. Every family there dreamed of going to America, or places like Australia, Norway, New Zealand, or any other free country that would receive them. But while waiting, they seemed content. The adults found a way to make money for their families, the children went to makeshift schools and played, they created churches and worshipped the Lord Jesus with praise and thanksgiving in their hearts.

That camp's population was nearly 15,000 at that time with people of the Karen tribe, the Pa-O tribe, Burmese Buddhists, and Muslims. We enjoyed a wonderful service with them, singing and preaching. Nearly two hundred people came to our service. They had a full choir, and it was obvious that they rehearsed much. Even though we could not understand most of their tribal language (not Burmese), their spirit bore witness with ours. It was very evident that they loved the Lord Jesus, and we enjoyed our time of fellowship with them.

Note: Two years later, half of this refugee camp burned to the ground and many were killed. I watched the images and videos of the homes burning to the ground over network television. Again, the people who survived lost everything they possessed. But some of them made it to America. And they are serving the Lord here.

It was late afternoon and, as we got ready to leave the camp, several ladies from the church brought two children to our truck. No one had informed me about them. They said, "This is Sheri and her little brother, Senecal." They were barefoot and their clothes were torn and soiled. Someone had shaved Sheri's head, trying to help her. Infectious puss oozed from bulging sores across the top of her head, through what was left of her scalp. Both children were almost delirious with high fever and trembled with pain and fear.

Sheri was determined to take care of her little brother. But she was so weak that she could barely walk. The men told her that we would help and take them to a doctor in the valley. But she did not want to go with us. She fought us. Finally, the men just scooped her up, and her little brother, and put them in the back of the truck. Sheri looked like she was going to cry. But she was too weak to do even that.

I said my farewells to everyone and jumped into the back of the truck and sat on the bench next to Sheri. She recoiled immediately and pushed herself away, off the bench, and onto the floor of the truck bed. As the other men jumped in with us, she took a squatting position between the benches, looking forward and holding on to the railing below the cab window. I motioned for her to come back and sit with me. But she would not come.

The driver put the truck in gear, and before we even left the property, Sheri fell from her squatted position and hit her head on one of the benches. Again, I motioned for her to come to me. But she was too scared. And she kept her eyes on her brother who was already on Pastor Steven's lap. The bumps and curves in the road were torture for Sheri. She would fall, get back up, and then look again at me. I wanted to just reach out and grab her.

When we came up the mountain from below, I was amazed how fast the driver was rounding the curves. Now, on the way down, he was driving equally as fast. In one dangerous curve he was forced to brake hard without warning, throwing everyone in the back forward. Instinctively, I reached out and grabbed Sheri's arm to protect her. Still, she would not come up on the bench and sit with me. So, I took her hand and placed it on my knee and told her to hang on to me. She did so but kept her eye on me. Through the next few curves, I put my hand on top of hers, and held on to her.

With all the tossing and turning, braking, up and down and around, Sheri had become nauseous, and without warning, she vomited all over my leg and shoe. I tapped on the window of the truck cab, motioning to the driver, and he stopped on the side of the road. Sheri jumped out of the truck and went into the bushes, pulled her outer shirt off, and cleaned herself as best she could. I grabbed her soiled shirt and threw it out in the bushes.

She ran and retrieved it. Then she turned to check on her brother. She climbed back into the truck and wiped the vomit up with her shirt. One of the men put her shirt in a plastic bag. Because it was now nighttime, and the mountain air was cooler, Brother Reedy was wearing a hoodie sweatshirt. He took it off and gave it to Sheri. She quickly put it on and threw the hood over her head. I think she was more grateful for the head cover than the warmth.

Again, we started up and Sheri went back to her squatted position, clinging to the railing ahead. But I could not tolerate the situation any longer. I reached out for her, and this time she came to me. She climbed up on my lap, curled up in my arms, put her head on my chest, and slept through the remainder of the journey.

The rest of the trip is still a bit of a blur in my memory. Traveling down the mountain at night, you can see the lights of Tak Province and the city of Mae Sot below. What a sight! But I didn't see it. Sheri's diseased scalp was just below my nose, her head on my chest, and I could literally feel her heart beating against mine. I could also feel her fever. Her little brother was with someone else, but my mission was to keep that girlsafe and secure. All the way down the mountain I stared into her hooded face and talked to God about my new friend.

It's not easy for me to fall in love and then walk away. It seems like I do it every day when I'm in Old Burma. The children and young people, college students, business owners, street vendors, farmers, taxi drivers, Buddhist monks and nuns, hotel personnel, beggars, policemen, and military soldiers: I love them all. I love them for Christ's sake. I love them because of Christ. I am fully aware that I have changed in the last ten years while going to Myanmar. But I did not change myself. I know that God is no respecter of persons. He loves all and "...is not willing that any should perish..." But when He called me to Myanmar, He put in me His love for that nation and those peoples. He called me to love them for Him. It is a special thing for me.

I can honestly say that I have never met a Myanmar person that I did not love immediately. I think it is an evidence of the calling. And I think that every missionary and every pastor ought to feel the same passion for those to whom they are called.

One year when I returned to see Saya Htein Win Ei, we crossed the wide Ayeyarwady River by boat, between the larger village of Aung Lan and smaller Thayet. Our boatman was the biggest, darkest Burmese man I had ever seen. He was huge in every imaginable way. His skin was leathery from constant exposure to the sun. And he had a stern, intimidating countenance. But when I began to address him, it was obvious he knew no English words at all. With my limited Burmese vocabulary, I did my best to befriend him. And he responded. With very few words, but just smiling, shaking hands, patting each other on the shoulder, and being kind, I gained a friend. There is a language that is unspoken. It is the language of love. Sometimes we speak that language with our eyes. Sometimes people understand that you care for them by a simple but meaningful touch.

We were walking through a neighborhood of Insein Township, part of Yangon Division. Suddenly I could hear singing. Just a single voice, and I could hear the strumming of a guitar. The man I was with at the time wanted to forget about it and go on. But I wanted to see where the voice was coming from. The song was melodic and sweet. My ear drew me inside a dark alley where a ten-year-old boy, totally blind, was playing a song, never missing a note or a beat and singing along beautifully. I didn't want to scare him, because I sensed he could not see. So, when he was finished singing, I gently said, "Mingalar bar!" He looked up and smiled. I said, "Beautiful song!" He answered, "Thank you, sir!"

We listened through several of his songs and sat and talked awhile. His mother appeared and we witnessed to them about Christ. From the moment I laid my eyes on that boy, I can honestly say that I loved him. I will never forget him. And, as I told him about the joy that I have in singing for Jesus, he put his faith and trust in Christ for salvation. And so, did his mother.

In the middle of a field surrounded by goats, we preached the Gospel to several families sitting in a circle under a tarpaulin hung between tree limbs. As we approached them, they asked us to come sit with them. One of the preachers took his place with the adults. But there were three small children sitting on the ground, over to one side. I took a seat next to them. There was an old guitar and I asked if I could play it. Strumming simple chords on the worn-out strings, I sang a familiar Christian hymn.

When I was finished singing, a four-year-old boy came to my shoulder and smiled from ear to ear. I invited him to come to me, and he instantly jumped on my legs and curled up on my lap like a bird in a small nest. I don't know how he knew that it was okay to come to me like that. We had never met before and I had never been in his village. His straight black hair was cut in bangs across his forehead which seemed to frame his big dark and shining eyes. I thought he was very handsome. I stroked his head and back a little, and he became so comfortable and secure that he fell asleep. I had to put him down when it was my time to preach, but afterwards he came right back to me.

I learned that his father was dead. His mother was sick. His feeble grandparents would soon be caring for him. He cried when I left. I did too. I have wondered, now after ten years, could I find him again?

I was visiting a village on the exact opposite side of Myanmar and a small Burmese boy became my shadow. Where I walked, he walked. Where I sat, he sat. When I stood, he wanted me to hold him. When I put him down, he climbed up my legs, over my back, and sat on my shoulders. The villagers watched it and laughed hilariously. I know exactly where he's at. I will search for him next time I am there. Maybe he will remember me, maybe not. But I know this: his parents became believers.

I preached in the Shwe Pyi Thar township of Yangon Division where GLBM missionary Lal Ram Hngak is planting a new church congregation. A small, frail twelve-year-old boy came to me as I was sitting on the floor along the wall. He was skinny with drawn cheeks and dark circles under his eyes. And, when he kept poking me in fun, it was obvious that he was a tease. So, I grabbed him, pulled him down with me, and tickled his ribs gently. He jumped up and sprinted out of the building. But soon he was back, and I tickled him again. This time he stayed, and never left me. He sat on my legs with his head on my chest, and I held him. I learned that his father is dead. His mother is poor and depressed. I helped them both. Wouldn't you? I will again!

We traveled after dark to another small village where people were waiting to hear the Gospel. We took our shoes off, climbed up into a bamboo hut where the only light was two small candles. We sat on bamboo mats, and I explained Bible salvation to those people who had never heard it before. That night eleven souls came to Christ, including a young boy who sat speechless by my side. Perhaps eight years old, he took my Bible in his hands and slowly leafed through its pages. He never asked a question. But you could see desire in his eyes. He was a handsome boy and I wondered what he would look like behind a pulpit. He followed me outside to the van. And, as we stood in the darkness and talked with the men, almost unbeknownst to me, he slid under my arm, and put his arm around my waist. When I realized he was there, I looked down and into his eyes. He had a question: He asked, "You come back?" And I fell in love again. Wouldn't you? Well, wouldn't ya?

We visited a small orphanage that gets its funding from a secular NGO. The children live with a woman who is their caretaker, but their existence is meager. They have no beds; their clothes are few and seldom clean. And, looking at them, they seem undernourished. While we were there, we watched them eat their dinner – a pot of boiled chicken feet. One beautiful little girl came to me and asked if we would like to have some of their dinner. She wanted to share what she had with me. And, I have to say that I thought about it. I surely didn't want to offend her. I have chewed on chicken feet before. They say that it is a great source of protein and calcium. But, like fried bat, boiled snake, "Filet of Fido," and other such tribal delicacies, I would have to be extremely hungry to choose it. When we left the orphanage, I said goodbye to everyone, and especially that little girl. But, as we were pulling away, I spied her running out of the house, waving and trying to get our attention. I cried out, "Stop!" I jumped out of the vehicle and ran to her, picked her up and hugged that little girl's neck. Wouldn't you? I will never forget her. So what happened to Sheri and Senecal?

We finally made it down the mountain and, now back in the valley again, we stopped at a roadside park where there are restrooms and a beautiful waterfall. Most everyone was nauseous, a bit sore, and generally worn out. It was still a good forty-five minutes into the city, and we all needed a break. I had to wake Sheri. Her face was almost glued to my shirt with drool. Fully exhausted and sick at the same time, she was still weak and shaky. I hopped out of the truck and reached out to help her and her brother down. Then she took my hand and never let go. We walked through the park to the waterfall with everyone else, and that's where I took the photo of Sheri and Senecal, her in Reedy's orange hoodie.

Somewhere in the process I learned the story of Sheri and Senecal: Their mother had died three years before and their father remarried another woman from the village. She did not like his children. So, he threw them out of the house. Sheri and her brother wandered until they found the refugee camp, a place where they could find a little shelter and scavenge for food.

We were soon back on the road, and within forty minutes we arrived safely again to the church and school. Waiting there was a married couple who were going to take care of Sheri and Senecal. They would carry them to the clinic, treat their infections, and introduce them to their new home.

I have to say that I did not want to let go of them. I watched as the dear Christian couple took the children by their hands and led them to their vehicle. Sheri kept looking back over her shoulder at me. I wanted to run after her. But there was a plan, and it was good. I couldn't put those children through more turmoil than they'd already been through. I had given them nothing. I had sacrificed nothing for them. But I was connected in some way. I watched as they got into the vehicle, drove away and out of sight. I wept. And I wondered if I would ever see them again.

The story of Sheri and Senecal is a picture of God's love for all of us. Under the inspiration of the Holy Ghost, the Apostle John wrote that Jesus Christ was He

"...that loved us, and washed us from our sins in his own blood" (Revelation 1:5).

The prophet Isaiah said, *"But we are all as an unclean thing, and all our righteousnesses (*or those things we do that we think are good) *are as filthy rags; and we all do fade as a leaf; and our iniquities, like the wind, have taken us away"*(Isaiah 64:6).

Thank God, just two verses later, that same prophet goes on to record,

"But now, O Lord, thou art our father; we are the clay, and thou our potter; and we all are the work of thy hand." The Lord finds us deeply defiled in our own condition, cleanses us in the only way acceptable with Almighty God, adopts us into His family, and changes our lives.

Just recently, now years later, I inquired about Sheri and Senecal. I am told that after they were taken into the school and orphanage, they prospered. Their lives completely changed. Sheri is a beautiful young woman with long, flowing black hair. And Senecal is a strong young man who wants to serve the Lord. Friend, you may find yourself today as Sheri and Senecal. Sometimes life itself can deal you many discouraging blows that no one can explain. But our own choices sometimes bring us to the place of clinging to things in which there is no hope. I promise, you will find a friend in Jesus Christ. If you will let go of your false hope, that which you are clinging to, that which has brought you no peace and no comfort...if you will reach out and take the hand of the One who is reaching out to you, the One who genuinely loves you and proved it on the Cross of Calvary, He will cleanse you from your sin, take you into His family, and change your life.

CHAPTER ELEVEN

"...*What man is there that is fearful and fainthearted? Let him go and return unto his house, lest his brethren's heart faint as well as his heart.*"
Deuteronomy 20:8
(Dramatically, and somewhat evangelistically, presented)

There had been a misunderstanding in the village. And I had been taken. The possibility of arrest had occurred to me, but I had not given it much thought. For reasons only God knows, I had great peace and I knew was in the perfect will of God. He told me to come to Myanmar. No one could persuade me otherwise. I didn't know why, but I had obeyed. Even when they were questioning me over and over, I was not afraid. I am in no way trying to make myself a hero of any kind. But God was doing something. I didn't know what it was. Over the years, I have learned that I can trust Him.

When the officers of the Immigration Department and Military Intelligence were finished interrogating me, they said that I must return to the city of Yangon. Sadly, I could not stay in Aung Lan. And, for me, it was a long, painful ride back down the river. Starting out in mid-afternoon, it would be early morning before we would arrive there again.

They said that I could stop at a local restaurant to get something to eat before leaving town. Unbeknownst to me, Pastor Htein Win Ei, my host, had sent a message home and now, arriving at a small roadside café, his family and all the orphans and students met us there. I could tell that they were all scared and some were weeping. The boys put several tables together and I sat opposite Htein's wife, Dashi Kha Tom. I will never forget the look of heartbreak and disappointment in her eyes. A government agent with a very stern countenance sat at a table nearby and glared at me without ceasing. I knew that Htein had been jailed and beaten several times before for starting his ministry without government permission. I asked him, "Sayar? Will you suffer more persecution because of me?" I will never forget his answer: Unpretentiously he said, "I may experience a short time of unpleasantness."

Sayar Htein said that we needed to fill the car with petroleum before leaving town. We stopped in front of a house set far from the road, and I wondered what we were doing. It did not look like a gas station. I gave Htein 10,000 Myanmar kyats and two men grabbed a short section of green garden hose, walked through the tall palm trees and brush, and disappeared behind the house. They came back to the car with a large red can of fuel they had siphoned from somewhere and filled our tank.

Soon we were on our way, heading south along the Pyay Road, and Htein nudged me and said, "They will take you again!" I answered him, "What do you mean?" He said, "It is their plan; they will take you again outside the village, along the roadway. I asked, "Is there another way?"

Htein is such an easy-going person that it is difficult to imagine him nervous or agitated. I call him "The Watchman Nee of Burma." After discussing the matter, he and I thought it wise to get off the main road and go through the hills as we headed southward. Turning left and up a steep hill, the road soon became one lane and then dirt and gravel. It curved upward through dense jungle and, even though we could not see the valley below, it became evident that we were on top of a mountain. The road's surface was like grandma's old washboard, and I thought our car would surely fall apart in pieces. But I just love a good adventure, and this was turning into one for sure.

Matthew 4:16 talks about people who sit in great darkness..." And, if there were any families who lived along that road, as evening and darkness settled in all around us, I was completely unaware of them. There were no lights anywhere. The darkness became overwhelming. There was no moon, and no stars. If it wasn't for the lights of our forty-five-year-old vehicle, we wouldn't have been able to see anything at all.

Any single source of light becomes brighter than ever when in complete darkness. And our source of light was revealing the extent of the darkness. It was everywhere around us. People who know me best say that I have a gift for geography and direction. Of course, don't ask my wife about that. She would tell you that it is my pride that keeps me from asking directions, and that could be. But, as I travel alone, I seldom need a map or GPS to find my way on any Interstate Highway in America. I just get in the car and go. But, honestly, that night along that road, I had lost all my bearings. I kept thinking that we might come upon a house, a general store, or a gas station. But there was nothing up there at all. It was complete wilderness, and utter darkness.

Then, suddenly our car lost all power. The engine stalled. The headlights and dashboard lights went dark. We rolled to a halt along what seemed to be the shoulder of the road. And there we sat, seemingly helpless.

You need light to see when you are working on a car engine– at least, most of the time. I know that any graduate of Paris Island can disassemble a Colt .45 or M16 Rifle without light and even while blindfolded. But our driver was no Marine. And he was no mechanic. But he was, indeed, trying to get us back to Yangon. The engine was still hot, and it was extremely challenging to let his fingers feel their way through what was under the hood. I had a small pocket flashlight in my bag that had served me a long time without any problems. But, on that night, yes, as soon as I turned it on, the tiny light bulb flickered with a micro-explosion, and it would not work at all. You would think that any old heathen taxi driver would smoke nicotine sticks and have matches in his pocket or glovebox. But not our driver. Then I thought of my cell phone, tucked away in my backpack. But when I found it, the battery was dead. We were in total darkness.

Pastor Htein Win Ei is not Burmese. He is of the Asho Chin tribe. Whereas most Chin tribes are hill peoples in Myanmar, the Asho are flatlanders or valley dwellers. Htein and his people live along the Ayeyarwaddy River in Magwe Division. But, like all Myanmar peoples, the men traditionally wear traditional longyis, rather than long pants. Htein wears a longyi almost exclusively. And there have been times when I was envious of his freedom of movement in them. It is like a wrap skirt. It allows great freedom, and in the heat of their country, it is light and airy, a wonderful sensation when you are desperate to feel a draft from any direction. I have tried them and own several of different colors and fabrics. I think, however, that they are best suited for men with a slender, more athletic build. And, even though I have seen rather large Burmans filling a longyi to their utmost capacity, they may not be so comfortable or practical for those of us who are more blessed, or well-rounded.

Our driver continued to fumble around in the dark, trying to fix the car. And I decided that the back seat of our small Japanese wonder was an acceptable place to spend the night and wait for sunrise. But those hills, even in the Burman jungle, are cold at night. And the coldness went right through me. I thought perhaps I could open the trunk, get my suitcase, and wrap up in some more clothes, or use one of Htein's longyis as a blanket. But the darkness was overwhelming. So, for the moment I was content to curl up and shiver.

Only one of perhaps several things could have made the night more challenging: I was soon to be confronted with two of them.

Paul the Apostle said, "I speak as a man." And I hope you will forgive me as I speak, or write, of carnal necessities. As King David was faced with the need to "cover his feet" in a cave, I was eventually forced from the false security of my backseat refuge to take the pause that refreshes.

Running my hands along the back of the seat in front of me to the door and then finding the handle, I opened the door and put my feet on the dirt road beneath me. I couldn't really see the road, but I took a couple steps away from the car. I thought that I knew where the driver was, probably in front of the car, under the hood. I had no idea where Pastor Htein had gone. My necessity was turning into desperation. So, out in the darkness I went.

But what direction was the side of the road, and how far was it? I decide to gamble. I would go straight out in one direction, away from the car and, turning about, straight back again. In my mind, it was simple. I stepped slowly and purposely. I did not count my steps. But, in retrospect, it may have helped. When my feet finally perceived grass, stubble, or brush of some kind, I took my usual, yet daring, and inconspicuous position. Relief was immediate. But when my ears perceived an unnerving presence in the darkness ahead of me, indistinguishable as it was at first, the essence of my necessity changed.

I thought perhaps it was my imagination running wild because of our circumstance. But I heard the sound again. And it seemed a bit closer. "Grrr." I thought, "Couldn't be! Nah!" But then again, "Grrrrr." Suddenly, the sound of brush or braking twigs directly in front of me was unmistakable.

In my mind, I tried to make light (no pun intended) of it. I thought to myself, "If I am to be eaten in Old Burma, as my Buddhist friends believe, I will come back. However, I thought, after the digestive process, I could end up as a Rhododendron or palm tree.

There are tigers in Old Burma. Also monkeys with long, intimidating fangs, not to mention a host of other critters that all make impressionable sounds. They are highly territorial. Matter of fact, not far north from where we were is one of the world's largest tiger preserves, originally started and funded by an American naturalist.

Just a year ago, a young Karen farmer was killed and eaten by a large male tiger in the southern part of Myanmar. After years of being hunted to almost extinction, the tiger population is growing. But, also, there are still herds of wild elephants. I am told that if an elephant decides you should die, his mind cannot be changed, and your death is imminent. All these things were going through my mind as I was trying to finish my business at the side of what I thought was the road.

So, I turned toward where I thought the car was, and I could see nothing. I tried waving my hand in front of my face. I couldn't see it. But, with another growl, this time yet closer, I knew that I needed to proceed without delay. My feet wanted to run, but my head was warning me to proceed with caution.

I stuck my right foot out and tried to feel my way. The ground ahead of me didn't feel like roadway. It had only been a couple short minutes since I left the security of the car, but my venture into the unknown seemed much longer. I heard it again, "Grrr." Now, my nervousness was turning to fear.

I did not want to panic. I had the feeling of being stalked, and I thought that crying out might make me sound like prey and quicken an attack. So, I proceeded cautiously and deliberately, stretching my foot in different directions, until I perceived what I thought was definite roadway.

"Htein!" Htein!" In a muffled voice, slightly more than a whisper, I called to my pastor friend. "Htein! Where are you!" There was no response. I was beginning to shake.

I took one step at a time, feeling my way along in the utter darkness. One step. Then another. Then again, "Grrr!" Another step: a little bigger, a little farther this time. "SAYAR HTEIN! Are you there?"

(I am aware that I am quickly approaching content of a more graphic nature than the most daring of preachers might tackle in either pulpit or prose. But please bear with me as I attempt to explain and paint the picture of our adventure that night in a way that will keep most of my readers from blushing.)

Remember, Htein Win Ei, like most Burmans, wears a longyi instead of pants. Most men in Myanmar who dress in longyis will squat on the ground like a woman, when relieving themselves. People in many other countries, even in Eastern European villages, like in Ukraine, do the same.

Even Bolivians in South America would understand this. Sometimes your mind plays tricks on you. Especially in the quiet darkness, sounds seem to be amplified. It had only been a few seconds since I had heard the last growl. But the deafening silence was unsettling. I was supposing that my sabre toothed pursuer was so close that I could feel his hot breath on the back of my khakis; that craving a change of diet, he would take his once-in-a-lifetime chance to dine on white meat, clean me like a fish with one slash of his claws, and drag me off to his favorite place for a midnight snack. So, even though I could see nothing ahead of me in the darkness, I hastened my step, hoping to find the car, even if I was to run headlong into it.

Again, I called out for Sayar Htein. And again. But there was only silence. And I kept stepping.Suddenly, and without warning, I fell head over heels. In the chaos of the moment, I was sure I had been snatched, or pushed, or enveloped like a fly in a trap. With my arms flaying in every direction, trying to catch myself, but swinging punches at everything and yet nothing, I screamed like a chimpanzee running for its life.

Then I realized - something, or someone, was punching back. It was Sayar Htein! In the darkness, as I was trying to find the edge of the road, Htein chose to squat in the middle of it. And, hearing the same growls that I was hearing, he was hastening his highway hiatus when I fell over him. The ensuing rumpus inspired in both of us a struggle for survival and a chorus of the new hit single entitled, "Screeches in The Night." We almost beat one another, each of us thinking that the other was the tiger.

We finally realized our error, stood to our feet, and like any self-respecting preachers, straightened our clothing until we realized the tiger was still out there. Helping each other back to the car, we dove into the backseat and waited until our driver slammed the hood closed, jumped behind the wheel, and fired up the old Toyota. If there was indeed a tiger in the bushes, perhaps a leopard, monkey, an Asian bear or barking deer, we may have scared it off with our screaming. We never saw it, and the lights of our vehicle couldn't find it. But you'll never convince us it wasn't there!

There have been several times during mission trips when a close encounter with some dangerous creature elevated our heartrate: Like the time my pastor stood with us on a mountain near the Thai border and a deadly neon red centipede climbed his britches leg with intimidating speed. There was the day I was driving across country with our preacher boys in the back and we stopped at a picturesque lake after hours of driving. We parked the truck and walked through the grass at water's edge until Brother Reedy yelled, "Snake!" Exactly where we had walked, a large Burmese pit viper slithered out of the grass and could have bit any of us. Brother Reedy heroically dealt with the serpent by flipping it into the water with his bamboo Mosaic rod, made special for him by Htein Win Ei's young men.

Then there was the time that I was walking through the jungle, holding a conversation, and not looking directly in front of me. Most of the time, I don't focus at eye level. I look at the ground in front of me. But, on that day, I walked into a large web that hung between trees, and ended up with banana spider, larger than the circumference of a grapefruit, on my face. It covered my face. My face! What did I do? I screamed like a little girl, swatted it off, and stamped it to powder in the dirt below me. Banana spiders are huge, but harmless.

Don't get me wrong. There are, indeed, dangers in Myanmar. At the Bethany Baptist orphanage, a ministry of Thaung Lian's church in Yangon, one of his young orphan girls was in the bathroom on the 2nd floor of his new building. She was sitting on the toilet when she saw movement at her feet. It was a large King Cobra. It raised up in its typically aggressive posture, and the little girl screamed. She ran out of the bathroom, somehow avoiding the snake, and alerted the preacher boys in their 3rd floor dormitory. They came and killed the snake, then prepared it for dinner.

CHAPTER TWELVE

Smuggling Bibles For the Burmese

"I rejoice at thy word, as one that findeth great spoil."
Psalm 119:162

Saya Thaung was overdue, and we were all worried. There was always risk in carrying Bibles from Thailand. But, at that time, there was no other way to get them for our church members. Our country was closed, isolated from the entire world. There was so much distrust. Government informers were everywhere, and I myself used to be one.

I had not been a member of the church long. Matter of fact, I had not been a Christian long. But I was growing spiritually, and like others I wanted my own Bible. Many of our church members already had Bibles because of Saya Thaung's previous trips. He had made the journey twice before. But some of those Bibles went to the church plants far away in the provinces. So, our church people who owned Bibles shared them with others.

Because of their graciousness, we passed them around. One family would have a Bible for a week and then give it to another family. But now, if Saya Thaung was successful, we all would have Bibles. It all depended on Saya Thaung bringing them from Thailand.

There were those who begged him not to go. I was among those who were concerned. I had a bad feeling about this trip. I don't know why. The plan had been successful before. But the Bible was considered contraband like anything else the General's regime deemed as subversive to the government and the Burmese culture. I had been praying. I was amazed to think how God changed me, that I would pray for Saya Thaung, or pray at all.

For most of my life I would go to the pagoda and light candles, kneel and chant the prescribed saying. But now, I was praying for my pastor, a man who had been my enemy. And it was from my heart.

In each of his previous trips, Saya Thaung went to the border and crossed the Moei River to the city of Mae Sot. There, Bibles were waiting at a Baptist Church. Containers of Scriptures were being shipped from America to Bangkok and then brought to Mae Sot by truck. With the help of some of the Myanmar Christians in

Thailand, Saya Thaung would bring the Bibles across the river to the Myanmar side, and then bring them back to Yangon. Gathered in the church, we all prayed and begged God to keep our pastor safe. He had been gone five days already, and not even Mann, his wife, had heard any news.

There at the border, Burmese soldiers with AK-47s patrolled the river and were stationed behind sandbagged machine guns. Mostly, they guarded the bridge. The Friendship Bridge, between the border cities of Mae Sot on the Thai side and Myawaddy on the Myanmar side, had been closed for several years. This created hardship on trade and commerce, as well as those who lived on one side of the river and worked on the other. It divided families.

So, the people had devised ways of traveling back and forth. Local businessmen ferried thirty or more people at a time in long, narrow riverboats. Some just waded the river balancing packages on their heads. Others paid young men to tug them across on large innertubes. Lines of people waited to cross, carrying armloads of goods. Clusters of people lived along the river and under the bridge in tents. Some lived in small hovels, quilted together with pieces of cardboard or plastic. And then there were those who were even more unfortunate: they spent their nights scavenging the city streets for dumpster food and their days hiding from the sun under just a piece of fabric draped over a bush. It was over this river that Saya Thaung would bring the Bibles.

Young people from the Thai church helped him load the heavy boxes into a chartered skiff and, with a gratuitous nod and wave goodbye, Thaung gave the boatman a gesture who pushed away from the bank. In the rainy season it would have been impossible to transport the Bibles in this way. It is then that the river rages, making such a crossing perilous to the most courageous and skilled. But it was a short trip across, and a Karen preacher was waiting on the other side to help Saya Thaung get his precious cargo to the bus station.

Myanmar buses travel almost the entire country on single-lane highways, crossing mountain ridges, rumbling over precarious bridges, and fording muddy rivers. Linking the smallest of villages and large cities for business and trade, they haul both passengers and cargo around the clock. The economy buses stop at every burg and road crossing along the way, even some front yards, making the journey long and tortuous. But one can travel halfway across the country for a mere 6,000 to 8,000 kyats. For the more successful or endowed, the Express or VIP buses are luxury on wheels and translate to just a few dollars more.

As in many other Third World countries, officials can sometimes be induced to service by money. Myanmar is no different, and at times and in certain situations bribery is even cultural. Every long-distance bus has two drivers, one on duty and one who sleeps until his shift starts. Then there is a purser or two, checking tickets, handling money, and assisting passengers with luggage.

After speaking with the purser, and paying a small incentive, the boxes of Bibles would be placed in the cargo hold area in the bottom of the bus. There was

2,000 Bibles. It was the largest shipment yet. And Saya Thaung realized that, if successful, his people and those of many other churches would be empowered to do more for God.

The bus would travel up over the Karen State mountains, through the Thanylin River valley, across Bago Division, and finally into Yangon. The journey would be long and there would be many military and police checkpoints. It was a huge risk for Saya Thaung, and now for the bus driver and company. There was no way of telling how many times the bus would be stopped and searched. They might encounter Immigration officers or Customs agents. But the decision was made to allow Saya Thaung to ride underneath, in the cargo hold with his Bibles.

The current temperatures were more than 100 during the day and no less than 90 degrees at night. Equal to the heat was the debilitating humidity. And, being an Express Bus, they would only stop twice on schedule, to pay tolls, or when halted by officials.

Thaung Ngain Lian was born and raised in the Chin Mountain village of Tedim, near the Mizoram, India border. Temperatures are much cooler there, especially at night. But Thaung had taken his education in the Philippines and lived in Yangon for some time. He had become accustomed to the energy-sapping heat and humidity, but inside the cargo-hold of the bus would be like an oven.

I remember the first time I met Thaung Lian. I was the Chief of Police in our township. My family had been highly respected for generations. I was proud to serve my community. It didn't mean that we were rich. Everyone in those days struggled. But I tried to act like I was rich. I had much authority and I wielded it for all to see.

I recognized that Thaung was Chin, not Burmese as myself. I assumed that he was also probably Christian. The Chin people were long ago evangelized by missionaries, a hundred years before the present regime. Even though there was war between us at one time, the Burmese and Chin people had come to an amicable agreement. But that he should be on my street where I lived, and distributing Christian scriptures in a Buddhist community, infuriated me. I addressed him directly:

"What do you think you are doing?"

"Sir, I am a Christian pastor."

"Where is your church? We have no church in this community. It is not allowed."

"I am sorry, sir. But I did not know that there is a law against being a Christian in Dagon Saikkan Township."

I remember that I responded to him sharply and said, "There is no law against being a Christian. But you cannot distribute literature and you cannot disrespect Buddhism in this country. There is a strong law against that."

He responded, "Sir, part of being a Christian is proclaiming the Good News of Jesus Christ to all."

I scolded him and strongly warned him about seeking converts in our community. He was not disrespectful but told me that his God had commanded him to spread the message of Jesus, and he would obey Him rather than men.

A week or so passed. I was not thinking about this Christian preacher or his church. But, in my travels, I stopped at a corner grocery. The patrons were talking about the new church in the community and one of them had a gospel tract given to him by Thaung Lian. I was told that he was going door to door and visiting families, inviting them to his church services. Again, I was infuriated. I thought, "How dare this man ignore my warning!" But I thought that, if I let him alone, he would probably become discouraged and leave our community and go back to his mountain.

Weeks passed and, everywhere I went, people were discussing this Christian preacher and his church. They asked me, "How long will you tolerate this man and his church? His followers are growing every week."

I thought that if I did nothing, I might lose the respect of the people in my Township. Week after week his group became more visible. With the urging of my favorite monk, I decided to act.

There was about thirty people who gathered with me on a Sunday morning, just a block away from where Thaung Lian's church was meeting. He lived with his young wife and baby boy in a rented wooden building; their living quarters were upstairs, and the church assembled below.

As we gathered on the street a block away, we could see people entering the building. Soon we could hear them singing. Their songs sounded joyous. But they did not sound Burmese or Buddhist at all. In my heart, I wanted to know why they were so happy. But the people around me were becoming angrier and I knew I had to act.

I instructed them to pick up stones. Buddhist people in Myanmar know about stoning. They do not brag about it, but, infrequently when warranted, it is done. I had never done it before. And, I must admit, it made me uncomfortable.

The church singing stopped and I could hear Thaung Lian preaching. I heard every word. He spoke with authority, and he spoke with love. The people standing around me could hear it also. But they were not there for preaching. They wanted to drive this man and his followers from their neighborhood. And so, we waited on the street outside the building. The church service had obviously concluded. And, yet no one was leaving the building. We could hear them talking and they still sounded happy. They had no idea or warning of what was going to happen to them. And when they finally began to exit the building and walk into the street, Thaung Lian and his wife, baby boy in her arms, were among them. They were talking and laughing freely.

I gave the order that has haunted me ever since. But even before I spoke, a man reared back and threw a fist-sized stone at Thaung Lian, hitting him squarely in the forehead. Blood instantly gushed from the wound; he staggered and cried out. I thought he would collapse. But he collected himself and, as the stones from others rained down upon his small congregation, he shouted and told his people to run. Some ran back inside the building. Some hid by the corners of the house. The people in the street used all their stones and shouted profane denunciations. But they finally stopped. And, when Thaung went to talk to them, they all ran away.

The townspeople were all extremely pleased with me. But I was not so happy with myself. I could not sleep that night. Yet, the following week we stoned them again. This time we rained stones on their building, on the outside walls and tin roof. The sound must have been deafening. But they kept singing.

Another week we stoned them in the street, while they were walking to church. But they kept coming. I could not understand what possessed them. And, what made them happy, even when persecuted?

Then there was the day that my superior called me to his office. He had heard reports, not so much about Thaung Lian and his church but, about the stonings. He wanted me to handle this thing quickly.

I went to Thaung Lian's house with two younger officers, but he was not home. His wife said he was visiting in the community. But we saw him walking down the street and, as he approached us, we arrested him. We put him in handcuffs and took him to our township jailhouse. He did not resist at all. I was hoping he would. But he did not.

I kept him in prison a short time. I threatened him with more time in jail, with fines, and released him. But when he would not cease to teach and preach, I arrested him again. And this time I beat him with a steel rod. He cried and begged me to quit. But I did not. Bruised and bloodied, I sent him home. I thought surely, he would leave our community. But he did not. Several times I jailed Thaung Lian and beat him. But it seemed like the more I abused him, the more he would preach his Bible. In all my years as a policeman, I was never so frustrated and confused. I thought it was because I was not sleeping well. I was sick, not as before, but this time I wondered if I might die. When I first experienced the discomfort, I tried to ignore it. I did not want to complain. But every day it became worse. I needed to work, but it was becoming increasingly difficult. One morning I rolled out of bed and fell on the floor, doubled up in pain. When I finally got to my feet and stood straight up, I tried to wrap my longyi around my waist, I almost fell on the floor and my wife had to help me. I was determined to go to work. But in the next few days, I could not so much as get out of bed. Soon my wife convinced me to go to the hospital.

Doctors said that I needed surgery and the recovery would take a few weeks. I was hesitant, but I had no choice. But I wondered how my family would do without me. In Myanmar, most of us must work every day. If we don't work, we don't eat. And so, it was with my family. Yet, my wife insisted that they would be fine.

I remember waking after surgery. The pain was overwhelming. My doctor did not tell me that there would be this much pain after surgery. But they were giving me something that helped me sleep.

The next morning when I awoke, Thaung Lian was sitting by my side. I almost jumped out of bed because he scared me. I was afraid of him. I was in a compromised condition. Waving my hand at him, I said, "What are you doing here? Are you here to hurt me? Please leave me now!

"Sir, I want you to know that I am praying for you. Our whole church is praying for you." "Please! Please leave me. Get out of here!"

He did leave. But he came back. Again, and again, he returned to my side. And he prayed for me. His words were filled with love. I learned that he and his wife took food to my family. I couldn't understand how he could love me. I said, "I stone you; I beat you; I throw you in jail. And you love me!" I began to weep. Then I reached out for his hand, and I asked, "What is this thing you have inside you that I do not have in me?" He said, "It is Christ!"

So, I became a believer! And I realized that I was not so much persecuting Thaung Lian as I was fighting his message and the God he served. Saya Thaung, my pastor, has taught me the Scriptures, forgiveness, grace, the power of God, and soul winning. Now, when he goes to the street, I go with him. I have won several families to Christ and brought them to church with me. My desire is to serve God and be faithful in His church.

Now, on the new church property, we met and prayed. The first church structure we built was again two floors. The church met upstairs this time. Saya Thaung and his growing family lived in a small room downstairs. Outside that small room, we prayed and begged God for our pastor's safe return from Thailand.

I remembered reading in the Book of the Acts of the Apostles, how that while the people prayed for Peter, he was outside knocking on the door. As I prayed, I wanted to hear a knock at the door, fully expecting Saya Thaung to appear. But he did not come.

Saya Thaung had climbed into the lower cargo hold of the bus and carefully slid in, wedging himself between the boxes of Bibles and the floor of the passenger compartment above. The driver revved the big diesel engine, and smoke and fumes filled the preacher's already insufficient quarters. He thought, "I can do this. I have to do this!"

Leaving the small station, the bus rolled out onto the street, lurching from side to side as it turned. Saya Thaung would need to find something to hold on to, to keep from hitting his head and knocking himself out. And he had not thought about earplugs. The sound of the engine was extremely loud in his space. Regardless, the bus picked up speed, moving westward toward the ridge of mountains on the horizon.

The Dawna Range of mountains stretches north and south between the Karen cities of Myawaddy and Kawkareik. For years, the only way to traverse those mountains was an extremely curvy road of mostly dirt and broken asphalt. Barely maneuvering the hairpin turns and potholes, buses and trucks traveled it daily but slowly and sometimes at precariously. Trucks could be seen stopped along the way, pouring water on their brakes. As Saya Thaung's bus climbed the hills and rounded the curves, Thaung had everything he could do just to keep from bouncing around in his tiny space.

There was two checkpoints on the flat, one manned by military and one by police, between Myawaddy and the mountains. Saya Thaung could hear the officers asking questions. Some of them entered the bus to request passenger identification papers. But they never opened and searched the cargo hold. When the bus engine revved again and Thaung could sense the movement of the bus, he was thankful that he was not discovered. He had one goal, one burden: to get those Bibles home, no matter what.

He was glad to get out of the mountains. Again, he could sense when the bus entered more level land. But his relief would be short-lived. He knew that their first stop would be in the small city of Kawkareik. There possibly he could get out, stretch, and relieve himself, if not get something to eat.

But as the bus stopped and the air came off the brakes, Saya Thaung's relief turned to fear as he heard the demanding shouts of officers and the scurrying feet of passengers hurrying off the bus. His mind rushed with thoughts: "Will they search the bus? Will they open the door to the cargo hold? If so, will they find me? Then what? Will they take my Bibles?"

Suddenly, the heavy horizontal up-swinging door to the cargo hold pulled open and light came flooding into Thaung's compartment. He squinted to get his focus and to see who was outside. When he saw the uniforms of the soldiers, he looked for a way to hide but there was no place to go. Two soldiers grabbed him by the feet and ripped him from his hideaway, dumping him on the dusty ground. They began to kick and spit on him. He yelped like a puppy, but they seemed to enjoy his cries.

An officer with three stars on his shoulder came and barked some orders, instructing his soldiers to pull the boxes of Bibles out of the bus. Thaung cried, "No! Please!" They kicked him some more, laughing and spitting on him as he lay helpless on the ground. Again, the officer gave an order to his men and they jerked Thaung to his feet and took him to a small building.

The next thirty-six hours were filled with constant interrogation, then beatings, then more questions, calling him the most demeaning names in the Burmese language. The officer would get so close to Saya Thaung's face that he feared he might be bitten. Finally, when Saya Thaung was fully exhausted, they put him in a solid concrete, stand-up, torture cell. There was no room to sit down, or even bend his knees. As nighttime came along, his tiny space was filled with mosquitos that bit him on the face and he could not as much as raise his hand to swat them away. Weeping and begging for relief, the soldiers came again, opened the door, dragged him out, and beat him again. Disrespectfully, they spanked his butt with their hands and beat his back with a steal rod.

Dizzy and feeling like he would surely faint, the officer asked him more questions, most he could not answer. The soldiers then picked him up and threw him back into his tiny concrete box and left him for the night.

Sometime during the night, Saya Thaung must have fainted because, in the morning, his knees were bloody with the skin torn right off them. Back home in Yangon Division, we continued to pray. I probably made a dozen trips to the church, to find out if there was any news. Another day passed and, in my spirit, I knew something was wrong. I felt helpless and I feared the worst. I knew how the Burmese soldiers could be. And, to make matters worse, Saya Thaung's trek would take him through the middle of the Karen-Burmese Killing Fields, the place where our civil war was the bloodiest. My history with my pastor was still haunting me. And, fearing the worst for him, I felt a strange sense of guilt, like I was a part of it.

I could not sleep that night. I wanted to go to my pastor. But I didn't know where to start looking for him. So, I went to the church. And I just sat there, outside the front door. I waited and prayed.

That next morning, the sun was just coming up over my left shoulder and I heard a phone ring. The church door was shut, but I heard some of the conversation, and I heard Mann sobbing. I jumped up and rushed inside to see the tears running down her face.

"He's okay!" she said. "We need some men to go pick him and the Bibles up at the bus station." "I'll go!" And, with that, I ran out of the building to organize the men. I cannot describe the joy I had when I saw my pastor standing at the bus station. He was bruised and looked like he had not slept in a long time. But he was ok!

We hired a truckman to haul us and the Bibles back to the church. The boxes filled half the room in the downstairs part of the church. But they would not be there long. We would now need to distribute them to our own people first, then a dozen waiting pastors out in the provinces. They and their people would be so excited! But what had happened to Saya Thaung? His bruised face, his bloodied knees, his torn clothing, the way he walked with a limp: we all knew that it was a miracle of God that brought him home.

Saya Thaung told the story:

"I was wedged inside the tiny concrete torture cell, and I was barely conscious when I heard the Captain's voice and saw the flash of soldiers uniforms outside my enclosure. The door was opened, and the soldiers gently helped me out. I was too weak to stand. So, they carried me to the small building, washed my wounds, gave me a little food and water, and let me rest for a while.

The Captain - the one with three stars on his shoulder - he came to me with one of my Bibles in his hand. Very humbly, he said, "Please forgive me. I stole one of your Bibles."

I said, "Excuse me, sir?"

"I took one of your Bibles and began to read it. This book talks about how the world began. It is amazing! I have never read anything like it before."

"Sir, the Holy Bible explains, not only about creation but, how mankind fell away from God, and why we need a Savior. The Bible teaches us about Jesus Christ, the Savior of the World."

The captain asked if he could keep the Bible. I said, 'Please do!' And, then I asked him if I could have the rest of my Bibles. He said, "Oh, yes! I will send you to Yangon with all your Bibles."

So, he instructed his soldiers to gather the boxes of Bibles. They stopped a truck going to Yangon, loaded the Bibles, and kindly sent me on my way. The truck brought me straight to the Yangon Bus Terminal. Praise the Lord, here we are with God's Word for everyone. How good is the Lord to us!" Someone said, "But Saya, what those men did to you, it is shameful and a crime!" Saya Thaung just smiled and said, "Many have paid a great price for the Word of God. Now it is our turn to do a great work for God with what we have received."

CHAPTER THIRTEEN

Too Burmese to Believe

*"And he is the propitiation for our sins: and not for ours only,
but also for the sins of the whole world."*
1 John 2:2

"Shhh. Momma, please don't tell him I'm here." "Chit Te Maung, she's in here!"

"Momma! Please! You don't understand."

Chit Te Maung burst into the room, grabbed CC Tan by the wrist, and demanded that she come home. Her mother did not understand, but she would suffer a beating that night. CC's mother had seen her bruises before. And she knew that Chit Te Maung was an angry man. But, in her mind, it was a woman's duty to obey her husband no matter what.

CC Tan had been beaten many times. Her husband was known in the community for his temper. And he was a drinker. When he became full of Burmese whiskey, his anger was uncontrollable. Even though Chit Te Maung was small in stature, he was a scrapper. Especially when he was into the booze, people knew to stay away from him. He had been in many street fights. He had even gone to jail for fighting.

On this night he was drunk. And he was particularly angry because, despite him forbidding her to go to her "meeting," CC Tan had returned to the Christian teacher who was filling her head with sacrilege. His friends had told him that they saw her coming from his house.

There were reports in the community about Christians. But they were very few and, if Burmese, they were disloyal to their own people. The area monks warned about them. Faithful Burmese were not even to talk to them.

Chit Te Maung was raised in a staunch Buddhist family. His elder brother was a monk, a high priest teaching in some of the most respected monasteries in the province. Chit Te Maung did not want to tell his brother about his wife's curiosity about Christianity. It was enough for him to deal with in the local community. If she should convert to Christianity, it would bring utter shame on him and his whole family.

One night, after supper, there came a knock at the door of their home. Standing outside the door was a Burmese man and woman, dressed in the traditional men's longyi and lady's thummy – wrap skirts, respectively. They were smiling as friends, but Chit Te Maung did not know them. When they introduced themselves, he knew the polite thing to do was to invite them inside their home. But he did not want to.

"Please, come in!"

The stranger introduced himself as "Than Zaw," a Christian pastor – the teacher who had been teaching Chit Te Maung's wife. Chit Te Maung's first impulse was to throw this man and his wife out of the house and into the street. But such an act would bring shame. He knew it was not the Buddhist way. Chit Te Maung didn't know that his wife was visiting a pastor, a Christian minister. He did not know of any "church" in their whole community.

Chit Te Maung asked the man and his wife to sit down. And, as they took their places on the floor, CC Tan ran out of the house and down the street, almost losing her flip-flops along the way. A nearby "laphetyay saing" (Burmese grocery and café) was just a few doors down. She purchased a fresh bag of the best Burmese tea leaves and rushed home to boil water and serve her guests as best she could. CC Tan knew that Than Zaw had come to talk to her husband about the Lord Jesus. Her heart was pumping so fast that she could hardly speak. "I have no time to talk," she told the cashier. "I have to get home right away!"

"You are a Christian minister, sir? Chit Te Maung asked. "Where is your church? There is no church here. We are Burmese; this is a Buddhist community."

"Yes, Chit Te Maung, that is true. But we have started a new church here. And your wife has visited us on several occasions."

Than Zaw knew that CC Tan had been beaten for coming to their services. Matter of fact, Chit Te Maung beat her every time she came to church. He thought she was attending some kind of teaching class, perhaps English school – because everyone wants to learn English. But when he discovered that she was attending Christian Bible studies, it infuriated him. How would he explain to his family and the people of his community?

"Where is this church? I have never seen a church here!" Chit Te Maung wanted to ask this man, "What gives you the right to start a church in our community?" But he held his peace. It was evident that this man and his wife had come in a friendly way.

CC Tan entered the room with a pot of fresh tea and ceramic cups. Placing them on a tray on the floor between them, Than Zaw and his wife could see her hands shaking.

"Please, won't you have some?" she asked.

"Kyay zu htin bar de!" (Thank you very much!)

It had been a nice visit, and Chit Te Maung seemed to listen. But inside he was bristling.

When Than Zaw and his wife left the house and disappeared down the street, Chit Te Maung began to scream indecencies at his wife. Than Zaw had not only come to their house uninvited, but he had tried to convert him to Christianity. In Chit Te Maung's mind, Jesus was the god of the Western world, the white people. He would have nothing to do with this god. Buddha was a god. And, someday, if he remained faithful to Buddhism, through many cycles of life, he would become a god also.

That night, Chit Te Maung threatened his wife like he had never done before. He told her that if she shamed him like this, he would kill her. She was not allowed to return to this "church," and Than Zaw and his wife were never to come to their house again.

But they did come! Many times. Each time, they would bring a gift. Sometimes it was a small bag of rice, or some fruit. Once they brought a two-liter bottle of genuine Coca Cola. They would talk about the weather. When it was rainy season, there was flooding. In the dry season, it was hotter than a two-dollar pistol. Than Zaw said it wasn't as hot as the place people go who have never believed on Christ.

It was an extremely hot Saturday afternoon. Than Zaw stopped at the house to invite Chit Te Maung to church. "I told you, Saya. I'm not coming to church. You're not going to convert me, or my wife."

Chit Te Maung didn't know that his wife was standing right behind him. And, immediately CC Tan said, "I already have accepted Jesus as my Savior."

Chit Te Maung was infuriated. He flew into a rage and acted like he was going to hit the preacher. Instead, he ran out the door into the street and disappeared into the darkness.

"What will he do, CC Tan?"

"I don't know, Saya. I have been praying and fasting for my husband."

"Me too. Both my wife and I have been praying with tears. We believe that the Holy Spirit is convicting his heart."

"Thank you, Saya! Whatever happens, I will see you in church tomorrow morning."

Than Zaw welcomed his people into his house the next morning. The room was filled with children and married couples, all former Buddhists, and Muslims too. There were no chairs to sit on, only thin bamboo mats on the floor. The people sat "Indian-style," shoulder to shoulder. The young church had no piano or organ, not even a guitar. But they sang from their hearts. Than Zaw had put together a small hymn book of translated songs, like "Amazing Grace" and "Jesus Paid It All." Their singing could be heard outside the building and down the street.

No Christian pastor ever loved his people more than Than Zaw. He and his father were both converted from Buddhism, and they paid a price for doing so. They had been shunned, stoned, and driven from their family's village. But both men had started separate churches in different villages, faithfully preaching the Word of God and winning people to Christ with no salary, or support from any missions group.

Than Zaw is pure Burmese. That means that he is not part Burmese and part Chin, or Karen, or some other Myanmar tribe. And, in Myanmar, if you are Burmese, you are presumed to be Buddhist. Buddhism to Old Burma is as Roman Catholicism is to Italy. Even more so, Buddhism is not only Myanmar's religion, but also their culture. And that culture dates back thousands of years. In the Burmese mind, to think of a Burmese- Christian is like trying to comprehend a child plagued with Hutchinson-Gilford Progeria Syndrome, the rapid and unnatural appearance of aging. It's an anomaly.

Then Zaw stood before his converts with his Bible open and he was explaining "the love of God which is in Christ Jesus our Lord" (Romans 8:39). Suddenly the front door to Than Zaw's house burst open with a loud sound like an explosion. It was Chit Te Maung. And he looked over the group of believers, saw his wife, and grabbed her by the hand, pulling her from her seated position. When she resisted him, he grabbed her by the hair and dragged her out of the house. Than Zaw and the believers tried to stop him, but finally CC Tan surrendered to her husband's rage and went home with him.

The children were crying. The other women were stunned. Some of the men wanted to find Chit Te Maung and beat him as he had beaten his wife. Instead, they began to pray.

The Psalmist speaks of the angry man in Psalm 22, verses 24 and 25: "Make no friendship with an angry man; and with a furious man thou shalt not go: lest thou learn his ways and get a snare to thy soul."

The word "angry" in these verses denotes a man whose emotions can be seen on his face. He is so disturbed that his nostrils flare. The appearance of his eyes is distorted. But the furious man is hot with displeasure. He is incensed. The heat of his indignation develops as sweat beads on his face, like poison seeping from a bottle or like venom from a snake. Men can also become so enraged that they begin to physically shake or even weep.

After dragging his wife home and beating her until her face was bloody and swollen, Chit Te Maung had no relief from his anger. All night he paced the floor with his anger seething from his profane mouth. He could not sleep. He reached for his bottle of whiskey. But he was shaking so much that he could not put it to his mouth. Instead, he flung it across the room, the glass bottle breaking against the wall and shattering in bubbling pieces across the floor. CC Tan sat weeping, curled up on the floor on the opposite side of the room.

The next morning, Chit Te Maung had worked himself into such a state that he could not even go to work. Suddenly there was a knock at the door. And, when Chit Te Maung looked to see who it was, he did not repulse the pastor. To CC Tan's surprise, he asked him to come in.

He said, "Saya, I need help! Please help me."

"Chit Te Maung, you think that Jesus is only the God of White Men, but the Bible says that He died for all. He died for you!"

"Mar kaung bu! Mar kaung bu! I am NO GOOD, NO GOOD!" Chit Te Maung began to sob.

Pulling his Bible from a shoulder bag, Than Zaw turned to the New Testament and the Apostle's Book to the Romans. He began to read in Judson's Burmese Bible, "...there is none that doeth good, no, not (even) one." He continued, "For all have sinned, and come short of the glory of God."

For the first time Chit Te Maung was listening. He was thinking about the words Than Zaw was reading.

Than Zaw read on, "God commendeth his love toward us, in that, while we were yet sinners, Christ died for us."

Shaking and yelling, Chit Te Maung interrupted, "BUT THAT'S NOT FOR US; WE ARE BURMESE!" "NO! YOU'RE WRONG, Chit Te Maung! Why did God give this Book, this Law?"

"I don't know!" Chit Te Maung hung his head.

"Look here, Chit Te Maung: Romans 3:19. God gave it "that every mouth may be stopped, and the whole world may become guilty before God." Why? Why do we need to understand our guilt?

Again, Chit Te Maung hung his head, as if surrendering, and said, "I don't know, man! I don't know!"

Then Zaw continued, "So that the whole world will understand that we must all confess our sin and turn to Christ – so that we can be SAVED. Chit Te Maung, God wants to save YOU from your sin and give you peace in your heart. The Bible says, 'For God so loved the world, that he gave his only begotten Son, that WHOSOEVER believeth in him should not perish, but have everlasting life.' Chit Te Maung, God sent his Son into this world, not to condemn the world, but so that the whole world through him might be saved. Chit Te Maung, would you like to be saved?"

Tears running down his face, Chit Te Maung looked at his wife and said, "I'm sorry! I'm sorry. I didn't understand!" He looked back at Than Zaw and said, "Please tell me what to do!"

That day Chit Te Maung believed the Gospel and turned from his culture of religion to faith in Jesus Christ. He confessed his sin and his need of a Savior. Saya Than Zaw will tell you that Chit Te Maung has become one of his most faithful church members and a powerful witness for Christ. Chit Te Maung and CC Tan are happier and more in-love than ever before.

CHAPTER FOURTEEN

Thankaiyar

"So shall he sprinkle many nations; the kings shall shut their mouths at him: for that which had not been toldthem shall they see; and that which they had not heard shall they consider."

Isaiah 52:15

"Momma, momma! Come quickly! Quickly momma!"

"What is it, Sandar Tun?"

"Momma, look! Foreigners?"

The inhabitants of Thankaiyar village had never seen foreigners from any nation. Certainly, they had never seen anyone with white skin. Sandar Tun and her mother were naturally hesitant to come close. But, when they saw Saya Peter with us, they came running and approached us warmly.

Peter Van Siang Lian is a Chin preacher who graduated from the Southeast India Baptist Bible College in Bangalore. I first met him on Facebook. He had seen my posts through another Friend's page. So, he contacted me immediately.

Almost every week I receive dozens of messages from men and women in India, Pakistan, Nepal, Singapore, the Philippines, and even African nations. They all invite me to visit their ministry with the hopes that they can partner with GLBM. But, as gently as I can, I tell them "I am not coming!" And, they will say, "Oh! But why, sir? Please come!" I say to them, "I will pray for you and be your friend as much as my time will permit, but I know my calling and my hands are full in Myanmar."

My father used to say, "Son, you can be a small fish in a big pond or a big fish in a small pond. Which will you choose?" In my ministry his saying translated to me like this: I can make a small impact in many places, or I can make a large impact in one. I have chosen, with God's help, to make the largest impact in the place where God has placed my heart. That is Myanmar.

When Peter contacted me, I must admit, I was leary. He was from the Sagaing Division in Northwest Myanmar, along the Manipur border. He had what I thought was a small ministry in a village called Kanan, two hours north of Kalay, a major city near the Chin State border and known for its trade among the Chin people. I had chosen not to work with the Chin people because I thought they were already well evangelized. The city of Kalay has hundreds of churches from various denominations.

I had met some families in Yangon who were originally from the city of Tamu, just an hour north of Kanan. They were from the Kuki tribe, and I was stunned to learn that most Kuki are Jewish and considered by Jerusalem scholars to be a Lost Tribe of Israel. I was intrigued and immediately wanted to go there and preach the Gospel if possible. But, in the early days of my Myanmar ministry, the area was closed to foreigners and I was forbidden to travel there.

Now, Peter was inviting me to come to Kanan, and I was tempted. So much so that I did some homework and investigated who he was. It did not take me long to find a pastor who knew him, another Chin preacher who was a former Bible professor at Peter's college. He told me that Peter was one of the most "Fundamental Baptist" men he knew. That was good enough for me.

So, I consented to visit Peter and when I arrived there, I was shocked. He and his young family were living in a small room in the back of his father's store. Together, they had started a church and built a boarding school and dormitory housing more than a hundred children. Peter was teaching the Word of God to those children, and one of the first things he asked of me was to baptize his converts.

Peter's father was my senior by just a few years, but his health was not good. I learned that he had put everything he owned at Peter's disposal and by himself financed the dormitory. I would become like a brother to this dear man. I fell in love with him. And, when suddenly he passed away, Peter would become like my son. I helped Peter raise the money to erect his church building. And when he acquired a dozen orphans and his student body swelled to 160 children, GLBM helped him build another dormitory with living quarters for he and his family.

During one of my visits, Peter asked me if I would like to visit a small village where he had a vision to start another church. The village was called Thankaiyar, it was Burmese, Buddhist, with about 400 households. There was no church of any denomination there, and never had been. Most of the residents had never heard the Gospel or the name of Christ.

As the bird flies, Thankaiyar is approximately twelve miles from Kanan. It lies between mountain ridges in a valley that is carpeted with rice paddy fields as far as the eye can see. A one-lane, straight as string, dirt road is the only entrance to the village and, during rainy season, it is often covered with murky water. As we drove there in a borrowed van, our driver sometimes had to estimate where the edge of the road was. I wasn't thrilled with the idea of falling off the road or sinking into the snake and leech-invested water.

We could only proceed so far in our van, and then we had to get out and walk across a foot bridge, then up a hill into the village. Every house in Thankaiyar is built high on stilts with bamboo, some larger than others.

Walking through the village, I could see that we were attracting a lot of attention. I did not see many men; I thought they were probably working. But the women and their children greeted us with big smiles and laughter all along the way.

There was a couple other Americans with me, including GLBM Missionary Tim Davis, and Peter led us to a larger home. We took our shoes off and climbed the narrow steps into the thatched shelter where a crowd of people was gathering. Ladies and children sat on one side of the room. And, on the other, there was the men, a whole line of them, and more were coming. I went down the line of men, stretching my arm and hand out to each in the culturally Burmese fashion. Then I sat down among them, and they welcomed me warmly.

Saya Peter and some of his men sang a couple hymn songs. The Thankaiyar men sat stone-faced and silent. Of course, they would not the songs. As we were strangers to them, also everything they would experience about Christianity that day was also brand new.

There is a large Buddhist temple in the village, and they have their own government school. But, in all my visits to Thankaiyar, I have never seen a monk. They are there, and they probably collect their daily offerings in alms pots each morning like elsewhere in Myanmar. We certainly made enough noise and drew sufficient attention within the village. But they have never come to greet or challenge us.

After the brief singing, Saya Peter said to me, "BaGyi, it is your time!" Another words, it was time for me to preach. So, I stood in my bare feet and introduced myself, giving the greetings from America. I explained why we had come and that the God whom I serve had sent us to them with a message. I then asked them if I could give them that message. I looked over at the line of men to see their faces smiling and their heads nodding consent. It never occurred to me that they might be offended or refuse to listen to the Gospel of Christ. In all my trips to Myanmar, I have always found the people to be warm and gracious.

I did something I had never done before, but it seemed as though the Holy Ghost was nudging me to ask Saya Peter's assistance in a particular way. As I preached the Word of God and read each verse in English, I asked Peter to scoot around the room and to show each family the words of the Scriptures that I was reading in the Bible of their own language. The Burmese Judson Bible and the King James Version are remarkably similar, being translated from the same reliable manuscript. I wanted them to see the words of God with their own eyes.

These people did not know me; they knew nothing about my God or His book. There was no reason why they should believe me. How would they know that what I was telling them was the Word of God? We had to show them. And, as Peter sat with each family, those who read followed every word as he pointed with his finger. I watched as smiles and hints of belief and confidence appeared on their faces. I did not have to spend much time teaching them about sin. They all recognized the depravity of man. But I spent most of my time describing the impeccability of my Savior and His love for them.

I gave the floor to Saya Peter and asked him to explain to them how to become a Christian. He gave a short invitation to receive Christ. Nine souls professed faith in Christ. They bowed their heads before all and asked Jesus to come into hearts, forgive their sin, and be their Savior.

Of course, we were not certain how many understood and genuinely turned to Christ from their idols and spirit worship. But in the weeks and months ahead. Most of those dear people, not only came to church services, but bravely took their stand for Christ in believer's baptism.

After we departed from Thankaiyar, the Village Chief, or community chairman, went behind us to every house and warned the people, saying "This is a Buddhist village. If you convert to Christianity, you will be forcibly removed from the community." Thankaiyar's new converts told Peter what he said. So, Saya Peter immediately went to the Chief's house, knocked on the front door, and said "Sir, you cannot do this!"

"Well, I can do anything I want," said the Chief. "This is my village, and I am the boss!"

Saya Peter answered, "No, sir. I have here a copy of the new Myanmar Constitution which guarantees that we as citizens have freedom of religion. This government document promises that we are free to choose our religion. If you do this, we have powerful friends, and we will get lawyers and sue you in court and perhaps you will not be Chief anymore."

The Chief was stunned. But the following week when Peter returned to Thankaiyar, the Chief approached him and said, "If you want to have a church in my village, I will sell you some of my property and you can build it there."

The Chief took Saya Peter to a prime corner lot in the village. Saya Peter asked, "How much will you ask for this property?" The Chief said, "1,973,063.0000" Burmese Kyats, which equals $1,500 US dollars. GLBM wrote the check.

Among the new believers at Thankaiyar was Sandar Tun and her parents. Sandar Tun soon moved to Saya Peter's boarding school in Kanan where she was among more than a dozen new converts whom I baptized. Also, among the converts in Thankaiyar was a young man and his wife who grew spiritually very quickly. He became Peter's shadow and disciple. After some time and training, he became the new pastor in Thankaiyar.

CHAPTER FIFTEEN

Learning to Wait

"And it shall be said in that day, Lo, this is our God; we have waited for him, and he will save us:this is the Lord; we have waited for him, we will be glad and rejoice in his salvation."
Isaiah 25:9

I was born and raised in the small Sagaing Division village of Minhla, near the city of Kalay. Our family was active in church, and we went to many church meetings and Chin festivals. It seems that I always wanted to be a preacher. But there were not many opportunities for a young preacher boy in our village. When I went to meetings with my parents, I heard missionary stories, and I dreamed about one day leaving home and going somewhere to serve the Lord.

In 1999, I was in 10th grade and studying for what we call matriculation. 10th grade is the final level in Myanmar high schools. If you pass the matriculation test, the door opens for college and all the best things our country has to offer. But it is so difficult that many students do not even attempt it. Many fail the test and never try again. I always applied myself in school and did well on tests, but everyone is afraid of this test. I studied every night until I fell asleep on my books.

I knew I had prepared as well as possible but, like many others, I was still extremely nervous. I knew I needed God to help me. I remember BaGyi Bob saying that people do not get saved until they realize they need a Saviour. It was during this time of my life that I realized I needed Christ. I was sixteen years old, and I asked Jesus Christ to forgive my sin and save me.

The test took all morning and, afterwards, I went straight to what I called my prayer mountain. I prayed and fasted the rest of the day and night until morning. I had begged God to help me pass the exam. But I told the Lord, "Whether I pass or fail, I will go on to Bible school and study Your words. I want my life to be used in the ministry for Your glory."

The results of the Myanmar matriculation tests are not immediately known. It takes several months for the grades to be posted. So, I went on to the city of Yangon and enrolled in Bible school as a freshman. In a short time, the matriculation test results were published, and I was informed that I passed the test with sufficient score enough to enter a secular university and perhaps become wealthy someday. But I had promised God that I would serve Him with my life.

During my four years of Bible school, there were teachers that spoke of the "fundamental faith" as opposed to those who were liberal or modernistic. I accepted the "fundamental faith" as my own. Regardless of what would happen or where God would lead me, I believed every word of God's Book.

In 2003, I graduated from Bible school and, with the urging of my principal, moved to Rakhine State to do missionary work under his authority. He sent me to the small remote Buddhist village of Khwah Son in Min Pya township. There were only seventy residents in the whole community. Because I had learned much English in school, I volunteered to teach English at two government schools. I received no salary or compensation for my teaching. But as my relationship grew with the Buddhist leaders, they allowed me to teach the children Christian stories and songs.

It was during this time that I met my future wife. Her name was Tan Tan Ye, and she was Buddhist. But she always came to my meetings with the children and the church services where I was preaching. The loved to hear the words of God. Soon she believed in Christ, and I led her to the Lord.

During my second year on the mission field, Tan Tan Ye was baptized, and we got married. In 2005 we returned to Yangon. In my mind, I wanted to study more. My Bible school principal said to me, "You listen to me! God wants to use you on some mission field. But, if you want more education, you should go to Seminary in the Philippines, and I will buy your airplane ticket."

Tan Tan Ye has always been a selfless servant and walked with the Lord since the day she became a believer. We went home and prayed. Tan Tan Ye returned to Rakhine State and stayed with her Buddhist family for three years while I studied in the Philippines. Her family had many questions. I could support her; I could not even support myself. And I didn't know how I was going to pay for my schooling. I traveled to the Philippines by faith. But, after one month, the seminary hired me to clean the campus buildings. I was able to pay my school bill, send some money home, and graduated with a master's degree. When I returned to Myanmar in 2008, my wife and I reunited in Yangon, and I taught two years in the Bible school.

I received an e-mail from a friend in Mae Sot, Thailand. She said that there was a missionary who was desperate for a Burmese translator and wanted to know if I would come. After discussing and praying with Tan Tan Ye, I left her in Yangon and went to Thailand to help the missionary reach the Burmese Buddhists there. After one year, I sent for my wife.

Our existence in Thailand was meager. We lived very simply and did not have many worldly things. It was there that our son, William, was born. We felt that we were so happy and blessed, but the ministry there was not easy. There were many struggles and disappointments. Nevertheless, we labored loyally with that missionary for seven years, always praying that God would someday send us back to plant a church in Myanmar – a place where there was no Gospel witness.

Soon after I moved to Mae Sot, Dr. Bob DeWitt came to preach at our church and school. People called him "BaGyi Bob." He was from America, and I never knew anyone quite like him before. I had met a few other Americans, but BaGyi ran and played with the children. He would let them climb on him and he would sit with them for hours. They loved him and he obviously loved them. He preached with a passion for souls and loved to go into the remote Burmese villages. Tirelessly he would climb up in bamboo huts, sit where the people sat, and ate what they gave him. When he would talk about his people in Myanmar, he would weep. Tears would roll down his face. He said that it was not him but God's love in him. But I knew that God had given BaGyi to Old Burma.

I introduced myself to BaGyi Bob. I said, "My name is Lal Ram Hgnak, but people call me 'Pastor Steven.'" BaGyi said, "Good! I will call you Pastor Steven."

Tan Tan Ye said to me, "My dear, BaGyi is the man who can help us go back to Myanmar and start a church." I knew she was right. So, one day, I shared my vision with BaGyi. To my utter surprise, he said, "Yes, I will help you!" But he also said that we would need to be patient and pray much.

In those coming years while working in Thailand, every time we had a need, it just seemed like BaGyi was there. When my father was ill and near death, he gave me enough money to travel home and see him. BaGyi would stop at our house and play with our son, William. William was not easily approached by adults. Somehow, BaGyi won my son's heart.

Late in 2017, my wife and I packed everything we had, hired a bus to take us across the border and back to Yangon, and BaGyi was there. He paid for everything. We found a house to rent in one of the most growing communities of the province - hundreds of thousands of Burmese Buddhist families without a gospel witness. Before we left Thailand, BaGyi promised us $300 monthly support while starting our church. He paid our monthly rent on six-month contracts for the past several years. When my wife was sick and needed to go to the hospital, he sent us financial help. When I could no longer see my Bible and was having regular headaches, BaGyi took me for an eye exam and bought me glasses. BaGyi always said that the help was coming from GLBM. But I learned that he paid for all these things himself from his own personal support.

We had heard stories of many Myanmar preachers being persecuted by neighbors and government officials. But we have never yet experienced such a thing. After moving to our community, we started the Grace Baptist Church. We knocked on doors, distributed Gospel tracts, had church services in our home, and started a weekly football club for neighborhood boys. Before playing football, we studied the Bible. The club became so successful that the boys began coming to our house all the time. The Buddhist families loved it and some of them have been saved.

Two years ago, BaGyi was in Myanmar and he called me on the phone. He said, "Steven, I want you to bring your wife and children to my hotel in Yangon." I said, "BaGyi, it is far. Very expensive!" He said, "Tell the taxi driver that he will get paid when you arrive."

We left the house early in the morning and arrived at Hotel 63 in Botathaung Township at 10:00 AM. BaGyi was already out and about and we waited for him in the hotel lobby. When he appeared, he said, "Saya, I want you take you to lunch, so then we are going shopping. I want to spoil your wife." I said, "Excuse me, sir!"

BaGyi took us to the Golden Duck Restaurant, and we feasted until we were ashamed. Then he took us to the most expensive mall in Yangon and asked Tan Tan Ye to pick out a dress, something that she "could not live without." When she did so, BaGyi said, "Now please choose a second one!" Then he asked her if she needed shoes. Then he bought four new dress shirts for me. Then he took my children to a toy store and let them pick out one special gift, whatever they wanted. My children love BaGyi Bob. My wife said to me, "Fifteen years ago, my father died. Now BaGyi has become my dad!"

Last year, we began to look for property in our township on which to build a church. When BaGyi Bob arrived in Yangon, we traveled to look at several different neighborhoods and building lots. I was very anxious to find a permanent location for our church. One property looked good to me but was not perfect. BaGyi Bob said, "Please be patient!" During his next trip, God directed us to another property, much better than the first, and again GLBM wrote the check. BaGyi said, "Put a sign in front that says, 'Future Home of Grace Baptist Church'."

The people in our township are extremely poor. I have taught our people and they give what they can. But, as it was impossible to purchase property, it would take a miracle of God to build a church on that lot. BaGyi said to pray and trust God.

In November of 2019, BaGyi Bob brought with him a team of nearly thirty Americans, many from the New Manna Baptist Church of Marion, North Carolina. They went to the city of Kalay, near my birthplace, held an evangelistic crusade under a thousand-seat tent, distributed 150,000 full-color gospel fliers, fed thousands every night, and saw nearly a thousand souls saved. Praise the Lord God!

GLBM brought all the students from the Cornerstone Baptist College in Yangon. And BaGyi asked me to come along also. I worked the street with the New Manna team members. As I answered their questions and shared my needs, God burdened their heart. They went home and raised $20,000, sent it to us through GLBM, and we have just moved into our new church. Hallelujah! God is good!

BaGyi Bob says, "God does stuff! Just wait and trust Him." I have learned that waiting is not easy. But learning to wait is worth it.

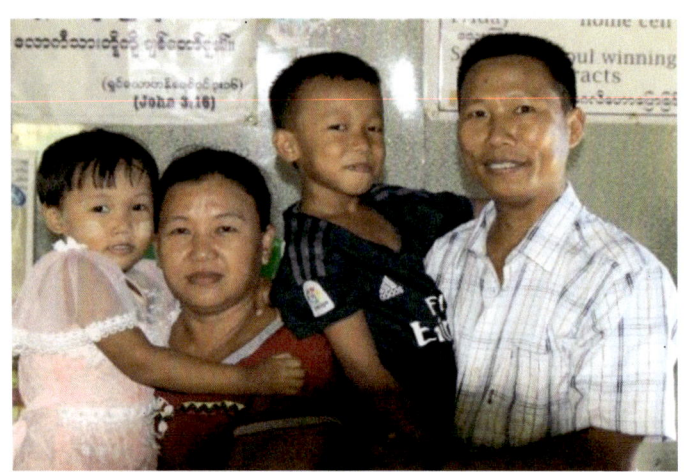

CHAPTER SIXTEEN

Lifting the Lame and Loving Lepers

*"And as ye go, preach, saying, The kingdom of heaven is at hand. Heal
the sick, cleanse the lepers, raise the dead, cast out devils:
freely ye have received, freely give."*
Matthew 10:7-8

I was preaching a Missions Conference in a small church in central
Mississippi and the Pastor asked me, "Brother Bob, have you ever met Tommy
Tillman?" I don't know why, but I had not. The pastor wrote the name of his
biography on a yellow sticky note, put it in my hand, and simply walked away. On
the paper were the words, "Embracing the Untouchables by author Stephen
Fortosis." I stuck the note in my pocket and didn't think any more about it.

When I emptied my pockets that night, out came a few coins, my
pocketknife, and that little note. I wanted to get online and see what the book was
and if I could order it, but I was staying in a missionary apartment at a children's
home all that week and there was no internet available and an extremely weak
wireless phone signal. So, I put the small yellow sticky note in my briefcase, you
know – the catchall pocket - and completely forgot about it. Several months later,
in another state and another meeting, I came upon that note again. This time, I had
Wi-Fi and, getting on Amazon.com, I found and ordered the short paperback book.

When I returned home, the book was waiting for me. It was one of those
books that you cannot put down. I read it cover to cover in just a short time,
weeping between chapters. Few books have affected me so deeply as reading about
Tommy Tillman. Giving their lives to the Lord completely, Tommy and his wife Jo
Ann became God's answer to the lost whom no one else seemed to care about.
Beginning at the seaports along America's Gulf Coast, Tommy found a way to share
the Gospel with Communist seamen docked with their massive cargo ships. Later,
God called him to go to Asia. For thirty years he has given his heart and life to the
thousands in Thai leper colonies who have lost all hope. Tommy learned that rotting
flesh and the loss of limbs was only part of the devastation created by leprosy. He
saw their children living in sewers and being sold into prostitution. He saw the
loneliness and shame.

One day Tommy knocked on a man's door and was invited to come inside. As he began to tell the man about salvation in Christ, the man stood up and left the room without explanation. Twenty minutes later, as Tommy was still waiting for the man to return, he appeared with a plate of fresh cooked food. Both of his hands had been eaten away by leprosy and where his nose had been just a hole in his face. With his handless wrists, also full of leprosy, the man placed the plate of food on the table and invited Tommy to eat.

Tommy said that he looked down at the steaming hot food, bowed his head, and prayed for God to keep him safe and allow him to eat every bite. When he was finished eating, the leper was weeping and explained that others had come and asked him to listen to their words. They would not eat his food. Tommy led the man to Christ that day.

Years later I was in the city of Malawmyine with GLBM's Missionary, Peter Judson. I asked God to let me go there and, when He did, Peter asked me if I would like to go to the leper hospital. I did not know there were lepers in Malawmyine. I immediately jumped at the chance to preach to the lepers. I remembered the lepers that Jesus healed. And I remembered Tommy Tillman's story. But really, it didn't matter to me if the patients had leprosy, or AIDS, or any other dreaded disease. They were Myanmars, and that meant that they were my people.

But honestly, I was not prepared for what I experienced. In this hospital there were several wards. There was the ulcer ward, the surgical ward, the amputation ward, and the terminal ward. The divisions of patients became more severe as you went deeper into the facility. But, truthfully, the stench of rotting flesh was thick and could be smelled right away.

The saddest thing to see was the children. A few visitors had come to see family members who were patients, there was a little boy who was following me and hovering about. Every time I turned around, he was there, and nearly getting under foot. I thought he was with the visitors, but I quickly realized that he was a patient because one of his feet was bandaged and blood was seeping through the gauze. As I sat down, he stood there and stared at me. I finally just invited him up on my lap, and he was so excited. I did not know much about leprosy. At the time, I was under the impression, false as it may be, that the disease is not contagious if the ulcers are dry and not oozing with infectious fluid. However, I did keep an eye on where his foot was and what it touched.

The deeper I went into the leper hospital, the more burdened I became and yet, the more comfortable I was. Entering a large ward, men and women sat on beds that appeared to be nothing more than wooden plank tables. There were no mattresses, or even thin padding. The patients had only a small pillow for their heads and a lightweight blanket for the cool of the evenings. Yet when we entered the room, they smiled with exuberance, greeting us warmly.

Coming through the door, I waved to everyone and greeted them, shouting "Mingalabar!" They all returned the greeting and, because one of us was carrying a guitar, a man asked, "You sing for us?" I walked through the room, talking to every patient, joyously greeting them, and finding out how long they'd been there and what their prognosis was. We sang several Christian hymns, and then I preached. After explaining the Gospel as simply and thoroughly as I could, I invited them to believe and turn to my Saviour. Many did so.

The next ward was full of women. But there was one man, a Muslim, who was being visited by his entire family. On one side, his ankle was bandaged. One the other side, his leg had been amputated to the knee. When I greeted him and his family, he responded to me in such a way that I knew God was going to save him. God did save that man, and his wife and oldest son also believed the Gospel.

Three beds down, on the same side of the room, was a young woman who had also lost her leg. One of the hospital workers told me that her situation was dire, and her family had deserted her, but when we approached her, the smile she displayed won us all over. I was amazed that she could smile like that while enduring such affliction and trial. We spent almost an hour with her, and she wept with many tears as she prayed with us, asking God to forgive her sin and give her new life.

Note: The following year, we returned to that same hospital, and she was still there, glad to see us and still rejoicing in Christ, her Saviour. The following year, she was gone. I inquired and discovered that she had been healed and released. God can do anything!

Also in that same ward was a Burmese woman whose head was shaved, and she had leprose sores all through her scalp. As I approached her, she wept. I could not help myself. I reached out and took her by both her hands. I said, "Please let me pray with you!" She agreed. So, I did something I had never done before and have never done since then, I held her hands in my left hand, put my right hand on her head sores, and prayed for that dear lady. She spoke enough English that I could understand her, and I will never forget her words. She said, "BaGyi, why you do like this? No one does like this for us?" I don't know why I did it, but God told me that it was okay, and it was!

In the last ward, all the way back in the far corner, was two older women. They were both full of leprosy. As I spoke with them, my heart broke. I could not keep the tears from my eyes. One of the women was a Christian. As I approached and introduced myself, she became overjoyed, asking me to tell her friend about Jesus. She said, "Oh, man of God, I have talked to my friend about the Lord many times, and she is such a strong Buddhist. She will not believe. Perhaps you can persuade her to believe in Christ." The nurse said to me, "She will die soon."

There have been many moments in my Christian life and ministry when I felt totally inadequate. This was also such a time, but the Lord told the Apostle Paul that God's strength is made perfect in our weakness (2 Corinthians 12:9). Yes, I believe it! So, saying a silent prayer to myself, I did my best to make Christ real to her. I showed to her the Scriptures. I gave her my personal testimony. She smiled through it all, and then clearly rejected my Saviour in favor of her family's Buddhism and idols. I felt awful. Her Christian friend begged her to believe and wept as I walked away.

The following year I returned to the leper hospital and looked for those two women. I found only one. The old Buddhist woman who was the weaker of the two had passed away, but not before trusting Christ. When I entered the room again, the old Christian woman saw me coming and began to shout the good news. The following year, she was gone also.

Pastor James wrote that our life is like "a vapour that appeareth for a little time, and then vanisheth away." Despite how it feels sometimes, we do not inhabit this life for long in the light of eternity, and what we do with our life and time on this earth matters a great deal. We can live our life for ourselves or others. I have learned that life lived for yourself is lonely and empty.

I met several Buddhist monks in that same leper hospital. They were patients and, like the others, were eager to sit and talk with me for as long as I would stay. Two monks occupied the same room. Both acknowledged that Jesus Christ was the Saviour of the world, the one Gautama promised would come. They joyfully listened to the Scriptures and prayed to invite Jesus into their hearts.

In another ward was an older monk who was obviously feebler and sicker. He lay on his bed and acted like he was not listening to my preaching. When he could no longer forebear the truth of God's Word, he sat up and shouted, "It is not true! It is not true! Eternal life is not by grace! You have to work."

I lifted my Bible in the air and answered him in front of everyone, "That is not what my Bible says! It is by grace alone." *"For by grace are ye saved through faith; and that not of yourselves: it is the gift of God: Not of works, lest any man should boast."* (Eph. 2:8-9)

He shouted back, "Not true, not true! You must work!"

I asked him, "Sir, how are you working for your eternal life?"

He said, "My suffering is my works. Because of my suffering, someday I will become a god."

Burmese people never disrespect a monk. They are the most respected individuals in Myanmar society, but the others in the room began to shake their heads as if disagreeing with the old man.

An old Karen woman was sitting in the corner and very faintly uttered, "But, he has the Book!"

Long ago, before missionaries came to Myanmar in the 1800s, it is said that the Karen people believed that white men from the West would come to their land and bring a Book. And that book would tell of a Saviour.

I asked the old monk, "How do you know these things? Is this what the

Buddhist scriptures say? Can you show me in your book?"

He said, "Sir, I cannot read." With that, he laid back down and never said another word.

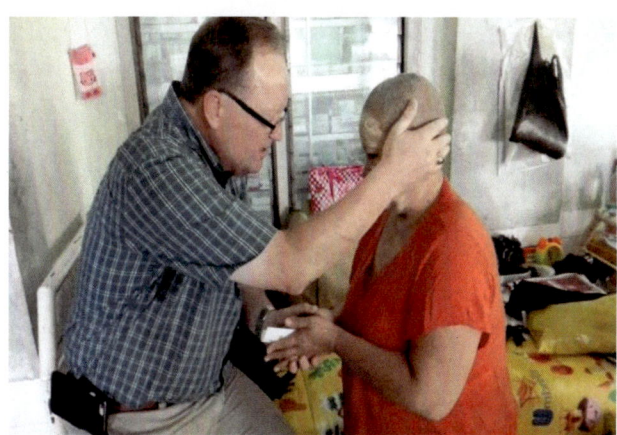

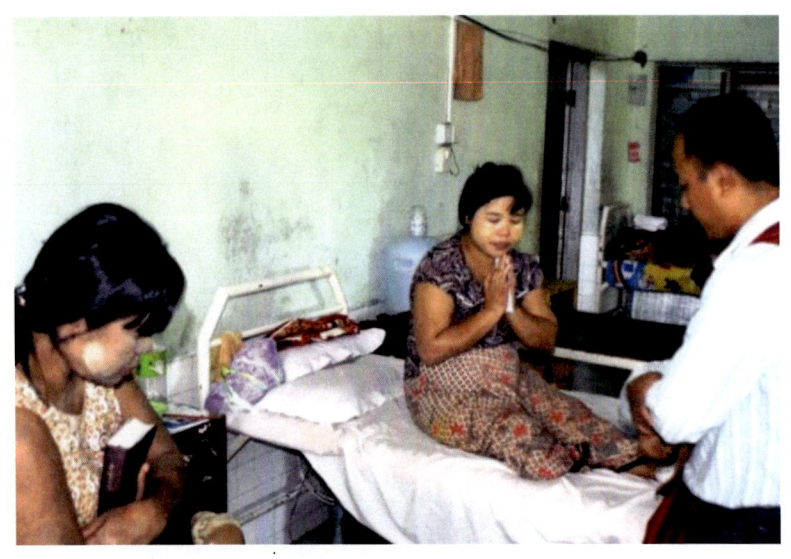

BaGyi Radar

"O Lord, I know that the way of man is not in himself:
it is not in man that walketh to direct his steps."
Jeremiah 10:23

While preaching across America, I have visited many communities where Myanmar refugees and immigrants now live. It is documented that for the past thirty years, they came here just like the Italians, Irish, Germans, and so many others, and settled in hundreds of American cities, first taking up residence in the worst parts of town, working entry-level jobs, but eventually owning their own homes and starting businesses. They have a wonderful work ethic. I have found them in almost every major community of New York State. I have crossed paths with them in almost every state and in Canada.

Some of my traveling companions have said that I have a way of finding Myanmar people. It is true that I have driven into cities like Philadelphia, the many communities of southern New Jersey, then Hartford, Connecticut, Louisville Kentucky, several cities of Indiana and North Carolina, and found them immediately. I don't usually check with Google or the Internet. I don't ask anyone. As it happens, I usually hear about them from someone or pray about it, drive down the highway, get off at a random exit, and run headlong into "my people." It just consistently happens. Someone has said that it is "BaGyi Radar."

Years ago, I brought thirty young people from a church in New Jersey to Albany New York. We put up a tent on the edge of town and I preached a weeklong revival meeting for Pastor Glenn Hamilton with the express purpose of starting a ministry to reach Myanmar people with the Gospel. Our team canvassed the streets of downtown Albany all day for a week and found them. We held Vacation Bible School meetings all over town, on street corners, city parks, front porches, and wherever we could get a crowd of people together. Not only did we find the Myanmar people, but we also brought van loads of them to the tent meetings every night.

One afternoon, I was on the street when two of our New Jersey young ladies came running to me, saying "BaGyi, please. Please come now!" I followed them to an old three-story apartment building that looked like it might fall over. They led me upstairs to the third floor where a door was already cracked open. The girls had been knocking doors in that building and came upon a family from Myanmar that didn't understand the Burmese or Karen languages.

When I knocked on the door, it pushed open to reveal a wide-eyed young father, crouched in the far corner of the room with his wife and two little girls. He had taken up his defensive posture and was trembling in fear like the rest of his family. With great caution, I slowly approached the man, offering my hand in the usual Burmese fashion. He mumbled something that I did not understand, and I backed away.

I tried to greet the man in Burmese, saying "Mingalabar, nay kaung lar?" or, by translation, "Hello! How are you?", but he did not seem to understand. I thought that perhaps he couldn't understand my accent. Maybe I was pronouncing the words incorrectly. Then I tried to greet him in the Karen language: "O su aw clay!", but the man made no response. I turned around and said to one of the young ladies, "Please go get Miss Debbie. Go as fast as you can!"

We waited for a few minutes and the girls returned with Miss Debbie, the daughter of a former missionary who had served for years in Thailand. I explained the situation and asked her if possibly they were Thai people.

Debbie thought that perhaps they were too small in stature. She said, "I think they are of the Kayah tribe."

The Kayah people live in their own Myanmar State along the Thailand border. They, like the Karen people, fled Myanmar during the rule of the Burmese Generals. Debbie's family had the opportunity to work with them much in western Thailand, and they learned their language.

The small Myanmar man was still trembling; his wife and children were hiding behind him. Debbie reached out to the man and greeted him in his native tongue, and the man began to weep, almost collapsing in her arms. She learned that they had been dropped off by an Immigration Department worker not 24 hours before we found them. They were given one twin mattress, two pillows and a blanket, a small amount of money for their first groceries, and an address to visit for help. They had spent their first night in town huddled together upon that one small mattress on the floor, and they had already heard the shouting of alley fights and gunfire on their street. They were scared to death.

Most of the people who we rounded up for the tent meeting were Karen and Chin. There were a few Burmese people. Our tiny Kayah family came also, because we were the only people they knew in the whole city of Albany, and God had directed us to them. They heard the preaching, they accepted Christ as their Saviour, joined the church, and began serving the Lord with their new spiritual family.

In Hartford, Connecticut, I got off a random Interstate Highway exit, turned to the right, then left, then right again, and ran headlong into "my people." The street and apartment courtyard were full of them. I pulled my car over to the curb, rolled down my window, and shouted "Mingalabar!" Instantly, dozens of Myanmar people came running to me. They invited me into their apartment, fed me, and I preached the gospel and sung the songs of my Saviour for several hours.

Farther south, I was in New Jersey with Pastor Dennis Higgins and we drove through town with the idea of finding the Myanmar refugees. Uncanny as it sounds, we went right to them. I helped Dr. Higgins start his ministry to Myanmars and it is still operating today.

I arrived in Frederick, Maryland to preach for Pastor Fry and the Ambassador Baptist Church. I was traveling with a friend, and we arrived in town early. I was craving the greasy taste of Waffle House and so we decided to get a bite to eat before the service that night. As we walked into the restaurant, I spied a young lady behind the counter, leaned over to my friend and said, "She is Chin from Myanmar!" Sure enough! We sat down at the counter, and she came to wait on us. I said, "Mingalabar, nay kaung lar?" She was very happy to meet us, and that encounter led to meeting the entire group of Myanmar immigrants in the area.

Thaung Lian was in the States with me, and we drove to Minnesota to preach for Pastor Joe Grimaldi. He had started the Midwest Bible Baptist Church in Rochester, and the church began to support GLBM.

While we were there, I mentioned that I believed there were many Myanmar people in the St. Paul/Minneapolis area. Pastor Joe asked me, "Do you know where they are?" I said, "No!" I had never been in Minnesota before. Again, he asked, "How will you find them?" Thaung Lian spoke up and said, "Oh, don't worry. BaGyi will find them."

So we departed the next morning and drove from Rochester, the home of Mayo Clinic, north on Highway 52, and arrived in St Paul about 75 minutes later. As we connected with Interstate Highway 494, Pastor Joe asked me, "What exit do you want to take?" I answered, "I don't know yet."

I have known Joe Grimaldi since he was pastor of Calvary Baptist Church in Allison Park, Pennsylvania. He is not one to fly by the seat of his breeches, so to speak. He likes things meticulously planned out. But he went along with me. I said, "Just keep driving! I'll let you know."

So, we passed exit after exit, and I finally said, "Get off here."

Joe said, "Now what?"

I said, "Take a right at the bottom of the hill."

Joe said, "How do you know?"

I said, "I don't know."

He just shook his head.

I continued, "Now take a left. Now right. Another left."

As we turned left, the street was full of Myanmar refugees. I don't know how, but it just happens like that, everywhere I go.

We got out of the vehicle and distributed Burmese gospel tracts to every Myanmar person we met. We talked with hundreds of people. I still have a photo of Joe and I standing together with a man from Myanmar whom we led to Christ on the street in St. Paul, Minnesota.

Several years later, Joe Grimaldi moved back East and became the pastor of the First Baptist Church of Kenmore (Akron), Ohio. He asked me to come there and preach a missions' conference. I told Pastor Joe that I believed there were Myanmar people living in his city. He said that he didn't think so. The conference lasted five days with the church meetings each evening. First Baptist is on the southwest side of Akron, and I drove from the church, north past the old Akron Baptist Temple and then connected with the Interstate Highway, route 76. Driving eastward, I exited on Route 8 and went, getting off at Route 261 or East Tallmadge Avenue. There, just west of North High School, I found hundreds of Myanmar refugees, and many pure Burmese. I stopped and talked to a few folks, then returned to First Baptist Church and told Pastor Joe that I found them. The next day we drove back to the North High School area and began distributing Burmese Gospel tracts and scriptures.

Talking with a Burmese married couple, they invited Pastor Joe and myself to their home. They lived just a block away in a small apartment building. They asked us if we would stay and eat lunch with them. Of course, I said yes. When I am in the United States and miss my Myanmar people, there is nothing I like more than spending time with them here.

We sat down at a large table in the middle of the room and our hosts brought to us bowls of "Kyay Oh." It is a popular Burmese noodle soup made usually with pork and egg, sometimes chicken or fish. Pastor Joe looked at me with grimacing eyes, as if to say, "Is this going to be alright?" As he put a spoonful to his mouth, I nodded approval, and with surprise he exclaimed, "This is really good!" We were unashamedly gorging ourselves on a second bowl when a Burmese, saffron-robed, monk entered the room. I immediately stood to my feet, greeted the man respectfully, and invited him to sit next to me and join us. The monk was full of questions for me, and I answered him politely because I knew he was curious about our presence and our purpose with his people. I found out later that our hosts were his family.

While I ate my third bowl of Kyay Oh, I told the monk that I was preaching meetings at Pastor Joe's church and asked him if he would honor me by coming to hear me. He politely said that he would try to come. I finished my soup and we excused ourselves to return home and prepare for that night's meeting.

The following day was Sunday, and the evening service would be our last service of the week. A Filipino missionary from Thailand was traveling with me and we had been praying that our new friend, the monk, would come to the service that night. Just before the service began, into the back of the sanctuary came the monk with a young Buddhist disciple. I immediately left the platform and ran to greet them. They took their seats on the back row of the church and my Filipino missionary friend sat next to them.

Throughout the singing, I was overjoyed to see the monk looking through the hymnbook and trying to follow the notes. But I was equally amused to see Pastor

Joe's entire congregation breaking their necks to see a saffron-robed, shaved-headed, Buddhist monk in the back of their church house. As I began to preach my message, the Filipino leaned over to him and showed he and his companion the scriptures in his own Bible. They followed along.

I cannot remember the message I preached that night. But I know that I preached on salvation. I know that I made it plain and pointed, stressing that there is no other way to God and everlasting peace but through Christ.

As I was preaching, suddenly the Filipino missionary disappeared with the monk's young disciple. I didn't know what was happening. I watched the monk, and his attention was no longer on me so much as what happening at his feet.

In the middle of my preaching, the monk's young disciple turned to the Filipino missionary next to him and said, "If what he is preaching is true, I want to be saved! Can I be saved right now?" Immediately the Filipino missionary and the young man slid out of their seats to their knees, at the feet of the Buddhist monk, and prayed together. That young man got saved right there and then.

When the service was finished, church members were exiting the building and I spoke to the monk. He said, "BaGyi, I so much enjoyed your message about faith." I said, "Saya, may I give you a Burmese Bible?" His eyes opened wide with excited expectation. I said, "I will show you where to begin reading. Perhaps as you read and study, I will be able to help you find faith in Christ as your friend did tonight." He answered, "Yes, BaGyi! I will look forward to that."

I asked the monk, "Saya, you called me BaGyi. How do you know to call me by that name?"

He answered, "Ah, yes! You were in Fort Wayne, Indiana and visited our Burmese Buddhist temple there. You took Bibles to the monks in the temple. Before I came tonight, I called to them on the telephone and asked about you. They told me, 'Yes, BaGyi came here and gave to us Holy Bibles. He stayed with us for hours comparing the teachings of Jesus and Gautama. You go hear him; he is a good man!'"

CHAPTER EIGHTEEN

Dala'

"For our gospel came not unto you in word only, but also in power, and in the Holy Ghost, and in much assurance; as ye know what manner of men we were among you for your sake."
1 Thessalonians 1:5

"Slow down, BaGyi!"

He said that we were going to walk to the Dala' Ferry. Exactly how far? He didn't really say. It was eight o'clock in the morning, the sun was beating down on us, and it was already hotter than...well, like BaGyi says...hotter than a two-dollar pistol. It gets hot back home in the West Virginia hills, but the humidity in Southeast Asia just wears you down.

The preacher boys from the college had just arrived at the hotel with Saya Thaung Lian, and each of them carried a heavy box of Scripture booklets containing the Gospel of John and the book of Romans. We were all looking forward to getting out on the streets of some place called Dala' and distributing God's Word.

"How far is it, BaGyi?"

BaGyi hollered back, "Not too far! Just a short stretch of the legs."

Oh, my goodness! He's more than sixty years old. I've never seen an older man go like he does. I'm eighteen years old, and I can't keep up with him. BaGyi says that it's not a strong body that pushes a man forward, but a strong spirit. I guess so, but that day, I sure did wish he wasn't so strong!

We left the hotel on foot, carrying the Scriptures on our shoulders. We were going across the river to distribute Scriptures in the village of Dala'. BaGyi said we would take a ferry boat across. I thought that sounded so cool! But he never said how far it was to the ferry boat. In the heat, and on foot, it was a long way.

We met in the hotel lobby, prayed together, and when BaGyi said "Let's go," he just took off, through the double glass doors, and started walking down the street. Each preacher boy had a box of Scriptures, and I had my shoulder bag and a bottle of water. BaGyi was already way ahead of us, and I was in the back of the line.

From the Hotel 63, located at Merchant Street & 63rd Street, it is just a block away from Strand Road, a major thoroughfare through the city on the southside of Yangon. It runs along the Yangon River all the way down to Monkey Point where the river divides and empties into the Bay of Bengal. Along the riverside there are shipyards, stretching for miles and as far as the eye can see. Big cargo ships are docked, one after another, with acres of ocean containers stacked high in every direction. The huge trucks that carry those containers are parked in the street, lined up for miles on both sides of the road. As we walked along Strand Road, we walked among those trucks, zig zagging in and out, and around them.

It was a little intimidating for me. BaGyi made it look like it was nothing. We finally reached a place where there was sidewalk, but the concrete was in pieces and heaved up, making it a veritable obstacle course. It made me think of jumping on steppingstones in the water creeks back home. You really had to watch your step!

"BaGyi! Show down, please?"

"I don't think he hears you, Caleb!" said Isaac Khong, one of the preacher boys who was balancing a heavy box of Scriptures on his shoulder.

Isaac Khong is from southern Chin State and, after he graduates, he wants to plant a church among the Burmese Buddhists. I asked him where he will go. He answered, "I have a place in mind. Maybe God has already put it in my heart. Or maybe he will send me to another place. Wherever God wants me to go, I will obey Him."

We walked past a private high school called the Sein Kant Kaw Pwint. I was told it is for those who can afford a good education. Saya Thaung said that most cannot. The students, all in green and white uniforms, watched us closely. They pointed and giggled as we trekked by with our heavy loads. They must have wondered who we were and what we were doing. I wanted to stop and talk to them, but BaGyi was getting too far ahead of us. I just waved at them, and they waved back.

Still walking along Strand Road, we passed the Riverview Hotel, and then the 59th Street Mosque. There were quite a few Muslim men standing outside, and they really looked at us strangely. I wanted to give them copies of our Scriptures, but I wasn't sure how they would react and BaGyi and the preacher boys were getting still farther ahead of me. The truth is that everywhere you look and everywhere you go in Myanmar, there are people who need the Gospel. I guess it's like that back home in America too. I saw a sign for a café called "Bite Me Foods and Coffee." I thought to myself, "What a great time for some 'Air Con' and refreshment!" We were all huffing and puffing, but BaGyi kept walking.

On the river side of the road was a huge Buddhist temple. It is the Botahtaung Pagoda. It sits right in the middle of the shipping terminals. I guess the sailors need a place to pray like anyone else. These temples are huge, shaped just like a big Hershey Kiss, but they are gold colored. And they say it is real gold.

We walked for possibly two miles and, finally, Saya Thaung suggested that we take a city bus the rest of the way. Soon a bus approached that was going our direction and we all hopped on-board with our boxes of Scriptures. That bus, like most Yangon city buses, was packed with people like beans in a can. And even though there were not enough seats for everyone and there was no "Air Con," we rejoiced and relaxed for the next two miles or so.

The bus stopped several times along that short stretch of road that led to the ferry terminal. And it was so overloaded that it was difficult to even turn your head. When Saya Thaung signaled everyone to get off the bus, we wiggled and squirmed our way to the doors and jumped to the curb as quickly as possible, thinking that the driver might not wait for us to exit before starting up again.

Now, we had a choice between crossing four-lanes of rushing traffic, dashing between oncoming vehicles while carrying the heavy scriptures, or climbing four sets of long and steep stairways to cross Strand Road via a crosswalk. In Myanmar, pedestrians do not have the right of way. Very few people get hurt, but it seems to me that the chances of getting run over are higher there than standing in the New York Stock Exchange during the first few minutes of a sudden bullish Market.

We finally arrived at the Ferry Terminal and needed to purchase our tickets quickly. The next boat was departing soon. Of course, we all had to show our Passports, fill out some paperwork, and answer more questions than I thought was necessary. I also thought it was a blessing that the ticket line was short. However, as we left the ticket office and walked outside, the line to board the ferry looked like a day at Kings Island Amusement Park. I thought we would surely miss the boat.

Wouldn't you know it? While we waited in line, some young Burmese children approached BaGyi and attached themselves to him at the hip. He did not know them, but they held his hand and put their arms around him as if they were his own. He didn't mind. When it was time to board and the line started moving, they just followed him right on the boat and stayed with him. Maybe they had tickets; perhaps they did not. With the sudden rumble of the engines and a plume of blackish smoke, the boat moved gently away from the pier. We found seats on the top deck and I stood on the railing to see the muddy water roll away behind us. The journey across the river took about a half hour. The view from the ferry boat is spectacular. The city of Yangon looks different from out there on the river, and I wondered how Missionary Adoniram Judson perceived it in the early 1800s. Of course, the tall buildings of downtown have changed the skyline much since then, but the lay of the land is still the same. Old Shwe Dagon, the most famous of all Burmese Buddhist temples, adorns the apex of the city and points, not to Buddha but, to Heaven, just as Judson wrote about.

I have not traveled as much as BaGyi but, on the mission trip with him, I saw enough of the country to know that there is no place in the world just like Myanmar.

It is not just the temples, the bright colors, the food, or the Buddhist culture. Framed by a horseshoe of high mountain ridges that surrounds the great Ayeyarwaddy River valley in the center, the Myanmar landscape is beautiful. In the valley of rolling hills, massive rice fields stretch beyond sight, great herds of water buffalo roam freely, and ox carts carry massive loads of sugar cane to market. In every direction, golden pagodas pepper the landscape and glisten in the sunlight like fields of fireflies on a humid night in June. Astonishing and unexpected massive mountains of rock, protruding from the earth like fingers of a man's hand, stretch into the sky and dominate the horizon. From the mountains to the seashore, from the cities to the primitive villages, from the large rubber tree plantations to the small settlements of thatched-roof bamboo huts stilted over algae-greened water, I loved it all, but that which makes Myanmar special is the people themselves. They are openly warm, friendly, gracious, and serving.

The ferry boat slid into its dock at the village of Dala' and we followed the crowd off the boat to the end of the ramp where we huddled together to receive instructions. BaGyi's kids had disappeared in the crowd. We divided into teams, divided up the Scripture booklets, and prayed together again before stepping out into the community. As soon as we turned toward the street, a half dozen Burmese men surrounded us, asking where we were going and offering their taxi services. But there were no cars or trucks. Rather, a line of horse drawn carriages and their drivers lined the street on the far side. It amazed me that traveling just a short distance across the river, from city to village, was like a journey back in time. The men surrounding us had motor scooters and three-wheel bicycle taxis, but didn't want to ride. We had purposed to walk through the village, distributing our Scriptures door to door and face to face. Nevertheless, several of the men stayed close to us, hoping we might change our minds.

One of the motor scooter drivers assessed the situation right away and picked BaGyi as our group's leader. He said, "Saya, you want to go bamboo village?" We didn't know what he was referring to and Thaung Lian, the only person among us who might know, had already moved far down the street. I'm not sure that even BaGyi understood exactly what the "bamboo village" was. But he agreed to go, and he chose me to go with him.

The driver suggested that he call one of his friends who owned a bicycle taxi with a sidecar. But BaGyi insisted that he could ride with the driver on the back of his motor scooter. Another driver came with his scooter for me, and off we went.

I guess it's just a natural thing for a foreigner to be a bit apprehensive at times like this and wonder about legitimacy. I had all kinds of thoughts and questions as we biked through the village. First, we didn't know where we were being taken. Second, I wondered if we were going to be robbed, but BaGyi has a sense about these things and seems to know his people. He always thinks the best of them. I guess that is part of the love God put in him for the Burmese people.

Our drivers took off quickly and sped down the main street of Dala' until we turned left on a narrower concrete lane that led through the village. The streets were so narrow that other scooter drivers had to pause for us to pass. More than several times, I had to be careful to keep my elbows close to my body or get them torn off by a passing biker. I must have left fingernail prints on my driver as I clung to him with the wind blowing in my face and an occasional bug hitting my forehead like the windshield on my truck back home. We were following behind BaGyi and his driver and I could see him waving to people as we passed by. How they turned their heads in amazement!

Down river, on the far side of Dala', we came to what they call the bamboo village. It is the older section of town, where all the river fishermen and their families live along a canal. They occupy modest houses, built close together on small lots. Some of the families live right on the water and dock their fishing boats in their backyard. Mangy mongrels patrol the streets and park their carcases in the middle of the roads, many of which are lined with high piles of garbage. The stench of rotting fish and raw sewage fills the air.

Yet as we walked through the village, there was a welcoming atmosphere. Young children played in the street along the canal and responded fearlessly to our playful gestures. We greeted everyone with waves, yelling out "Mingalar bar!" As we approached, every person received the Scriptures, bowed graciously, and responded by saying, "Kyay zu tin bar de!" or Thank you very much!

One home was a bit larger and built on a corner lot that was fenced with thin chicken wire. Between two posts hung a wrought-iron gate that opened to a short flagstone walkway and led to a shallow porch. As we opened the gate, the old hinges squealed a high-pitched song that brought the resident to his doorway. His instant smile signaled approval of our arrival and he immediately invited us inside his home. His wife and daughter came to the front room, greeted us, and then excused themselves to go gather refreshments for us, their unexpected guests.

The man of the house was uncommonly larger than most Burmese men, both tall and broad. Unlike most Burmese who do not shave their faces but pluck an occasional long hair from their chins, he had a mustache and goatee. He spoke with authority and skilled English. The first thing he said was, "Gentlemen, you are from America, no?"

The man had worked as a merchant marine and traveled to ports of call around the world. He had sailed the high seas and learned, not bits, but chunks of English, Russian, Thai, Japanese, and Portuguese. He could hold an interesting conversation about history, geography, art, or music and keep his listener's attention. We were so impressed. When BaGyi asked him if we could share Christ with him, he immediately said, "Oh, I am saved!"

I think it even surprised BaGyi. The man didn't say "I'm a Christian." He didn't say he was a church member. He used the Bible word, "Saved!" He had led his wife to the Lord and all his children. BaGyi and I were almost speechless.

His name was Thagyamin, meaning "change." He told us the story of how his ship docked in New Orleans and how the sailors rushed the ramp to disembark and experience the vices and spices of the world-famous French Quarter. Even though he had a wife and a respectable family in Yangon, he had entertained promiscuous imaginations of the Cajun-kind across two hemispheres. Like his shipmates, he was ready to party. Several of the old salts were already drunk and one of them, a pony-tailed Filipino, had just been hurled to humiliation by a mechanical bull, whirling and twirling to the tune of "Jeremiah was a bullfrog."

Thagyamin wanted to enjoy his sensuous sashay in N'erlins, known as the Crescent City, but he loved his wife and children. There was a nagging nausea in his Burmese belly that wouldn't go away. So, he stepped out of the tavern and onto the sidewalk of Bourbon Street and wrestled with the internal voice that had obviously stowed away in his heart around the world. He had tried to silence it. A Christian in Yangon had spoken to him about Jesus Christ, his sin, and need of a Saviour. Across the Bay of Bengal and Indian Ocean, around the Cape of Good Hope, traversing the Atlantic Ocean, and into the Gulf of Mexico, Thagyamin attempted to muffle the voice of the Holy Spirit, but now standing on Bourbon Street, it was louder than ever. As a matter of fact, he could hear it better than ever. Really hear it. A street preacher was roaring the message of the redemption just a block away. Young people were passing out Gospel tracts to whoever would receive them.

Thagyamin was immediately drawn to hear more. He forgot about his shipmates inside the bar and walked the block to hear the preacher's words more clearly. There, standing with a Bible in hand, the preacher spoke about sin, salvation, and forgiveness. He described the unconditional love of Almighty God. He invited his hearers to come to Christ, to turn from their sin, and to trust the Lord completely for eternal life.

Thagyamin described the compelling conviction and how the tears ran down his face as he listened to the preacher's words. When the preacher saw it, he ended his oratory, walked to Thagyamin's side, and invited him to come to Christ. There, in the middle of the French Quarter, with music blaring, horns blowing, and partiers parading by, Thagyamin got saved.

It was an amazing story and we wanted to stay all day and hear more, but as John Wayne used to say, we were "burning daylight" and had to move along. So, we finished our refreshments, thanked them for their hospitality, suggested that we hoped to see them again, and said goodbye.

We had distributed almost all our Scripture booklets and, just as we turned the corner, we could see in the distance that our motor scooter drivers were still waiting for us at the other end of the street. Walking along, we passed a simple bamboo house, and the door was wide open. We could see at least one man and two ladies sitting on the floor, in typical Burmese fashion, and eating from small bowls. BaGyi waved to them.

The man immediately stood and came to the door, motioning for us to come. Instinctively, we approached the man and he invited us to come inside. As we stepped into his house, he asked us to eat with them.

Without hesitation, BaGyi immediately collapsed his legs and sat on the bamboo mat floor "Indian-style," and made himself at home. They put bowls of rice, goat curry, and watercress in front of us, and BaGyi started nibbling, but we had just eaten with Thagyamin and his family. I had to excuse myself. To be honest, I wasn't sure if it was safe or not. Nevertheless, they had set some kumquats out as well and I munched on them. As they finished up their dinner, they asked us many questions. Where are you from? Do you like Myanmar? Is this your first trip here? Why do you come to Myanmar? Ah! That's the question BaGyi likes to answer.

BaGyi leaned away from the food and said, "I come here because my God has put His love for the Myanmar people in my heart. He has changed my heart and my life, and He wants you to know Him too. I come here to explain about Him. If you will permit me, I would like to tell you about my God. His name is Jesus Christ."

They were so interested. With big smiles on their faces, they were eager to hear, but BaGyi had limited Burmese vocabulary and wanted these people to hear the Word of God clearly. So, he asked me to go and fetch Thaung Lian who was on the other side of the village.

BaGyi stayed with the family, and I hopped on one of the scooters and the driver took me to find Thaung Lian. When I arrived again at the Ferry dock, our team was already assembled and waiting to return to Yangon. I said to Thaung, "BaGyi needs you to come to him right now. The other teams had good news. They had led several people to Christ and were so excited to tell their stories.

Saya Thaung hopped on another scooter and followed me and my driver back to BaGyi. And, when we returned to the house, everyone was laughing and talking like old friends. Saya Thaung came inside and said, "Yes, BaGyi. What do you need?" BaGyi said, "Please explain the Gospel very clearly to these people, so that they can be saved."

So they believed and were saved. They joyfully, with thanksgiving, prayed to receive Christ as Saviour and Lord. The following year, BaGyi returned to the village and visited the family again. The next year, the family was not there any longer. Their neighbors said that they shared Christ with them and moved to another village, taking their faith with them. In Myanmar, like anywhere else, God directs us to many places and many people. It is always a joy, and sometimes it is a miracle of God.

CHAPTER NINETEEN

I'll Fly Away O'glory

"And I said, Oh that I had wings like a dove!
For then would I fly away, and be at rest."
Psalm 55:6

It was my dream to fly – literally. As a child I dreamed the same scenario night after night. I would climb up on the roof of my house and jump off. Not to worry though! I learned to swoop down like a bird with my arms outstretched like wings. I learned how to use the wind currents to lift myself higher and higher. Eventually, in my dreams, I became so talented at flying that I no longer needed to ascend to a rooftop or high point. I could merely get a running start, jump in the air, catch the winds, and soar like an eagle. Through the years of dreams, I was able to fly higher and for greater periods of time until it became as natural for me as walking.

In my dream, there was always someone watching me fly and they were always amazed. The attention that I received – in my dreams, that is – was exciting and very fulfilling to me, but I didn't do it for mere accolades or praise. In my dreams I learned how to use my gift for good, like a genuine superhero. The dream occurred almost nightly.

I think that many dreams are forgotten quickly, perhaps before we even wake, but some dreams stay with us longer. My dream has remained with me my whole life. Even after many years of maturity and even into my later years, the dream has returned.

My Burmese name is Kan Cetan Oo. The English know me as Martin Mitchell. I was born in 1917, in the month of May. My father was a Brit, a chief mechanic in the British Colonial Army, stationed near the city of Moulmein. That's what the local Mon people called it. The Bamar, or Myanmar people, call it Malawmyine, meaning "damaged eye" or "one-eyed man." There is a legend that a Mon king had a third eye in the middle of his forehead, and by it could see the affairs of all rival monarchs around him. The legend says that he married the daughter of one of those kings and that one night she got him drunk and was able to destroy his spy eye.

My mother was Burmese. They met along the beach at Kyaikkhami (the Brits called it Amherst) and had a whirlwind romance, falling in love almost overnight. I guess you could call it "love at first sight." Rudyard Kipling described the scene very well in the first few lines of his poem entitled "Mandalay:"

"By the old Moulmein pagoda, lookin' lazy at the sea There's a Burma girl a-settin', and I know she thinks o' me".

I think my mother's dream was to marry an Englishman. Back in those days, Moulmein had a large Anglo- Burman population, so much so that there was a section of the city known as "Little England." The Brits had occupied Old Burma since the first Anglo-Burmese War in 1824. By 1900, the "kabya," or Anglo-Burmans, were dominating business, trade, agriculture, and working in the rubber tree plantations that spread across southern Burma. For the most part, the Burmese accepted, and even respected the kabya, unlike the Anglo- Indians who refused to learn Burmese and still spoke Hindustani.

Burma. I even had freckles and reddish hair. And, because of that, I was the target of every cruel jokester at school and fought my way through many afternoon breaks. Not that I had a chip on my shoulder, as the Americans say, but I have never been a push-over. I always stood up for what I thought was right or just.

I was not the best student in school. The Burmese schools were not on the same level as European or American educational systems. But they did their best to provide a foundational understand of basic skills. But, for whatever reason, I did not apply myself. That would cause me a bit of suffering later.

When I was twelve years old, my father's father passed away in England. I had never met him or my grandmother. I guess they were not very adventurous and couldn't bring themselves to board a ship and make the month-long journey on the high seas, even to see their only grandson. We would get letters that were mostly outdated and often pre-read by prying eyes aboard whatever ship that carried them. I tried to learn something about my grandparents and their country from those letters. When my parents told me that we were going to move to England and take care of my grandmother, I was excited. Not because I wanted to leave Burma, and not because I wanted to meet the rest of my father's family. To be honest, I wanted to see an airplane. At school we heard stories about them, but no one had ever seen an airplane. They said that a man could fly like a bird. O, what glory it would be to fly! Those were some of the greatest days for Burma in modern times. The economy was thriving because of rice, rubber, oil, timber, and gems. Rangoon had become the largest cosmopolitan city east of the Suez Canal and was quickly becoming known as the "Jewel of The East." Still, if I was going to fly, I knew it wouldn't happen in Burma.

The "Cody 1" was developed by Samuel Franklin Cody in 1907 and flew by its own sustaining power at an Army Balloon Factory in Farnborough, England. It became part of the growing arsenal of the British Army and made headlines in newspapers worldwide, even in Burma. I couldn't afford it, and our schoolteachers discouraged it, but I would sit for hours making paper airplanes, trying to perfect their design and flight, and dreaming of flying a real plane someday. My classmates said I was crazy, but I had a dream.

So, we moved to London, England, to a community northwest of the city called Brent Cross. There, from my backyard, I could see the hot air balloons lifting into the sky from the Hendon Aerodrome. In June of 1932, the Society of British Aircraft Constructors sponsored its first invitation-only flying display. The fields were decorated with rows of brand new, state-of-the-art flying machines in preparation for the pageant of the new Royal Air Force. I knew then and know now that I shouldn't have done it, but I walked all the way from home and stuck my nose through the security fence to see them with my own eyes. Aww, did I ever get in trouble!

After moving to England, I excelled in school. I graduated from high school with honors, and still had my dream of flying someday. In 1936 I was nineteen years old and the sixth annual National Aircraft Display moved to Hatfield, England, to the de Havilland airfield. As part of a group of chosen young people, I attended the Display and, while there, made my application to join the RAF. To my utter surprise, I was accepted.

Air Force Basic Training was difficult for me, but I was driven to succeed. More than anything, I wanted to fly R. J. Mitchell's experimental Supermarine Spitfire. Built as a short-range, interceptor aircraft with a revolutionary elliptical wing, it achieved amazing speed and agility for its time. It was destined to become the primary weapon of the RAF Fighter Command, a capable opponent of the Luftwaffe's various fighter planes of WWII, and would be used by many other allied countries, including America, Canada, and France.

As in high school, by pure determination, I did well. And, because of my grades and quickly rising rank, I was chosen again, this time to train in the Hawker Fury, a biplane. Oh my! My dream had come true. I was flying like a bird. The rumble of the engine at my feet, the forward thrust when I pulled back on the throttle, the instant exhilaration of the wheels leaving the ground. It was glorious! I loved everything about it. Then during my first solo flight, I looked down from nine thousand feet, realized that I was all by myself and, for the first time ever, my life depended on me alone. No one had my back. Nobody was propping me up. I was flying...like a bird...all by myself.

It was the summer of 1940 and I had earned my wings and logged sufficient hours in my trainer biplane to qualify as a RAF pilot in the new Hawker Hurricane monoplane. It could fly faster, farther, and more importantly, it was competent to go up against the Luftwaffe's Messerschmitt 109. The Hurricane was a single seater in an enclosed cockpit over a cantilever single wing and a retractable undercarriage. Carrying eight wing-mounted Browning machines, it was the single greatest and most used air-defender of the British Isles at the time.

Germany invaded Poland in 1937, Czechoslovakia in March of 1938. By June of 1940 they had defeated the French and taken possession of their airfields. The Nazis now controlled most of Europe and Great Britain was the only power standing in the way of Hitler's goal of European domination. He could not invade England without first defeating the RAF. For months German aircraft had been making nuisance flights into English airspace, even buzzing the beaches, and coming irritatingly close to our airfields. But starting in the summer of 1940, everything changed.

In July, Hitler attempted to isolate England with a sea and air blockade, targeting shipyards and airfields. Officially, the Battle of Britain lasted only between July and September, but Hitler's blitzkrieg of the United Kingdom lasted ten months. Almost every night the air raid sirens blared their warnings and people would frantically run for the bomb shelters. They targeted, not only our airfields and the shipbuilding ports but, London factories as well, and there were a lot of casualties.

My father was assigned to the Army headquarters and our family lived comfortably, especially by Burmese standards. Parliament was pleading for workers in those factories connected to the war effort. My mother wanted to help and insisted that, even though she was pure Burmese and still struggled with the English language, she could get a job at a nearby factory, making electrical parts like dimmer switches, remote contactors, and starter buttons. I could hardly believe it; my mother was essentially making airplanes.

I was assigned to a first-response Squadron. The sirens would warn of the approaching enemy. The officers barked their orders, and we would sprint to our flying machines. Each pilot had a small team, and they would help us get into our flight gear. We would jump into our eggshell cockpits, push the throttles forward, and fling ourselves across the field and into the sky at 300 plus miles per hour. What a rush!

We were also aware that, after all our preparations, this was the real thing. No more simulations. There was no time for more practice runs. Ready or not, we were going to war. Even though we might be killed, flying for any reason was glorious. That was my thinking! Being honest, I did have several sleepless nights, wondering what it might be like to die.

By the time we got the alert, our approaching enemy was already halfway across the English Channel. To the vast flocks of hungry incoming German Messerschmitt fighter pilots, we must have looked like easy prey, but our birds were better than many people thought. We could climb fast, dive faster, and bank sharply. I'll never forget the mixed emotions and the feeling in my stomach when I shot down my first Jerry. In time, I downed a couple of their best fighter pilots and more than several bombers.

In most of our missions, our target was not the fighter escorts; it was the bombers. Many times, however, as we were attacking the bombers, we would need to protect ourselves from the fighters. Sometimes, depending on the strength of the enemy, we would group together in a Vic-formation. More times than not though, we would divide into three "finger-four" groups, thrusting ourselves toward our enemy like a spearhead. In that way we could back each other up.

We were not alone up there. Many useful Canadians came over to help defend Old Blighty, and they were mighty good flyers. Then there were the Yanks! You know? The young American pilots for hire who came over to help us before the U.S. entered the war. We referred to them as cowboys because of their grand spirit. They taught us about decorating our birds with little Swastikas, like notches on Wyatt Earp's gun handle. I told them that I was going to mark my plane with more "stikas" than anyone. I said, "Isn't that right, Brooklyn?" In my mind I can still hear his accent and how he would say, "You gonna get ya some 'stikas' tonight, Burma?" Another Yank blurted out, "Burma, you better watch your tailfeathers out there. Them Nazis will clip your wings and send you to Hell quicker than you can say Mingalar bar!" I asked, "Hell? What's that?" He answered, "Ah, it ain't nothin'! Just something outta the Bible." I said, "I'm Buddhist. I don't know about that stuff." I made a flippant gesture, turned, and walked away.

Almost every night at least one flier, sometimes two or three, would come back injured from an air battle. Some were more seriously hurt than others. We were glad they made it back in any condition. Some men never returned to England. Early in the war, I didn't fly every night, but as our planes and pilots became fewer, I was sent up more often, sometimes more than once a day. They talked about the law of averages; the more we would fly, the greater our risk of not coming back. I didn't mind. Still, I just wanted to fly.

In November of that year, my grandmother passed away. My commanding officer gave me leave to attend the funeral. I have to admit, I had never seen anything like that. She and grandpa belonged to the Church of England, but they never talked about their faith. I'm not sure that they had any. We had never become close, and there were times when I wondered if she accepted me as family.

There were not many of us at the funeral and the austerely huge church sanctuary made our few family members and friends look even more insignificant. I was very anxious to leave and get back to the Air Base, but my mother wanted to introduce me to a young lady she worked with at the factory. To my utter surprise, she was Burmese. She was a trained nurse, and when she could not get a position at one of London's hospitals, she was hired to run a small infirmary at the factory where mother worked.

"My name is Hla Bennu! I am pleased to meet you, Sir" she said with a strong smile. There was a warmth in her eyes that quickly brought my imaginations back to my homeland of Burma. I guess I was a bit stunned because I just stood there staring. She finally spoke again and said, "Are you okay, sir?" I finally answered and said, "Your name, it means "beautiful eagle," no?" "Yes, sir" she said. We talked for a while, and the time seemed to slip away. I looked at my watch and, even though I didn't want to leave, I had to excuse myself and get back to the base.

In the next couple of months, Hitler's winged warriors brought devastation to London and almost every family in England was affected by the trauma of war. The greatest pain for the Brits was not the injuries caused by bombs. It was the fear of invasion. Every family had an escape plan and kept a loaded shotgun by the door.

One night was particularly stormy and we thought that "Fritz" might not come. Myself, I thought for sure Command would ground us. Dark clouds had us socked-in with a low ceiling and sustained 40-kilometer winds coming in from the West. When the sirens sounded, we jumped into our flight suits and rushed through the driving rain to our parked planes. I was surprised to find my team already on the ground and my plane started and running.

Several of us took off together, wing to wing, and leaving the ground at the same time. I looked to my right and didn't see my wingman. I looked to my left and saw another plane. Even though I couldn't see through the rain hitting my windshield, I knew it was Brooklyn. I didn't want to leave the field without my wingman, but there was no time to wait. Brooklyn and I climbed to 9,000 feet in about 3.5 minutes, then on to 12,000 feet, doing our best to keep formation. Before we even got over water, the Jerrys were all over us. It seemed like they came out of nowhere. One Schmitty came from above me like a bolt of lightning, buzzing me so close I thought we were going to collide. I didn't see him coming, and I didn't see where he went. Another Jerry was heading right for me, head-on. Instinctively, I looked for my wingman, but he wasn't there. Then I saw Brooklyn and signaled for him to climb with me. I pulled back on my stick as hard as I could and climbed out of that mess. But Brooklyn didn't come with me. I looked everywhere for him. He just wasn't there anymore.

Despite the visibility and the fact that our opponents had caught us while we were still climbing, I got myself a Stika. I had taken a couple shells in my fuselage, and I was feeling a little draft up my pantleg, but my bird flew home okay. I was hoping to find Brooklyn back in the barracks, but the boys said they watched his smoke trail until he fell into the sea.

The next morning after roll call and breakfast, I walked out on the field to examine my bird and count my Stikas. I didn't have anything particularly against the Jerries. I'm not sure I ever met one face to face.

I heard that they are big boys. Of course, most of us Burmese, even some of the Anglo-Burmese, are quite "midgy." That's what the Brits say.

I missed Brooklyn. Like all the rest of the guys, I thought maybe there was chance of him coming back. We weren't supposed to dwell on those things, but the truth was that I was thinking more about death than I ever had before. Somebody said that Brooklyn went to Glory. I asked, "Where is that?" They said, "Don't you know? We're talking about Heaven." I still didn't know, but one thing I did know was that I didn't want to die. I guess it was because I didn't know where I would go.

The days and weeks crept on with monotonous cruelty. The air raids and the bombs that shattered ears and earth, the sirens blaring nightly in every neighborhood, the painful cries of mother and child – it was all so horrific! I did not want to kill people. I wondered why people wanted to kill us. All I wanted to do was fly!

A junior officer approached me as I was coming off the flight line, "Hey Martin! The CO wants you in his office right away."

"Yes sir, I'll go there as soon as I make my report." "No, man! He wants you to come right now!"

We had just landed from a mission, and I was looking forward to getting out of my jumpsuit, getting some hot tea, and then going to bed. What did my commander want with me? Did I do something wrong? Maybe my mind hadn't been as disciplined lately, but I was flying well.

"Aww, don't worry. I'll go see him!"

The messenger insisted, "That's an order, Mister! It sounds important." "Hey! Give me a minute or two to hit the latrine! Huh?"

Usually when you go to see the CO, you fix yourself up a bit, wash your face, comb your hair, maybe even brush your teeth. When I walked into the captain's office, I think I looked a little battle worn. I know I smelled like it. So, what was so urgent?

"Come on in and have a seat, Martin."

"What's this about, Captain?"

"Martin, I've got some bad news for you and I need you to get ahold of yourself."

"What does that mean, Captain?"

"Listen. I hate to tell you this. Your mom…I'm sorry."

"What is it, Captain?"

"Well, the factory where your mother works was bombed tonight. Your mother has been killed."

The captain's words went through me like a Burmese da. I felt a wave of heat go all through me, then a bit of dizziness. I sat back in my seat and just started weeping. I couldn't control the tears. The captain walked over and put his hand on my shoulder.

Wiping the tears out of my face, I looked up and said, "Captain, are they sure. How do we know it is true?"

He never answered my question. He simply said, "Son, I'm going to give you a week or two off. Go home to your father and bury your mom. Come back here when you have everything in order."

After my mother's funeral, my dad changed. You could see that his reason for living was gone. At one point, he was so depressed that he would sit in the house, stare at the wall, and say nothing – nothing at all. I would try to talk to him, but it was like he couldn't even hear me. The Army gave him an honorable discharge and he sat in his chair, day after day, and stared straight ahead.

My reaction to my mother's death was not depression. It was anger. Now I had a reason to kill Jerries. The war had become personal, and I was going to go back to my bird and kill as many Germans as I could.

I had seen Hla Bennu at the funeral. She was very warm and sweet. She wept and mourned, standing with us at the casket like she was family. I was aware that she wanted to spend time with me. She wanted to help us through our time of grief. But I wasn't interested in help or women. I wanted revenge.

My CO came to me as soon as I reached the base. He asked me, "Are you sure you're okay, Burma?"

"I'm okay, Captain! Honestly, I'm ready to get back in the war."

"I'm not so sure! Maybe you should take a few more days off."

"Honestly, sir. I just want to get back up there and do my job."

I was like a man possessed. I wanted to kill Germans. I didn't care if they were in the air or on the ground, but at the same time, I was deeply conflicted. My mother's Buddhist training kept telling me that it was wrong to kill. You know? There is a difference between the act of war, in fighting for your country, or people, and killing because you want someone to die. That's murder! Isn't it? I knew that the Hitler's Nazis and the Axis powers followed an evil agenda; I knew that they must be stopped, no matter the cost, but until now, it wasn't personal. Now, they had killed my beautiful, gentle mother and I would make them pay.

In just a few days I was back in the cockpit of my Hurricane and pushing the throttle forward again. It felt wonderful. There was no more fear. I had no thoughts of dying. As our Squadron left the field, I was obsessed with finding a target and pulling the trigger.

We were cruising at around 12,000 feet and, unlike many other days, the air over the Channel was crystal clear like the waters of Inle Lake near Thaunggyi. With virtually no crosswind, we were making good airspeed. We were trying to keep a tight formation while watching the horizon ahead. Suddenly, my wingman squawked, "Hey, Burma! Look. You can see the French coast far in the distance today!" He no sooner got that out of his mouth when someone yelled, "Twelve o'clock! Twelve o'clock high! Disperse!"

Before we even saw them coming, they were on us. The Messerschmitt BF-109s came from above, and as they swooped down with their wing cannons barking out a barrage of destruction, one of our planes exploded in mid- air. Another Hurricane whirled downward with its tail section completely severed from the fuselage. I remember seeing the eyes of the pilot as he hopelessly hurled toward the open sea. I instinctively climbed and spiraled away to my right, hoping my wingman would come with me. I reached my absolute ceiling, performed a critical wingover to get back into the battle, and looked around for my wingman. I looked over my right shoulder, then my left. I looked everywhere. He was not there, anywhere. I was alone, and I could see the dogfight happening beneath me.

Banking into an attack position, I was relieved to see my wingman, but he was doing his best to out-maneuver a fast pursuer. I had my own problem. Another enemy pilot had spied me and was approaching at high speed. I immediately went into a steep dive to flank my wingman's challenger. Not thinking about my own pursuer, but flying at redline speed, I squeezed the trigger and loosed all eight of my Brownings on the enemy's airplane. I remember seeing the pilot's face, and even his eyes, as he turned at the last moment to see me coming, putting his hand in front of his face as if to keep from seeing the unmerciful storm of my guns. Like a hot knife cutting through butter, I kept firing and my 50 cals cut his plane to pieces. At the last second, I pulled up sharply and looked over my left wing to see his shattered, blood-bathed cockpit, but no pilot remained.

A man should never enjoy the death of another, but I did. The bitterness of my mother's death had filled my mind and was destroying my heart. Having killed one German, I immediately set out to find another, but, as it was, one of their hot-shot Aces found me. As it was with my latest victim, I didn't see him coming until it was too late. As he dumped his 20 mm cannons on me, I could hear the bullets hitting and piercing holes in the fuselage of my plane. Trying to escape, I immediately pulled the stick hard to the right and went into a barrel roll. Suddenly, a searing pain was followed by own blood spurting and filling my britches leg as a round impaled my thigh just above my left knee.

I must have blacked out for a few seconds. When I came to my senses, my plane was plummeting toward the water below. Desperately pulling back with what little energy remained and realizing that I had a dead stick, I knew that my plane would certainly crash into the sea. I reached helplessly for the canopy release, yanked on it, and tried to smash the broken glass. But the hatch was jammed closed. There was no escape. I was going to ride my bird into the sea, a watery grave, and perhaps reunite with Brooklyn.

The last thing I remembered was the explosive impact into the water and the coldness enveloping my body until I was completely overcome and smothered in darkness. I don't know how it happened. I don't know who came to my aid or how I was rescued, but I woke in the hospital nearly two weeks later.

I had one thought, a single wish or desire. As my CO came to visit with me, I said "When can I fly again?" Giving me no consolation or commitment, he merely said "We'll see."

Despite a slight infection and the consequential delay in my healing, I reported for duty once again several months later. This time, my dream had come true. I was assigned to a different airfield, a new commanding officer, and a new fighter plane. To my utter surprise, someone in the RAF thought me worthy and put me into the Supermarine Spitfire program. The new planes had not even arrived from the factory yet, but I was chosen to fly one of them.

Vickers-Armstrong built the first Spitfires, promising to produce five planes per week to fulfill an initial order of 310 fighter planes at £1,395,000.00 British pounds or £4,500 each. Beset by deadline failures, the English government contracted with Morris Motors in Birmingham and construction began at the Cowley Plant in southeast Oxford. Then again, plagued with the problems of doubling costs, workforce strikes, and innumerable design modifications, a new plant was built right next to the Aerodrome and called the Castle Bromwich Aircraft Factory. I was well familiar with the Aerodrome from my days growing up nearby. So, I was doubly excited to be invited, along with other pilots, to tour the new factory and see our exciting new birds in production firsthand.

At the height of the Battle of Britain, demand for the Spitfire rose dramatically to the point that two other factories had to be constructed. Of course, Germany sought to destroy those facilities. The first bombing raid came on August 23, 1940 and the Jerries completely missed the factory. One month later, they tried again, and this time many of England's most experienced aircraft production workers were killed, but most of the production jigs and machine tools had been moved five days earlier and thus survived. So did the Spitfire.

The day that they began to arrive from Birmingham, I stood on the tarmac almost all day watching. What a lady! My Spitfire had the most beautiful lines of any plane I had ever seen. Powered by a Rolls Royce 24-liter, V-12 Merlin engine, it hummed like a bee and purred like a tiger. I was sent back to flight school to train on the new fighter. It was weeks before they allowed me to take her up. Then it was several more weeks before I was ready to fly a mission. Those weeks went by quickly, and I was happier, I think, than I have ever been before. However, my hatred of the enemy was still alive and well, and all I really wanted to do was kill Germans.

I got my chance on the very first mission we flew. The Spitfire was remarkably different than the Hawker Hurricane, but it was easy to fly. It was lighter, and therefore faster and more maneuverable. I began to stack up the stikas on the side of my plane and earned a bit of reputation to go with them. I won't say that I was an ace. I never earned that kind of title. But I heard that the Jerries were afraid of me. I hoped it was true.

I was glad for the day when news came that no longer would we wait for Fritz to come to us. We were going to fly into Germany. I was assigned as escort to our big Lancaster bombers, later to the American B-17s, and we were delivering special packages straight into Berlin. In May of 1941, an enraged Hitler ordered the incessant bombardment of London, killing 2,324 people and destroying 11,000 private residences.

As the ruins of London still smoldered, the war continued many other fronts. It seemed like the whole world was aflame. The Japanese bombed Pearl Harbor on December 7, 1941, dragging President Roosevelt and his reluctant Congress into the War. One week later, Bogyoke Aung San met with 227 influential Burmese and 74 Japanese officials in Bangkok, Thailand and created the Burma Independence Army. The Japanese had sought links with Allies in Burma to assist them in taking over the Golden Land. To them, they saw Burma as a launching pad from where they could control all Asia – the "hub of the wheel" so to speak. Aung San, a student activist who was family to the last Burmese monarch, was inspired by India's quest for freedom and helped to create an independence movement in Burma. Manipulated by a Japanese Army Intelligence officer named Suzuki Keiji, Aung San and the "Thirty Comrades," a group of motivated volunteers and one Buddhist monk, flew to Japanese-occupied Hainan Island and trained in the art of guerilla warfare. Now ready to fight, they crossed the Thai border into Burma alongside the Japanese invasion force, prepared to drive the Queen's army from their soil. Of course, in time, Aung San realized that the brutality of the Japanese was far worse than British control and extortion. Finally realizing his mistake and predicament, he joined his forces with the Allies to drive the "yellow devils" back to Tokyo, but not before many of his beloved Burmans were killed and a plot for his assassination planned.

During the Burma Campaign, the British and U.S. forces were assisted by

Indian Gurkhas and Belgium Congo medics. Their primary mission was to repel the Japanese and keep the Burma supply roads open to the Chinese under Chiang Kai-shek. I requested a transfer to the Burma War. I heard that the Yanks were using Curtiss P-40 Warhawks or Flying Tigers, an appropriate symbol and defender of the Golden Land. I really wanted to fly one, but my request was denied. And even though it never happened, I was still satisfied flying my Spitfire and killing Germans in Europe.

Looking back, I don't know how I survived the many missions we flew. They used to say that when your number comes up, there's nothing you can do. We "fly guys" stared death in the face every day. We never complained. Well, not much, but we surely had fatigue. I must admit that, like others, I became weary. There comes a point, no matter how you love to fly or how good of a pilot you are, exhaustion leads to mistakes and mistakes can lead to death. Several times I was pulled from the lineup, maybe because I appeared worn out, but now I can be honest. There were days when I was too tired to even pull myself into the cockpit. Many of the flyers became too sick to fly and shouldn't have. We did our duty, and we did it well.

On August 21, 1942, twelve American B-17s were dispatched to bomb German-occupied shipyards at Rotterdam, Netherlands. I was among those escort fighter pilots sent to protect them. We were to rendezvous at specific coordinates. As we spied the bombers on the horizon, we noticed a huge flock of enemy warplanes converging on them. What was supposed to be a secret operation had obviously been compromised.

The B-17s were ordered to abort the mission and turn for home, but it takes a lot of sky to turn a flock of those big birds around, and the Jerries were in pursuit. As we surged forward toward the oncoming waves of BF-109s, I noticed different German planes than I had not become accustomed with yet. They looked to be heavier in the nose, as if they had larger engines. They certainly seemed faster. Under their wings, they carried more and a different kind of munition. It was the Focke-Wulf FW190. Powered by the turbo-supercharged BMW 801 radial engine, it could carry greater payloads and more fuel, making it more formidable than its predecessor. I was flying a new MK IV Spitfire with the more powerful Rolls Royce Griffin engine. It was a 37-liter V-12 that produced 1,735 horsepower, driving four 10-foot propellers at a top speed of 423 mph. I was fairly confident.

Attacking the German warplanes, we tried to give our bombers time to escape. Still, one B-17 was severely damaged, but reportedly made it home safely. The B-17 Flying Fortress was a workhorse that could be shot full of holes fore and aft, and still make it home, but that day we were outnumbered greatly.

As they say, we put the pedal to the metal and speared ourselves headlong into the battle. Being a squadron of twelve healthy Spitfires, we split into three "finger four" formations and attacked the Jerries. Even though they had already accomplished their mission, scaring our bombers into running for home, they seemed very willing to stay and play with us, and they seemed to be experienced pilots.

I was positioned as the index finger in our attack group, which meant I was not the tip of the sword but watching the back of the plane in front of me, but when he took a couple 20mm rounds into his engine, the ensuing smoke indicated that it was my turn to attack. That's exactly what I did. I just hoped that someone had my back.

Our Spitfires could turn or bank with anything the Germans had. Once I got behind and in range of a fleeing Messerschmitt, there wasn't much he could do to escape me, but the new Focke-Wulf FW190 was just a bit faster than our planes. Whereas my Spitfire could sustain 400-plus mph, the 190 could do 425. Like the Hurricanes, our new birds were outfitted with the big Browning machine guns in the wings – two in each wing on the earlier models, and four in each wing on the later. It was a lethal combination. Then the RAF began to order planes with the new Hispano drum-fed 60-round guns. It was a great idea, but the Hispano seized up rapidly under both heat from firing and the cold of altitude. Those planes and all subsequent orders were refitted with four new .303 cannons in each wing. Those boomers would make an awful mess! On this flight, I was trying them out for the first time. I don't know what it is about the Luftwaffe pilots but, as before, a Jerry was coming right at me like playing chicken. So, I decided to take up his challenge and play his game. The longer you fly straight without turning, especially with a good tailwind, the faster you can go, and I poured it on. I came to know later that the FW190s were faster, had more firepower, and could perform well at altitudes up to 46,000 feet. I knew my limit was around 34,000. At the higher altitudes the 190's performance was a bit compromised.

Each of us flying at our plane's top attack speed in a nose to nose, head-on confrontation, with guns blazing a path forward, we turned at the last second. I veered to my right and, fortunately, he turned to his right and climbed. By chance, I chose not to turn hard, but went into a climbing spiral and came up behind him. He was still climbing: 18,000 feet – 23,000 feet – 28,000 feet. It looked like he might peel away, and I was ready. But he continued to climb: 30,000 feet – 32,000 feet. But then he slowed down. And, I thought, "Ah ha! I've got you, Herr Fritz!"

I had not looked behind me and forgot that he might have a wingman. I heard the fire of rounds. I felt the impact of them puncturing and shredding the fuselage of my plane. Then came a searing pain like no other I have ever experienced. I could sense the warm flow of my own blood surrounding my backside. I could barely move my hands and my feet were numb. The new Griffin engine was sputtering erratically, and I was losing control of the stick. I sensed a whirling deterioration of altitude. Somewhere in the process of crashing into the ocean, my second immersion into a supposed watery grave, I lost consciousness. How can it be that one person could survive two such experiences? I wondered for many years how it was possible and why my life was spared a second time.

Several weeks later I woke up in the No.4 RAF Hospital at Rauceby. I was being injected with a lot of morphine; so, I was in and out of consciousness. I guess I should be thankful for that. After more than a month, I opened my eyes one morning and saw Hla Bennu, the Burmese nurse who was a friend of my mother.

"I'm not sure what has happened."

Hla Bennu said, "You were shot down over the Channel and you've been here more than one month." Pointing to a small tent over my lower limbs, I asked her, "What is that?"

She answered, "I'm so sorry, Martin! You have lost your right leg."

Hla Bennu tried to comfort me as best she could, but the loss of my leg and the flurry of thoughts, bringing both anger and fear, was overwhelming. I said, "Get out. Go! Go away!" I screamed at her. Part of me wanted to cry, but I couldn't let myself cry. I was too angry, and the bitterness that had taken over my soul enveloped me even more.

"Please, I just want to help!" Hla Bennu said.

"Get out. Go away. I don't want anyone. I don't need anyone."

That same day, a nurse entered my room and brought some food. With my bandaged hands, I swiped it away and sent the tray crashing to the floor.

The nurse said, "You know? You're going to have to accustom yourself to letting people assist you. That young lady? The Burmese girl? She's been here almost every day since you were brought in. You should be grateful for a friend like that!" Then she left the room. She was right. Hla Bennu came every day and stayed for long periods of time. Despite my best attempts to dissuade her, she did her best to help me through the most difficult days of my life. I must admit, those days when she could not come, I missed her being at my side.

Not only had my leg been shot to pieces, leading to infection and then amputation, I was burned over half my body. Hla Bennu encouraged me through the many days when I wanted to die. Through the times when my pain was unbearable, and then through rehabilitation, she was always there. I wondered how it was that I survived and why. Why was it that I lived through a second crash? I had a lot of questions, but all I wanted to know was when I could fly again.

My hands were severely burned, and the bandages made feeding myself almost impossible. Extensive burns covered my left leg, but the doctors were hopeful that I could keep it. The doctors said that my face was burned but they didn't tell me how badly. Gauze covered my whole face with only my eyes showing and two small holes through which I could breathe. I could sense that most of my hair was gone and I had not seen my face yet. Part of me wanted to see it, but I was afraid. One day when they changed the bandages, I asked for a mirror. My eyebrows were gone. My nose was broken in the crash and, because of the burns, most of it fell off.

I learned that the practice of reconstructive tissue repair, or plastic surgery, has existed as early as 800 BC in Ancient India, but little was known of it among the British public before World War 2. There were only three plastic surgeons in all of England. I was informed that a New Zealander, based at the Queen Victoria Hospital south of London and far from my rehabilitation center, was the most accomplished, but I had little hope that the doctor would help me. However, without my knowledge, Hla Bennu worked to transfer me to that facility where I could get help.

One morning I was drowsing when the door to my room opened with a familiar squeaking sound. Focusing my eyes, I thought I would see either my nurse, the doctor, or Hla Bennu, but it was my CO. He said, "How are you doing, soldier?" I really didn't know how to answer him. I said, "I'm just looking forward to getting back in the air, sir!" He answered me, "The war is over for you, son! You need to concentrate on healing." I knew he was right. Even with new-fangled prosthetics, I knew in my heart that my dream of flying was over.

I don't know why Hla Bennu loved me, but it was obvious to me that she did. And I was becoming fonder of her, but I was ugly. How could I allow myself to have feelings for someone to whom I could give nothing? I was in the hospital for nearly nine months, and I fought those feelings every lucid moment. Yet I realized that, more than any other time in my life, I needed someone. The thought of living alone was almost as agonizing as never flying again.

My father passed away while I was a patient at Queen Victoria Hospital. I had not seen him in years, and when Hla Bennu informed me, I had almost no reaction. In May of 1945, all England was celebrating the surrender of the Third Reich. The war in Europe was over! I should have been thrilled as everyone else, but I was deep in depression. It was not that I was ungrateful for the help I had received, but I could not see any future ahead of me.

Doctors said that I could finally leave the hospital, but I would need to return regularly. Hla Bennu found a small apartment in London and helped me move there. She helped take me back and forth for multiple surgeries and procedures. It seemed like an unending process, and I wanted to give up often.

There was a small porch on the front of my apartment facing the street. Most of the time I used a walker to get out there because I had not yet mastered the use of a simple cane. My neighbors gave me a small wooden chair, and even though I could not sit for long without pain, I stayed on the porch for hours watching cars drive by and children playing on the sidewalk. More than that, as much as I hated to admit it, I waited for Hla Bennu to come. She came almost every day. Those days when she would not come, my spirit fell into deep depression.

Several years passed and I had come to depend on Hla Bennu more than I wanted to admit. I secretly loved her. I couldn't imagine living without her in my life. She would bring groceries from the market. She would rub my remaining leg with oils and give me medicine for the phantom pain of the leg I lost. Several times she found a way to take me to a park and we would sit and talk for hours, speaking to each other in Burmese. Even though I was in pain, I didn't want our time together to end.

It was in the winter of 1948 when she stopped coming. She never told me she was leaving, and she never gave me a reason. She had arranged for a nurse to come to my apartment twice a week. I was heartbroken. I spent my days on the porch hoping that she would appear. I spent my nights rolling back and forth in bed with agonizing pain. I had never felt so alone in my whole life. I spent many sleepless nights wanting to cry, but I could not. I was still angry and bitter.

My mind became a jumbled and twisted maze of thoughts. "How could she leave me? Doesn't she know how I feel about her? Maybe she did not? I never told her. How could I tell her that I loved her? Maybe she knew it, and that is why she ran away?" I blamed myself for everything and tormented myself every night.

I heard a knock at the door. It was late morning. I had not so much as left my bed, nor brushed my teeth. I had thought about boiling a pot of hot water for tea. I was too consumed with my sorrow, and to be honest, I was contemplating how to kill myself. The thought had occurred to me many times since I left the hospital.

Now I had no fight for life left in me. The knock came again. I tried to ignore it, but it was incessant. Then the thought came to me, "What if it's Hla Bennu?" I pulled myself out of bed, threw a robe around my shoulders, and reached for my walker. I got to the door as quickly as possible. But, when I opened it, no one was there.

That night I went to bed with a long, sharp knife. I held it in my hand for a long time, trying to talk myself into cutting my wrists or plunging it into my chest. I had never been that low in my whole life. And I wondered if there was a reason for me to live any longer.

Somewhere during the night, in the nerve-wracking stillness and loneliness of my bedroom, I fell asleep with the knife still in my hand. In the morning, at about the same time as the day before, I laid in bed unwilling to move, but suddenly I heard a knock at the door. This time, to the best of my ability, I hurried to the door. When I opened, it was not Hla Bennu, but a short, bald, gray-bearded man stood, holding a black book and a handful of small pamphlets.

Perhaps he could see the disappointment in my eyes. He said, "Is this a bad time to visit?" I said, "What do you want?" He said, "I would like to talk with you. Do you have a few minutes?" Well, I was desperate to talk to anyone. So, I said, "Please, come in, sir!" I apologized for not having much furniture to sit on, but I invited him to make himself comfortable as best he could.

He said, "I would like to talk to you about my Saviour, Jesus Christ."

I was always taught to be polite, but I wasn't in the mood to listen to a lot of religious talk. I told him that I wasn't feeling well, but he continued.

"Sir, I hear that you were a pilot and that we owe you a great debt of gratitude for your service in Her Majesty's Air Force."

I merely nodded. He said, "If I may ask, sir. How was it that you came to fly?"

I was searching for a way to stop this interview, but I had mixed emotions. It had been a long time since I had a visitor or had a serious conversation with anyone.

I answered, "It was always my dream to fly." "Did you learn to fly in Burma?" the man asked.

"I was too young then. There was no opportunity to become a pilot there. I came here with my parents, after my father was transferred back to England. I graduated high school and entered the RAF's junior flying program.

When Hitler invaded Poland and Czechoslavia, I guess the government knew they would need pilots. They never had enough fly guys, as the Yanks put it, you know!"

"We appreciate your sacrifice for England, sir. We are glad that you made England your home!" I snapped back sharply, "My home is Burma! I had hoped to go back; I guess I never shall." "What do you mean, sir?" the gentleman asked.

"I am sure that I will die here, maybe sooner than later!" "Are you prepared for that, sir?"

"What do you mean?"

The man began to open his book and fingered through its pages. He said, "I mean, do you know where you will spend eternity?"

I thought for a moment and then answered, "No one can know about those things. You just do the best you can, I suppose. I have lived a good life and I imagine it counts for something."

"Sir," he said, "I was introduced to Jesus Christ many years ago and He has filled my life and given me the hope of Heaven. I should like to explain to you how you can know Him also. Jesus was God Incarnate..."

I interrupted him and asked, "What does incarnate mean?"

He held up his book and said, "This is the Holy Bible, the Word of God. It says that Jesus was God, the Creator of the world and everything in it. The Bible says that Jesus created mankind, that man disobeyed God, and became separated from God, but Jesus became a man and died, making Himself the only sacrifice for our sin. The Bible says that we must turn from our sins to the Saviour, and that, if we believe in Him, He gives us everlasting life in Heaven."

Wow! That was a lot to comprehend, but I honestly thought about it for a minute. Then I said, "Why do men have to obey any god?"

The man was taken back, almost as if he was offended. He answered, "Do you obey your parents, sir?" Instantly, my anger flared. And I said, "My parents are dead, thanks to the Jerries!"

"Sir, God loves you and wants you to be saved!"

"Saved? No one saved me while I was flying my Spitfire! If there really is a God like you say, why didn't he save me and save my leg?"

"Sir, I don't mean to offend you. I came here to tell you that God is real and wants you to know Him. You cannot know God apart from Jesus Christ. He is the one and only mediator between God and men."

My patience had worn out and I was getting angrier with everything he said. I blurted out, "I'm a Buddhist. I was born a Buddhist, like my mother, and I will die a Buddhist. If there was a god like you say, why didn't my British father tell me about him? Hmmm?"

"Sir, please allow me to read to you from my Bible!"

"No, get out. Get out now!"

The man left without another word. I was angry all day after that. Hanging on to my walker, I paced back and forth in my front room. Then sitting again at a little table, I noticed a Gospel tract that the strange little man left for me. Without reading a word, I tore it into shreds and threw the pieces into the trash can.

I didn't know why I was so angry. I had chased off the only person to whom I had talked with in months. Now I was alone again. The days became unbearably lonely and boring, but I didn't want to see anyone. I had stopped sitting on my porch. I didn't even listen to the radio. I had no newspaper, no contact with the outside world.

Groceries were delivered and I had ceased going to the door. They simply placed them on the porch and some days I wouldn't even collect them.

Several more months passed inconsequentially. I had been a bit sickly, and on this day I slept later than usual. I can't even remember what day it was. I don't know if it was a Monday, a Tuesday, or Saturday. It didn't much matter. I didn't care. As usual, the window curtains were drawn closed, and the rooms were dark. I didn't want any light. Suddenly, breaking the silence of my loneliness and depressive mood, I heard a knock at the front door. My first thought was that it was the strange Christian man who had visited me before. I was determined to ignore him. Perhaps he would go away.

Whoever was out there kept knocking, and I was becoming angrier by the moment. I went back into my bedroom and laid down on the bed. They kept knocking. I covered my head with my pillow. They kept knocking. I yelled out, "Go away!", but they kept knocking.

Finally, I swung my leg across the bed, grabbed my walker, and scrambled as best I could to the front door. I grabbed the doorknob and flung the door open against the wall with a bang.

There stood Hla Bennu. And when I saw her, I just started weeping. She stepped through the door and put her arms around my neck and held me. She helped me over to a chair, kneeled next to me, and looked up at me, saying "How have you been?"

Her hair was longer now, falling over her shoulders. Her dark, shining eyes were so beautiful and warm, I just wanted to kiss her face. I didn't want to tell her that I had been so depressed that I almost killed myself. I just stared into her eyes, barely believing what I was seeing.

"Where have you been?" I asked her.

"Oh, Kan! I am so sorry for leaving you. Please forgive me!" "Why? Why did you go away?"

She looked away, then back at me. Again, she looked away.

"Tell me, Hla Bennu. Why did you go away? It has been so long." "I know," she answered. "I was afraid."

"Afraid of what? Of me? Why?" I was full of questions, but I did not want to drive her away again. "Kan, I was afraid you wouldn't love me!"

"What? I wouldn't love you?"

"Yes," she continued. "I have always loved you, and I wanted to take care of you, but I wanted you to love me."

"I do! I do!" I said it repeatedly. "I love you! I do love you. I have missed you so much. I thought that you would never...I thought you couldn't ever love me after..."

Hla Bennu put her fingers on my lips and said, "Will you marry me?"

I immediately said "Yes." But then she explained, "There is something you need to know."

"Hla Bennu, I know enough. I want you. You want me. I cannot be a whole man for you. If you will have me, I don't ever want to be away from you again."

I hadn't talked that much for years. I don't think I have ever spoken words like that in my whole life. But Hla Bennu had more to say, and she needed me to listen. I did.

"Kan, I have become a Christian."

"A what?"

"Really, my dear Kan! I have received Jesus Christ as my personal Saviour, and He has given me joy and peace like I have never had. I want you to know Him."

"Hla Bennu, you are Burmese! How can you be a Christian?"

"Dear Kan, Jesus died to pay for the sins of the whole world. Please let me explain how you can know Him like I do."

"Hla Bennu, did you send the man?"

"Yes, Kan. I did. It is one of the reasons why I went away. As a born-again Christian, I am not supposed to marry an unbeliever. I want you to know Jesus."

My head was hurting, and my thoughts were swirling like the propellers on my Spitfire. How could this be?

"Kan, we all have sin."

"I know that! Nobody is perfect, especially me."

"Jesus died in your place, to pay for your sin."

"If I say that I will consider this, will you marry me?"

"Yes, Kan. I went away because I knew that you would have trouble with this, but I have come to realize that I cannot live without you in my life. I want to be in your life. But you must put your trust in Christ. Please, Kan!"

We were married in a little chapel in a township north of London, but I did not accept Christ. The minister tried his best to convince me to believe, but I did not want forgiveness. I did not think I needed forgiveness. I had given my leg and almost my life for the people of England. Why did I need forgiveness?

Hla Bennu took good care of me. Through the RAF, she was able to find a wheelchair for me. She pushed me through the park, and we sat by the water feeding ducks. Most enjoyable to me was when she planned a trip to the Manston Airfield, way over in Kent, East of Canterbury, to see the test flights of the new Gloster Meteor, the first British jet fighter. With its revolutionary turbojet engines, it was the loudest aircraft I had ever heard, and I craved the exhilaration of soaring behind that kind of power. Being developed as early as 1936, it was not ready for warfare until the end of WW2. But the few Meteors that flew against German adversaries proved successful and became prototypes for future models, like the Hawker Hunter and Gloster Javelin. The Meteor became so effective in air-to-air combat that it was purchased and used by the nations of Egypt, Argentina, the new Israeli State, and Australia during the Korean War. Seeing them fly with my own eyes, I was in awe and grateful to Hla Bennu.

Everything in life became a challenge to me, but when Hla Bennu told me that we were going to have a baby, I had mixed emotions. How could I be a father to a child? I couldn't run and play at the park. How could we afford a growing family? I could not work like most men. In time, however, I became stronger physically and we had three children, all girls.

In 1947, England began to make provisions to move out of Burma. They helped Statesman Thakin Nu formulate and adopt the Constitution of the Union of Burma and he became the first Prime Minister. Subsequently, Burma achieved full independence one year later and an Embassy was established in London. Unbeknownst to me, Hla Bennu had contacted their office and a man came to visit me. He asked me to work for them, and I became a translator, making more than enough to support my family. I was thrilled. Again, I owed my life to my dear Hla Bennu.

For the most part, our lives were happy in England. Eventually we were able to buy a car which allowed me to move about more freely. We went from a small apartment to a townhouse, but climbing the stairs were exhausting for me, so we found a simple one-story home on the outskirts of town. We raised all three of our daughters, they went on to college, became successful in their own lives, and Hla Bennu and I became grandparents, but there was something missing in my life. I longed to return to what was now called Myanmar. But it was a tumultuous time there. Thakin Nu, honorably known as U Nu, had been deposed in a military coup d'état as General Ne Win became the leader of the new Burma Socialist Programme Party. His policies led the country into isolation, political violence, totalitarianism, economic collapse, and increasing Sinophobia, or hatred of the Chinese. Beside those things, the Anglo-Burmese population in Myanmar was decreasing.

Many of the older Burmese nationals remembered living under British authority and they didn't trust them. However, despite the consequences of my injury, handicap, and the loss of flying, life had become better than I presumed it would. My family made me happy, and just living alongside the love of my life was satisfaction enough for me – I thought. Every Sunday Hla Bennu would go to her church and return home to tell me of all the wonderful things that happened. Then she would say something like "Dear Kan, I wish you would give your heart to Christ." I would smile, she would giggle, and we would continue with life, but I was getting tired. I could feel it. I didn't have the stamina I used to have. I mean, after my injury, and through those years of recovery and depression, I experienced malaise, but this was a different kind of fatigue. I could not seem to get my energy back, no matter how much I rested.

So, Hla Bennu convinced me to go to the doctor. He gave me some supplements and did some blood tests. Thankfully, nothing showed up. I went on with my business as usual. Then one day, I broke a fever with shaking and chills. I spent the next two days in bed. Instead of emerging rested, I felt worse. I was losing weight without even trying. I wanted to call a monk and have him pray for me and perhaps light some candles at his temple, but there was no temple anywhere near our home.

Even though I was now in my eighties, I still went to the Embassy from time to time, translating both spoken and written words. One day I turned to answer the phone and caught my elbow on the corner of a desk. The impact ripped the skin open, and it bled. It bled a lot. It would not stop. We wrapped it with gauze, and I thought nothing more about it, but the next day, my whole elbow was bruised. From that time forward, my symptoms began to escalate. I had nosebleeds for no reason at all. I would wake up at night, my bedclothes soaked in sweat. It seemed like my bones hurt all over.

I returned to the doctor for more tests, and he immediately noticed some bruising on my arms and legs. He asked me, "How long have you had these tiny red spots on your skin?" I had not even noticed them. He then sent me for more blood tests. The diagnosis was unanimous among all concerned. I had myelogenous leukemia and they told me I might live five more years at the most.

I thought much about the things I might want to do. I had been given a good life, despite the challenges of my earlier years. I had even overcome my anger at the Germans and the trauma of losing my mother and my leg. I had not only fulfilled my dream of flying but had been given a family of which I was immensely proud, but something seemed to be missing. I still wanted to return to Old Burma.

I seldom talked about Burma to Hla Bennu. But I guess she realized the yearning in my heart. She still had family there and I think she, like me, wanted to be buried in the Golden Land. I didn't understand why she wanted to go back, but she did. I know it was not because of religion. We didn't know any Christians or churches in Myanmar. And, because I could not practice my mother's faith in England, my Buddhism had become just a cultural thing to me. Regardless, after several months of discussing it, we began to research how we could make the trip.

Initially, it seemed impossible. It was going to require much money, and we didn't have it. We would need to sell our home. Once in Myanmar, there would be no returning to, as they call it, Old Blighty. We wondered if we would ever see our children and grandchildren again, but times had changed so much. Now, with modern airlines, people could fly around the world in less than a day. It was amazing to us.

My blood cancer was becoming more physically challenging. My stamina, breathing, and attention span were all declining. Bruising and purpura, the gathering of blood under the skin from weakened vessels, was increasing. I knew that, if we delayed much longer, we would not make it to Old Burma.

Although she would not admit it, I think that Hla Bennu knew that my old RAF Squadron was going to help us. One evening, after supper, I heard a pronounced knock at the front door. Even in my weakened condition, she wanted me to answer the door. So, I did. It took me a few moments to get there. I said to her, "They might not wait for me, dear!", but as I opened the door, there standing in front of me was my old CO. Even though he had aged and been retired for many years, he was dressed in his old uniform. Standing beside him was a younger lieutenant with his wife. Behind them stood a beautiful little girl with the prettiest yellow hair I had ever seen. I addressed my CO. "Sir, what are you doing here? How did you find me?" My commander just stood there, saying nothing. I paused for a moment and finally said, "Please, please, come in!"

Stumbling, and almost falling over as I tried to get out of their way, I urged them to sit down and make themselves comfortable. This time, I had a sofa for them to sit on and I was mighty proud of it. I sat next to Hla Bennu, on the arm of her chair.

"Sir, what brings you here tonight?" I asked.

The lieutenant looked over at his wife as she fidgeted with her daughter's hair. Finally, my CO spoke up and said, "We have something for you, Kan! I want to introduce you to Benjamin Cohen."

There was an awkward silence. But I finally said, "I am pleased to meet you! You have a lovely family, sir!"

My CO interrupted, "Kan, we have a gift for you. The men of the Squadron have raised some money to help you return to Burma." He handed to me an envelope, and in it was £8,000 GBP.

It was the most money I had ever seen at one time, and I wasn't sure how to respond. I didn't even know if I should accept it. But I finally said. "I am grateful. Please tell the men that I appreciate this very much, but I am a little confused. How did you come to know that we are leaving England?" Again, they paused for a moment looking back and forth at each other. Then I asked the young lieutenant, "Do we know each other somehow?"

My CO spoke up and said, "Kan, this is Brooklyn's son!"

I felt like I had the wind knocked out of me, like time suddenly stood still and the world revolved in slow motion. Tears began to well up in my eyes, but gathering some quick composure, I said "I didn't know Brooklyn was married!"

The young man answered me, "He was not, sir! He and mother had plans to marry. But he was killed before they could have the ceremony."

"I am so sorry to hear this! Your father was the closest friend I had in England." I stopped and collected my thoughts a moment. "Perhaps he was the closest friend I ever had."

Hla Bennu reached out and patted my hand. She said, "I think I will go in the kitchen and make some hot tea while you are talking."

"My mother told me about you, sir. She said that Dad loved you very much."

No man had ever said anything like that to me before. I didn't know what to say and I felt a little embarrassed for my wife to hear those words, but Brooklyn had been my confidant, my partner, my equal, my friend, and many times my wingman. We had each other's back, so to speak. Instantly, the feelings of seeing his plane spiral out of control flooded back into my memory, and I was overcome.

"I hope that between the RAF and your father's American family, you and your mother were taken care of financially."

The young man smiled and said, "Mom always said that Jesus supplied our needs."

"Jesus?"

"Yes, sir! Jesus Christ, the Saviour of the world. Do you know Him, sir?"

The young lieutenant stood, waiting for an answer. But I did not know how to respond. I felt uncomfortable and I could feel myself becoming angry.

"Your father was a Jew! I know he was!"

"Yes, sir! My mother also."

"Then, I don't understand. What is this Jesus business?"

"Both my parents found the Messiah, the Lord Jesus Christ, and became Christians just before he died. My mother said that father wanted to talk to you about it, but then he was killed."

"Where is your mother now?" Hla Bennu re-entered the room, carrying a tray and tea service.

"Sir, two years ago, mother became ill and went to the hospital. The doctors found that she had a cancer. She passed away quickly without pain."

All at once I was filled with rage and it spewed out unrestrained, "How can you believe in a God like this? A God who does not love you enough to save you, who could not protect your father, who could not heal your mother? What kind of a God is that?" The young lieutenant started to interrupt, and I cut him off saying, "Your God, the God of the British, killed my mother!"

My CO reached out to put his hand on my shoulder as if to calm me, but I pulled away. Hla Bennu tried to say something. I cut her off. The young lieutenant took a step back and answered, "Sir, Jesus went to the cross to pay for our sins with His own precious blood that we might be forgiven and have everlasting life."

"Your parents don't have everlasting life; they died! My mother had no everlasting life; she DIED! She DIED!"
"Sir, Jesus is real. He loves you and wants you to know Him."

"I am Buddhist! Thank you for coming to see me. And thank you for your gift, but I am Buddhist. I was born Buddhist. I will die Buddhist. I don't want to talk about this anymore. Please leave us now."

I stood up, walked to the door, opened it for them to leave, then turned around and walked out of the room. I was furious and confused. How could Jews be Christians? In my mind, if you are a Jew, you are Jewish. If you are Burmese, you are

Buddhist. That is just the way it is.

When they were gone, Hla Bennu tried to talk to me.

"Dear Kan, I am Burmese, but you know that I am a Christian. Right?"

"I know that. I just don't know why."

"Kan, we have talked about this before. I am a Christian because I believe that Jesus is God and became a Man to die in my place. I confessed my sin to Him and asked him to forgive me."

"Why do I need to be forgiven? Just tell me that?"

Hla Bennu said, "The Bible states, 'All have sinned, and come short of the glory of God.' It is not that you are a bad person. The Bible says we are all separated from God because we are sinners and need a Saviour.

"So, you are a sinner too, Hla Bennu?"

"Yes, Kan. But I am a sinner saved by God's grace. He has forgiven me."

"I still don't understand. I have lived a good life. Why do I need the forgiveness of a God who has not proved himself to me?"

"Kan, don't talk like that! God proves Himself every day."

"I don't see the proof!"

Hla Bennu picked up her Bible, turned to Romans 5:8, and read, "But God commendeth (or proved) his love toward us, in that, while we were yet sinners, Christ died for us."

I said, "But why? Why does God want to forgive me?"

"Yes, He does, Kan!"
"But why?"

With a big smile on her face, Hla Bennu turned to Hebrews, chapter 12, and she read verse 10. Then she said, "He wants us to be partakers of His holiness."

"I thought you said we were nothing but sinners!"

"Kan, please, I don't want to argue with you."

"Okay. I don't want to talk about it ever again! I am Buddhist. That's it!"'

It was 2008 and we had wanted to arrive in Myanmar before March and be there for the Thingyan Water Festival in April, but our visas were delayed, and our departure was delayed. It was a good thing too because in April Cyclone Nargis came across the Bay of Bengal and cut a direct path through the southern half of Myanmar. It was a direct hit on the city of Yangon. The people had no warning and 86,000 died overnight. Hla Bennu said that her God protected us. I just smiled and thought to myself, "That would be the first time He protected me."

Someone suggested that we sail to Myanmar, the way they did in the old days, but I was becoming weaker by the day. Hla Bennu could tell that the leukemia was wearing me down. So, we flew with Emirates Airlines, from London Heathrow to Yangon via Dubai. Because I was sick, and because of the money given to us, we flew First Class.

After twenty hours of travel, we landed at Yangon International Airport and customer service agents met us on the ramp, then took us to Immigration and Customs. I did not know what to expect because of all the changes in Myanmar over the years. Armed soldiers were everywhere and, watching us closely, they made us a bit uncomfortable.

My mother's sister was my only living relative yet living in Myanmar and she was old and sick. Hla Bennu's parents had passed away in England, but she had a distant uncle who lived in Yangon Division. He met us at the airport and took us to his home in Dagon Saikkan, a township south of the city.

Even though my blood was Burmese, my body had become British, and I was not used to the heat and humidity. It was awful at first. Hla Bennu acclimated to it quickly, but I was having trouble, probably because of my disease. So, we began looking for our own home. Those with air-conditioning were generally too expensive and those without were in trashy neighborhoods. I really wanted to return to Malawmyine, but I no longer knew anyone there. After a couple weeks of searching, we settled on a townhouse in a community called Yuzanna Garden Village, near the Bago River and Thanlyin Bridge No. 2.

We were fortunate to get a unit on the end of the street, near a small market where the older men sat for hours, telling tales, and chewing Betel Nut. I had never tried the nasty mouth-reddening chew, but I was willing to give it a go for the sake of making friends. Not having the strength to hobble down there on crutches, I sat outside my front door and waved as the men walked by. I longed to go sit with them and, as they say, shoot the breeze.

Soon after getting settled, a neighbor walked by, I waved, and he entered the gate and we talked for hours. He invited me to come to the market and I confessed to him that, even though it was close, it was too far for me to walk on one leg. But I learned something about the Burmese people: they are amazingly resourceful and clever about solving problems and building things with their hands. In just a few days, my new friend made a three- wheel cart with a pump handle where I could propel myself down the street with my hands. It was a wonderful gift. But, when I saw what he wrote on the back of the seat, I was thrilled. It had a small British flag and read, "Spitfire 2."

Down at the market, the men loved to hear the stories of my World War 2 air battles. They would sit for hours and just listen. They tried to get me to try their Betel Nut, but I loved the tiny mandarin oranges. I think the Brits call them Clementines. My new friends teased me that I sweat more than them. They said it was because I was so white. They said I should try some thanaka, but I told them that it was for girls.

Sitting at the market one day, a Chin man came by, passing out small paper leaflets with Christian scriptures in them. He offered one to me and called it a gospel tract. I told him that I already knew all about that stuff and wasn't interested. I said, "Don't bother me. I'm Buddhist." The men around me laughed and patted me on the back, congratulating me for speaking up for Buddha.

A week later, the man returned. He stood just outside the market and began preaching his religion. We picked up stones and threw them at the preacher, called him rude names, and chased him away. He came back several times and one day a stone hit him in the eye, and he bled. He never returned. I joked with the men, "I guess his god is not powerful enough to protect him!"

My health began to deteriorate, and my weakness soon kept me from going to the market. Hla Bennu and I had saved a little money and she persuaded me to rent a hospital bed. When it was delivered, we put it in the front room. She said that the men could come and visit me. Every day I watched the men of the community walk by and I wondered if I would ever go to the market again.

I slept all the time, night and day. Near the end, I had lost so much weight that my clothes just hung on me and sometimes fell off. Hla Bennu tried to get me to eat something, but I had no appetite at all. Occasionally, the men would stop by, stand at the front door, and wave. There were days when I didn't have enough strength to even wave back. I knew I was dying, and the longer I lived, the worse I looked. Soon I didn't want any visitors. I told Hla Bennu, "Please don't let anyone in."

It had been a cloudy day and now, almost evening, dark clouds threatened rain. I told Hla Bennu, "I think it is a good day to die." She replied, "Please don't talk like that. I want to go to a meeting tonight and know that you're going to be alright while I'm gone."

"How long will you be?"

"I think it will only last an hour. An American preacher is here, and I want to go hear him."

"Oh, that's it. How do you suppose he even got here? You know the government won't allow foreigners to come here!"

"I don't know about that, but I want to hear him. Will you be okay?"

"Yes, go ahead if you have to. Don't worry about me."

It was nearing 9:00 PM and I was lying in bed, drowsing. I heard some shuffling about, and when I opened my eyes, Hla Bennu was standing over me and a white-skinned foreigner was behind her. She said, "Kan, this is BaGyi Bob. He is from America. Will you listen to him, please?"

I guess I didn't have much choice. So, with my wife's help, I sat up and swung my stick-like leg over the mattress and hung it down the side of the bed. The white man stepped closer and held his hand out for me to shake, holding his elbow with the other hand in true Burmese tradition. I wondered to myself who this fellow was.

"Sir, I have come to tell you about my Saviour, Jesus Christ. May I share some Scripture with you?"

"I am Buddhist. Please leave me alone."

I started to lay back down, and my wife stopped me. She said, "Please, my dear, he has come a long way."

I replied, "Not tonight, he hasn't. Is this the man at the meeting?"

"Please, Kan! For me! Please listen for me!"

"Sir, I have come all the way from America with a message for you."

"Okay, Yank, what is that?"

The American preacher stood by my side and opened his Bible. He said, "The God who created our world, you and me, and everything we know, wants you to know Him, but we cannot know God because of our sin."

"Sin? Are you telling me that I am a sinner? How do you know? You don't know me."

Hla Bennu stood against the far wall, looking downward at the floor, and mumbling something that I could not hear, but it was obvious she was not talking to me.

The American opened a small leather Bible and began to read in English, "All we like sheep have gone astray; we have turned every one to his own way; and the LORD hath laid on him the iniquity of us all." He continued, "Sir, I hear that you were a fighter pilot in the war."

"Yes, sir. That is right. I was a darn good pilot, too!"

"Thank you for your service and sacrifice for all of us. The whole world owes you a debt of gratitude."

"You're darn right, and not just me. There were a lot of us 'fly guys' in the war."

"Can you tell me about them, sir?"
"Who?"

"The men you flew with, sir."

"Well, there was a lot of them. Brits, Canadians, Aussies, and even some Yanks like you."

"You flew with Americans?"

"Yes, during the Battle of Britain."

"That's amazing! I didn't know that Americans fought in the UK during that time."

"Oh, sure they did. But they didn't have to. They volunteered, like my friend 'Brooklyn.'"

"Brooklyn?" the Yank inquired.

"Yes, he died."

There was a long pause. The Yankee preacher looked over at Hla Bennu and then back at me. He was clearly interested in my story, and I loved telling a story. So, I continued, "Brooklyn and I were best friends in the war. He was a Jew and always treated me as an equal."

The American interrupted, "A Jew?"

"Yeah. He was from New York City."

"How did he die, sir?"

"It was a cold, stormy night. I thought we would be grounded. We should have been! We got the call and took off into the wind. We had just got aloft when the Jerries jumped us from above. I thought I was going to die."

"Why was that, sir?"

"Let me finish my story. You want to hear it, or not?"

"Yes, sir! I really do," BaGyï insisted.

I continued, "We were still climbing to cruising altitude when the Jerries jumped us, and a German fighter, one of the new faster planes, came from above me and had me dead to rights."

"Dead to rights?"

"I mean, there was no escape. I didn't see him coming. I had no chance to evade. He had me in his sights, and if he had let his cannons loose on me, he would have cut me in half."

"Why do you suppose he didn't shoot?"

"Oh, he shot. I heard him shooting."

"Shooting at what?"

"It's not what. It is who!"

I was trying my best to keep my composure, but suddenly it all came back to me. In my mind I could hear the gunfire. I could hear the whistle of the plane engines as they whizzed by so close and fast.

I stopped my story and insisted, "I can't do this any longer. Please let me alone. Please leave me now."
"Yes, sir," said the Yank. "I will come see you again."

"No need. No need. Goodbye."

I didn't sleep any that night. The memories played in my head as on a gigantic movie screen. My wife tried to comfort me, but I was reliving every air battle. Most of all, I remembered something I had purposely put out of my mind. I knew that Brooklyn was flying behind me. He had my tail, as we say. When the Messerschmitt dove on us, the German pilot obviously had me in his sights, and something, or someone called him off me. Could it be …? I just couldn't think of that.

The next morning the American preacher returned – I think they call him BaGyi Bob for some reason. He stuck his head just inside the front door and said, "How are you feeling, sir? Can you finish that story for me?" As much as I wanted the Yank to go away, as much as I wanted to be left alone, there was something in me that wanted to tell the story, to relive that night, to face the truth about my friend. I said, "Come on in." BaGyi Bob entered the house and asked me if he could sit on the edge of my bed, since there was no other chair in the room. I consented, and he made himself comfortable.

"The Jerries came out of nowhere. One of them had me in his sights and could have easily shot me out of the sky."

BaGyi Bob asked, "What happened, sir?"

"Before I even knew he was there, he flew – I mean, like a rocket – over my nose and out of my sight."

"What happened to him?"

"I'm sorry. I just don't know. Maybe…"

"What, sir?"

"It could have been that Brooklyn shot him before he was able to shoot me. He had my back."

"Who else was there?"

"Nobody!"

"Sir?" BaGyi said. "You think that Brooklyn took your place, don't you? You think that Brooklyn paid the price for you to live and died in your place."

By this time, I was weeping uncontrollably. I could not even speak. BaGyi came close and put his hand on my shoulder. He said, "Sir, Jesus said, 'Greater love hath no man than this, that a man lay down his life for his friends.'"

I asked, "What else did Jesus say?"

"Sir, Jesus said, 'Believe me that I am in the Father, and the Father in me...'"

"BaGyi Bob, what does it mean?"

"It means that God the Father, the Creator of all, became a Man and His name is Jesus. He became a Man to become our sacrifice, to die in our place."

"Like Brooklyn?"

"Yes, sir. Paul the Apostle said that very few men would die for another, even if the person was righteous. Even less people would die for another man who is good. But God proved His love for us, 'in that, while we were yet sinners, CHRIST DIED FOR US."

It was becoming increasingly difficult for me to breath. My chest was hurting, but I didn't tell anyone. I asked, "BaGyi Bob, do you think Jesus died for me?"

He answered, "Yes, sir. I know that Jesus died for you. He paid the penalty for your sin. Like Brooklyn took the bullets that were meant for you, Jesus was nailed to the cross and died in your place. He was buried, then He rose from grave, and is alive forever more. Because He lives, sir, we can live also. Sir, do you believe this?"

"Yes, I believe it. What should I do?"

"Sir, just ask Jesus to forgive you. Thank Him for dying for you. Ask Him to come into your heart and give you eternal life. Will you do it now?"

BaGyi Bob took my hand and helped me pray. I had never prayed before. Even at the Buddhist temple, I never prayed, not like this. This time I prayed from my heart. And I said,

"Dear Jesus, please forgive me. I believe you died for me. I don't know why you love me, but I believe in you. Jesus, I know that I am an awful sinner, but I believe you gave your life to pay for my sin, and I want you, I mean, I ask you, to come into my heart and give me everlasting life. I know you have tried to come to me before, but this time I am coming to you, and I ask you to make me a Christian like my wife. Thank you, Jesus, for forgiving me."

"Hla Bennu, are you there? Hla Bennu, where are you?"

My wife ran to my side, and I looked into her eyes and said, "It's real, isn't it? I can feel it. Jesus is real."

I don't know what happened. I was just talking to Hla Bennu, and then suddenly I wasn't. Is this the place called Heaven? I'm not sure what happened, but I know this, I saw a very bright light. It was so beautiful! What is that? I think I see...Is that? Is that you, Brooklyn? Oh, glory! I can fly again!

RAF Spitfires taking off

RAF Hawker Hurricanes in-flight

Glossary of Burmese Terms with Pronunciation

A

1. A Boe Thail (ah´-bow-tile), a Mon Tribe man's name
2. Alaungpya (ah-lawng´-pee-ya), Burmese king of the Konbaung Dynasty
3. Akha (Ă-kă´), small disappearing tribe, living in Thailand and Shan State, Myanmar
4. Arakan (air-ah-can´) Historic name of the tribe which inhabits Rakhine State. The Burmese   called them Rakhine instead of Arakan or Arakanese.
5. Ashin Wirathu (ash´-shin War´-rah-thoo), Burmese Buddhist nationalist, fighting against the Muslim incursion in Myanmar
6. Asho (Ash-shoe´), or Khyeng, a Chin people group, mostly animist, living mostly in Magwe Division. Whereas most Chin peoples are hill tribes, the Asho people are river valley dwellers and their language is Asho-Chin with a global population of no more than 14,000.
7. Aung San (awng-san´), martyred Burmese General, national hero, and father of Aung San Suu Kyi.
8. Aung San Suu Kyi (awng-san-soo-chee´), Myanmar State Counselor, hero, patriot, champion of democracy and freedom, Nobel Peace Prize winner
9. Aung Lan (awng-lan), city on the Ayeyarwady River in Magwe Division, pop. 240,000
10. Aung Say (awng´-sāy), young girl guide in Bogyoke Zay
11. Ayeyarwady (ay-yaw´-wah-dee) Southeastern Burmese Division, like a State or province. Also, the name of Myanmar's major river, often called the Irrawaddy by Westerners.

B

1. BaGyi (bah´-gee), an older, respected gentleman, like an uncle or grandfather
2. Bago (Bah-gō´), formerly known as Hanthawaddy, is both a city and a Myanmar Division, northeast of Yangon.

3. Bamar (Bah´-mah), live primarily in the Ayeyarwady River basin of central Myanmar and speak the Burmese language. Their culture follows closely of the larger Burmese tradition.

4. Bayinnaung (Bæ´-yin-nǎwng), Burmese King of the Toungoo Dynasty

5. Betel Nut (bee´-tel), is the fruit of a type of palm tree that when ground and chewed like tobacco produces a deep red color in the mouth yielding adrenalin and producing euphoria. Its use in SE Asia is widespread and historic, but the World Health Organization has deemed it a carcinogen.

6. Botathaung (Bō´-tǎ-tǎung), a southwest Yangon city township.

7. Bogyoke (Boo´-jō), a stone bridge, General.

8. Bogyoke Zay (Boo´-Jō Zāy), large Yangon flea market (Zay = market in Burmese)

C

1. CC Tan (see´-see tǎwn), wife of Chit Te Maung

2. Chay zu tin ba de (chāy´-zoo-tin-bǎh-dāy)

3. Chin (Chǐn), Myanmar people group, speaking many different languages

4. Chit Myae (Chit´ Myāy), Asho Chin boy with guitar who sang Amazing Grace.

5. Chit Te Maung (chit-tāy-mǎung´), husband of CC Tan

D

1. Dala´ - (dǎ lǎ´), village in Yangon Division, across the Yangon River from downtown Yangon city.

2. Da (Dǎh´), a Burmese sword

3. Dagon Saikkan (Dā-gone´ Say´-cǎn), a southeastern township of Yangon Division.

E

F

1. Falam (Fǎ-lǎm´), a city high in the mountains of Chin State, near the Mizoram, India border. Pop. Nearly 10,000. Home of the Chin Baptist Convention. Originally settled by ethnic people called Tashon, also called Taisun or Tlaisun. Their language is Falam, or Kuki-Chin, derived from the Sino-Tibetan or Tibeto-Burman group.

G

1. Gadaw Ga (găh´-dōe găh), respect or homage paid to someone of higher stature

2. Galagodaatte Gnanasara (Găl-ăh-gō-dăt´-tāy Găh-năw´-săw-răh), Buddhist leader and politician in Sri Lanka

3. Gyaing (Yaing), river dividing Mon and Karen State, northeast of Malawmyine

4. Guatama (Burmese people pronounce it Gō´-tă-mă, others place the accent on the 2nd syllable), proper name of the Buddha, meaning "The Enlightened One."

H

1. Hakha (Hă´-Kă), capital city of Chin State, located at 6125 feet above sea level, also one of many Chin languages, otherwise called Lai.

2. Hanthawaddy (hân-thăw´wă-dee), former name of Bago (Pegu) and the historic name of the Mon dynasty

3. Hla Bennu (Lăh Běn-noo´), Kan Cetan Oo's Burmese wife

4. Htamein (Tă-māin´), ladies wrap skirt like a man's longyi.

5. Htein Win Ei (Tāne Win Ei´), pastor and educator at Aung Lan, Magwe Division.

I

1. Inle Lake (In´-lāy), a large, beautiful lake in the southern hills of Shan State, near the city of Taunggyi.

2. Insein (in-sane), township in Yangon Division, outside the city of Yangon on the north side.

J

K

1. Kabya (căw´-byăh), Burmese slang for mixed breed Anglo-Burmans.

2. Kachin (că-chin´), northernmost State in Myanmar and inhabiting tribe where Hkakabo Razi, the tallest peak in Myanmar and all southeast Asia rises to 19,321 feet at the southern tip of the Himalayas.

3. Kaladan (Căl´-ă-dăn), major river beginning in northeastern India and flowing south through Chin and Rakhine State, Myanmar

4. Kalagong (căl´-â-găwng), Mon tribe village on the Gyaing River,

known for the Japanese massacre that occurred there during the last days of WWII.

5. Kalay (Kă-lāy´), also found on maps as "Kale," a city located in western Sagaing Division, up-river from Mandalay and Monywa, near the Chin State border, pop. 400,000.

6. Kanan (Kă-năwn´), village in western Sagaing Division, on the AH-1 Highway and in that area also referred to as the Myanmar-India Friendship Road. Home of Peter Van Siang Lian.

7. Kan Cetan Oo (Kăwn-See´-tän Oo´), from "I'll Fly Away, O Glory"

8. Karen (Ca-rĕn´- accent on second syllable), a major Myanmar people group having originated in Mongolia.

9. Kaung de (kăwng´-day), Burmese for "How are you?"

10. Kaung Htet Kyaw (Kăwng´-tët-chōe), "adopted" pure Burmese teenage son of BaGyi Bob.

11. Kawkareik (Kō´-krit), small Karen-State city between Myawaddy and Hpa-an (Pă-ăwn´ – Karen capital)

12. Kayah (Kai-yăh´), a Myanmar tribe and tribal State in southeastern Myanmar.

13. Kempeitai (kĕm´-pă-tai), Japanese secret police known for brutality in WWII.

14. Kyaikkhami (Check´-a-mee), village in Mon State on the Adaman Sea.

15. Khaing Zar Myo (Kăīng´-zah-myoo), a Burmese girl's name

16. Khinny (Kin´-nee), nickname of Khine Htit Sar, one of six Mudon sisters

17. Khwah Son (kwăh´-sun), small, remote Arakan Buddhist village in Rakhine State

18. Konbaung (Kōne-baung), Burmese ruling dynasty of the 18th century

19. Kuki (Koo-Kee´), part of the Zo people group and known as Mizo in India, they are a hill tribe in India, Bangladesh, and Myanmar, considered by Jerusalem scholars to be a lost tribe of Israel.

20. Kyat (chat), a single unit of Myanmar currency

21. Kyaiktiyo (chaik´-tee-yoo), world's largest reclining Buddha temple

22. Kyawhtin Nawrahta (Chō´-tin Nō´-răh-tă), second given name of King Bayinnaung.

23. Kyaw Kyaw Aung (chō´-chō ăwng), Myanmar name of Peter Judson who is of the Pa-O tribe.

24. Kyay zu htin bar de (chāy zoo tin băh dāy), Burmese for "Thank you very much!"

25. Kyay Oh (chāy´-oo), Burmese noodle soup

26. Keng Tung (chëng tūng´), city surrounded by mountains of the Daen Lao Range in eastern Shan State, inhabited by Akha, Lahu, Shan, Wa, and Chinese peoples. pop. 175,000.

27. Krung Phet (crŭng pët), Thai name for Bangkok

L

1. Lahu (La-hoo), an ethnic group, mostly in China, secondly Myanmar, and throughout SE Asia, they are animists, Buddhist, with a minority being Christian. The Thai call them Muzoe, meaning hill tribe hunter.

2. Lal Ram Hngak (lăll răm năhk´ - pronounce the R in Ram as a rolled R, as in Spanish), alias Pastor Steven, pastor in Shwe Pyi Thar, Yangon Division.

3. Laphetyay saing (lă-pët´-yāy sâing), a Burmese market and café.

4. Leippya (Lāy´ pyă), a human soul

5. Lemro River (Lem´yoo), major watercourse in northwestern Rakhine State and southern Chin State

6. Lisu (Lee´-soo), a tribe or people group also known as Anung, living in Kachin State, but originating in southwest China.

7. Limonia Acidissima (lĭ-mō´-nyă ä-sĭ-dĭs´-sĭm-ă), the wood apple tree, growing on SE Asian

mountainsides and used to produce Thanakha.

8. Loi Mwe (Lō-Mwāy´), mountain village, southeast of Keng Tung, in eastern Shan State, near Chinese border. Site of Burmese military base.

9. Longyi (long-gee), traditional men's daily attire, a wrap skirt.

M

1. Mae La (Māy Lă), refugee camp, north of Mae Sot, Thailand

2. Mae Sot (mæ´-săwt), Thai city in Tak Province on the Moei River, the border between Thailand and Myanmar, opposite Myawaddy.

3. Maitreya (my-tree-yah, to be fully correct: roll the TR sound) – In Buddhism, the one who should come as the fifth and final Buddha. Gautama said that he would be a savior or messiah, a deliverer as such.

4. Malawmyine (mōw´-lōw-mē-yĕn), Queen city of Mon State, Burmese and British spelling and pronunciation as Moulmein (Mō-ūl´-mē-in).

5. Manaw (Man-nō´), another name for the Kachin tribal people.

6. Mar kaung bu (Mah cowng´ boo), Burmese for "No good"

7. Maru (Mae-roo´), Indian Chin people, mostly of darker reddish-brown

skin.

8. Mingalabar, or Mingalar bar (meeng´-a-la´-bah) The Burmese people love this traditional and universal greeting, meaning Hello.

9. Minhla (Min´-lăh), both a township and village, also a Chin people group with their own language.

10. Minbya (Min´-byăh), a township southeast of Sittwe, in Rakhine State.

11. Moei (Moo-ee´), river in Thailand, flowing south and forming the border between Thailand and Myanmar.

12. Mogok (Mō´-gŭk), a city in the Pyin Oo Lwin District of Mandalay Division, famous for its ruby mines.

13. Mon (Mōne), the tribe of people group of the former Hanthawaddy Dynasty.

14. Mong Lin (Möng Lin´), small Shan State village, north of Tachileik in the Golden Triangle.

15. Monghpyak (Möng´-pyäk), small Shan State village, north of Tachileik in the Golden Triangle.

16. Myawaddy (mē-yow´-wă-dee), located on the Moei River and border of Thailand and Myanmar, opposite Mae Sot.

17. Moorah (Moor´-ah), a Karen tribal name

18. Mrauk U (Meow-oo) ancient city and former historic capital of the Arakan people, on the Kaladan river, in northern Rakhine State.

19. Mru (Myoo), In the Burmese language, a transliterated "R" is often pronounced as a Y.

20. Mudon (Moo-doen), a city and township of Mon State in the Malawmyine District, and home of the world's largest reclining Buddha statue - pop. 89,123 (2019)

21. Myanmar (Mee-yan´-mah) The mya sound is prevalent in the Burmese language. "Myan" is often pronounced as a single syllable. Myanmar(s) refers to the collective peoples of the nation.

N

1. Naga (Nah´-gah), from Naga Hill in far northern Myanmar and Nagaland in Northeastern India. Naga people in India have modern cities and are largely educated. Naga villages in Myanmar are still mostly primitive and the people were head-hunters until recent history.

2. Nat (like gnät), a spirit

3. Nargis (Năr´-gis), catastrophic cyclone in 2008, direct hit on Yangon.

3. Naybugan (Nay´-boo-gahn), a Mru tribe village in northwestern

Rakhine, along the backwaters of the Kaladan River watershed

4. Nay kaung lar? (nee-kaung´-lăh), Burmese for "How are you?"

5. Ne Win (Nāy Win´), Burmese General and politician who enacted military coup and dictatorship in 1962.

6. Nyi Nyaih Shwe – nee y-eye´ shwee

7. Nyi Nyi (Nee Nee), Nyi Nyaih Shwe's mother

8. Naungyo (Năwng´-yoo), present day Ein´mē Township, Ayeyarwady Division, site of great battle between the Hanthawaddy and Toungoo Dynasties.

9. Nung Rawang (Nŭng Ră-wăng´), a small tribe of Mongolian ancestry, inhabiting far northern Kachin State, where the Himalayas join Myanmar near Mount Hkakabo Razi, not far from the China border.

P

1. Pagoda (Pă-gō´-dă), a Buddhist Hershey Kiss-shaped temple, usually gold in color.

2. Pai Lian Thang (pie lee-an tang – with short A sound)

3. Paletwa (Paw-lay´-wah), city in southern Chin State, near the Bangladesh border.

4. Pa-O (păw-ōh´), small indigenous tribe in China, Myanmar, and Thailand

5. Pegu Yoma (Pay-goo Yo-mah), Pegu is the old name of what is now called "Bago." The Yoma is a range of rolling hills, mountains, and forests between the Ayeyarwady and Sittaung Rivers in central Myanmar.

6. Peter Van Siang Lian (Peter Vän Sci-ăwng Lee-än), pastor at Kanan, Sagaing Division.

7. Prome (just like it sounds, proam), small Burmese empire and present day city of Pyay on the Ayeyarwady River.

8. Pya Thakin kaunggyi pe ba si (pyah´-ta-kin, kowng gee, pay, bah, see) Burmese for "God bless you!"

Q

R

1. Rakhine (Rah khine´) A tribal State or province in southwestern Myanmar, along the Bay of Bengal, the word also identifies with the Arakan people.

2. Rawang (see Nung Rawang)

3. Rohingya (row-hin´-jah), an ethnic Bangla people group.

1. Saffron (säf´-frăwn), a spice derived from the flower of the crocus sativus, deep red in color.
2. Sagaing (să-gaing´), a Burmese Division in northwestern Myanmar.
2. Salaam (Să-lăm´), sometimes spelled Salam is an Arabic or Muslim greeting meaning "peace" or "no harm," but sometimes denoting safety, protection from evil.
3. Sandar Tun (Sän-dăh Toon), a Burmese girl's name
4. Sami (also Samee) (Sam´-ee), city of southern Chin State
5. Saya (Say´-yăh), a teacher or preacher. (also Sayar in India)
6. Sein Kant Kaw Pwint (Sāne Kănt´ Kō Pwint), a private high school in Botathaung township of Yangon.
7. Sittwe (Sit´-twee) The capital city of Rakhine State, located on an estuarial island at the confluence of Kaladan, Mayu, and Lay Mru rivers, on the Bay of Bengal.
8. Shan (Shän), a major people group in Myanmar, much like the Thai people, and their State by that name.
9. Shwe Dagon (Shwee Dă-gōwn´), also spelled Dagon, is the world's largest Buddhist pagoda, rising to 325 feet. Tradition says it was built more than 2600 years ago. Its name means "golden spirit" (Dagon or Dagon was the West Semitic god of crop fertility and legendary inventor of the plow).
10. Shwe Pyi Thar (Shwee Pee Tăw), township in northwestern Yangon Division
11. Shwe Thazin (Shwee´-Tah-zeen) Burmese, meaning golden flower.

1. Tabinshwehti (tăh´-bin-shwee-tee), Burmese King and founder of the Toungoo empire.
2. Tachileik (Tătch´-leek), the Shan State Queen City of the Golden Triangle where the Mekong River meets the Ruak River and forms the border between Myanmar, Thailand, and Laos.
3. Tahan (Tă-hawn´), a community in Kalaymyo.
4. Tak (tăk) – a northwestern province of Thailand, along the Myanmar eastern border.
5. Tamu (Tä-moo´), border city with Manipur, India in Sagaing Division, large population of Jewish Kuki, pop. 69,000

6. Tein Nyo (Tane´-yoo), small village on the Kaladan River, north of Mrauk U.

7. Thagyamin (Tăw´-jă-min), Burmese man's name

8. Thakin Nu (Tăw´-kin Noo´), Burmese politician deposed by General Ne Win in 1962.

9. Thanbyuzayat (tăwn-byoo´-zae-yăt), Town in Mon State, known for the WWII Cemetery and the origin of the Death Railway.

10. Thankaiyar (tän´-kee-yah), small, remote village in Sagaing village.

11. Thanlyin (Tăwn-yl-yin), a small city in southern Myanmar.

12. Than Shwe (Tăwn´ Shwee), Nyi Nyaih Shwe's father.

13. Thanylin (tăwn´-yl-lin), river in southern Myanmar

14. Than Zaw (Tăwn´-zō), Burmese church planter in Sagaing Division and pastor at Nansanpu village.

15. Taunggyi (Tŏwng-jee), city surrounded by rolling hills and mountains in southern Shan State.

16. Thaung Ngain Lian (tăwng nine lee´-än), pastor and founder of Bethany Baptist Church, Yangon.

17. Thanakha (taw´-nah-kah), a white or cream-colored paste made from the bark of the Limonia acidissima, or wood-apple tree and used as make-up, especially among Myanmar women.

18. Thingyan (Thing-yän), annual water festival nationwide in the first week of April.

19. Tiddim, also spelled Tedim (Tĭh-dĭm´), second largest town in Chin city near Mazoram, India border at nearly 6,000 feet, pop. 89,000.

20. Toungoo (tūn´-goo), Burmese empire.

Note: "TH" sounds – a transliteration of the Burmese language into English does not sound out the H in TH spellings. Thus, Thaung would be Taung, and Thang would be Tang with a short A sound.

U

V

X

Y

1. Yangon (Yang´-own) Being the new name for Rangoon, it is often

wrongfully pronounced Yangoon, city population in 2021 census was 4,477,638 (but almost 9 million including the surrounding area)

2.   Yao (yow), an small ethnic people group, mostly in China and Vietnam, they are also known as Hmong in Myanmar and Thailand.

3.   Yaw (Yaw´), otherwise known as Nyaw and numbering about 20,000, the Yaw are primarily Buddhist, live in the Gangaw and Pokkoku Districts of Central Myanmar and speak their own dialect of Burmese.

4.   Yazeem (Yă-zeem´), Muslim man's proper name

5.   Ye Htut (Yee-tut´), first name of King Bayinnaung.

6.   Yet Le (yet´ lay), final day of a Burmese Buddhist funeral

7.   Yuzanna (Yoo-ză´-nă), a Burmese community in southern Yangon Division.

Z   Zomi – (Zoe´ Mee), literally meaning "of the hills," the Zomi people group include Zou,

Zokam, the Ya or Yaw, Jo or Jou peoples, and Zo in India. Their language is similar to Kuki

and Mizo.

Legend

1. Aung Lan
2. Dalá, Yangon
   Shwe Pyi Thar
3. Kalay, Kalaymyo,
   Tahan
4. Kanan
5. Keng Tun, Moi Mwe
6. Mae Sot
7. Malawmyine
   (Moulmein)
8. Mrauk U
9. Mudon
10. Nabugan
11. Tachileik
12. Tamu
13. Thankaiyar

Proposed Church Plants
(CBC graduates going soon)

14. Mandalay
15. Naypyitaw (capital)
16. Bago
17. Taunggyi
18. Magwe
19. Ayeyarwady Division

Myanmar is comprised of fourteen provinces: seven
Burmese Divisions, and seven Tribal States. 54,000,000
people and a land mass that is the largest in SE Asia.

THE GLBM VISION

Myanmar: The Hub of The Wheel in SE Asia – physically bordered by five countries and surrounded by twelve. GLBM seeks to train and equip an army of Bible-believing preachers and a new generation of young Burmese disciples, to send them to plant churches and reach the lost, not only across Old Burma, but to the surrounding people groups.

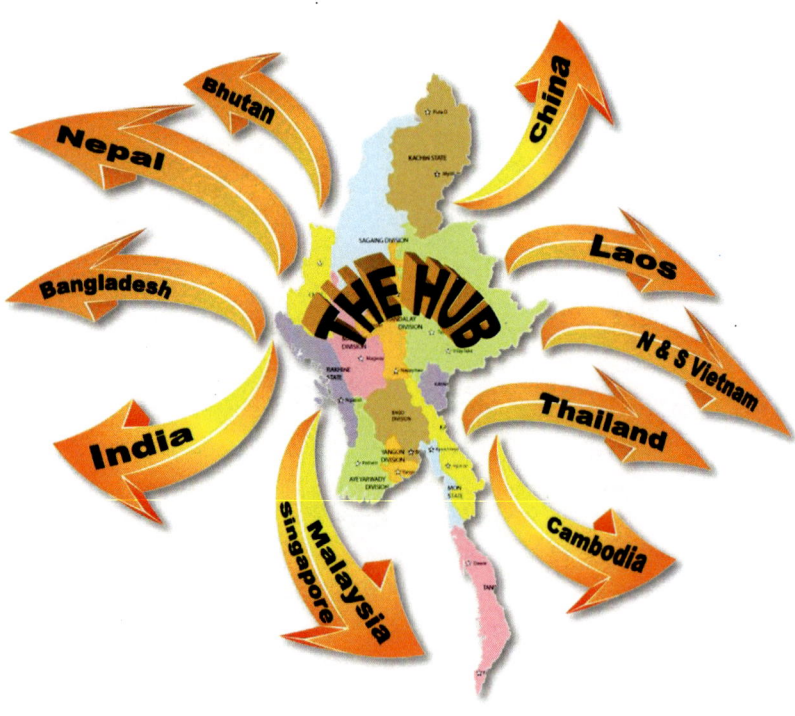

AFTERWORD

In these stories, I have presented people who made an indelible impression on my life as I did my best to manifest Christ to them. Some years ago, I wrote a Gospel tract, based on the testimony of a Burmese man who was converted to Christ and became an amazing witness to the Buddhists in his native Myanmar. The following is that tract in its entirety and it is full of Scriptures. It does not represent man's wisdom, but the truth of God's Word. My prayer is that, if you are without the Saviour or perhaps searching for truth, this final presentation in GOLDEN LAND CHRONICLES will answer your questions and lead you to Christ.

My name is U Saw Neing and I was born in 1965. I am pure Burmese with a very strong Buddhist family background. There has never been anyone in our family that became a Christian, but all have faithfully and blindly followed the teachings of Gautama for a lifetime.

DARKNESS AND CONFUSION

At six years old, I entered the monastery school and began to learn about the Buddha, the "awakened" or "enlightened one." I learned about his struggle for enlightenment and how he learned the answers of life through his own journey of suffering. I was taught that, as we are, he was; and as he became, we also can become.

Even though I had many questions that no one could answer, I became the most popular monk in my township and eventually reached my goal of becoming "high priest." I would speak to great crowds of people about the beliefs and practices of Buddhism, and many would give to me gifts and even bow down and worship me, but I knew in my heart that I was not a worthy person for such things. I wondered what I had to do to become worthy. It seemed that the more I tried to be worthy of such things, the more unworthy I felt.

I was physically fit, energetic, caring, generous, warm, and friendly to everyone I met. Yet I was miserable every day because I felt that I was in darkness and could not find the truth. Many people would come to me for help, counseling, and direction in life, and I would try my best to help them according to the teaching of Buddha. Even as I was speaking to them, there was emptiness inside my own heart and I felt that all I had accomplished was done in vain and amounted to "anata," or nothing.

TRUE ENLIGHTENMENT

I was invited to be a speaker in a Buddhist crusade in the Ayeyarwady Division of Myanmar. While traveling to this place, I met a friend who gave me a Christian Bible which I put in my bag. I was very excited and eager to read this Bible. After returning from the crusade, I thumbed through its pages and began reaching in the temple when no one was around me. It seemed that my eyes were directed to two verses found in **Matthew 16:26-27:** *"For what is a man profited, if he shall gain the whole world, and lose his own soul? Or what shall a man give in exchange for his soul? For the Son of man shall come in the glory of his Father with his angels; and then he shall reward every man according to his works."*

When I read these two Bible verses, they were like fire that burned in my heart very intensely and I wept because I knew that all I had been doing and all that I possessed were "anata" (vain or nothing) if I were to lose my own soul. Reading this Bible was like the sun rising in the morning, gradually turning a dark dismal night into a bright cloudless day. With each page I began to see and understand more. It made sense to me. I learned that this Holy Bible was inspired by God and given through many men of God over thousands of years and preserved to this day by the Holy Spirit of God so that we could learn about Him. I learned that the true Creator of Man is a living God and not at all like men and never has been. Now He was speaking to my heart by that same Spirit, through the very words of God recorded so long ago.

True Englightenment became mine through learning and believing these four truths:

1st LIGHT: THE TRUE NATURE OF THE LIVING GOD

He is Spirit. The Bible says, *"God is a Spirit: and they that worship him must worship him in spirit and in truth."* **John 4:24**

He is the Most High God. Abraham called Him, *"the LORD, the most high God, the possessor of heaven and earth."* **Genesis 14:22**

He is the most powerful of all earthly or heavenly spirits. *"That men may know that thou, whose name alone is JEHOVAH, art the most high over all the earth."* **Psalm 83:18**

He does not live in temples, shrines, or statues. The Bible says, *"the most High dwelleth not in temples made with hands."* **Acts 7:48**

He is eternal. Paul, the Apostle described God as *"…the King eternal, immortal, invisible, the only wise God…"* **1 Timothy 1:17** God told Abraham to call Him "YAHWEH" (LORD) or "The Great I AM." In other words, He is the Self-Existent One. He had no beginning and has no ending.

He is Holy. *"Holy, holy, holy, Lord God Almighty, which was, and is, and is to come."* **Revelation 4:8**

He is a Father. *"…there is but one God, the Father, of whom are all things…"* **1 Corinthians 8:6**
I learned that we cannot become God as He is because all human beings are born with a sin nature.

2nd LIGHT: THE TRUE NATURE OF MAN

Genesis, the first book of the Bible, says that God created the first man, Adam, as a three-part being, with a living body, soul, and spirit. But when Adam disobeyed God, he sinned against his Creator and his spirit died. He could no longer communicate with or understand God. Every man and woman from that point forward was and is born a sinner and separated from God by his sin.

"Wherefore, as by one man sin entered into the world, and death by sin; so death passed upon all men, for that all have sinned." **Romans 5:12**

God gave His Holy Word to the world through the nation of Israel and so many Jews believed they were special, different from others in the world. That same Bible makes it clear that all people, from every nation, are sinners in the eyes of their Creator God. The Apostle Paul said this:

"What then? Are we better than they? No, in no wise: for we have before proved both Jews and Gentiles, that they are all under sin; As it is written, There is none righteous, no, not one: There is none that understandeth, there is none that seeketh after God. They are all gone out of the way, they are together become unprofitable; there is none the doeth good, no, not one…For all have sinned, and come short of the glory of God." **Romans 3:9-12, 23**

No child needs to be taught how to lie or disobey, because we are born with a sin nature that we inherit from our parents. King David said, *"Behold, I was shapen in iniquity; and in sin did my mother conceive me."* **Psalm 51:5**

3rd LIGHT: THE TRUE DESTINY OF MAN

Mankind was created to live forever and commune with his Creator, but sin separated him from the Creator God and brought upon him the curse of eternal suffering.

"Know ye not that the unrighteous shall not inherit the kingdom of God? Be not deceived: neither fornicators, nor idolators, nor adulterers, nor effeminate, nor abusers of themselves with mankind, nor thieves, nor covetous, nor drunkards, nor revilers, nor extortioners, shall inherit the kingdom of God."

1 Corinthians 6:9-10

"...fear not them which kill the body, but are not able to kill the soul: but rather fear him which is able to destroy both soul and body in hell."

Matthew 10:28

"But the fearful, and unbelieving, and the abominable, and murderers, and whoremongers, and sorcerers, and idolaters, and all liars, shall have their part in the lake (HELL) which burneth with fire and brimstone: which is the second death." **Revelation 21:8**

SECOND DEATH??? Yes, the Bible talks about another death, worse than the first – not just a physical death but a spiritual death. NOT A CONTINUAL CYCLE OF LIFE, BUT ONE LIFE FOLLOWED BY A FEARFUL JUDGMENT BEFORE ALMIGHTY GOD.

"...It is appointed unto men once to die, but after this the judgment."

Hebrews 9:27

In the Bible's Old Testament, the Jews knew that sin needed to be paid for. Every day they would offer the blood of a lamb or bullock as a sacrifice for their sin. Also in the New Testament, there is a price for sin.

"For the wages of sin (the price, what we deserve) *is DEATH"* (spiritual separation from God forever). **Romans 6:23**

How then can we pay for our sin? Should we sacrifice an animal to God, or give our own blood, money or property? Can we earn God's forgiveness by doing good deeds?

The Bible says we cannot pay for our own sins by doing good works or giving anything. The forgiveness of sin and a relationship with the Creator God is a GIFT FROM GOD through faith in the living Saviour, the Lord Jesus Christ.

"For by grace are ye saved through faith; and that not of yourselves: it is the gift of God: Not of works, lest any man should boast." **Ephesians 2:8-9**

"Not by works of righteousness which we have done, but according to his mercy he saved us, by the washing of regeneration, and the renewing of the Holy Ghost." **Titus 3:5**

"The wages of sin is death; but the gift of God is eternal life through Jesus Christ our Lord." **Romans 6:23**

I had served among the temples and shrines of Buddhism all my life, trying to gain peace of mind and confidence of a better after-life, never having either. But the Bible made it clear: the problem was not in my head but in my heart. Despite a lifetime of meditating upon the principles of the Gautama, I knew I was a sinner and needed a living Saviour.

"How much more shall the blood of Christ, who through the eternal Spirit offered himself without spot to God, purge your conscience from dead works to serve the living God?" **Hebrews 9:14**

4th LIGHT: THE TRUE SAVIOUR OF MAN

As I turned the pages of my Bible and read in the New Testament, I learned that Yahweh, the Creator God, took the form of a Man named Jesus Christ, fulfilling every prophecy in the Old Testament of Himself. He was born of a virgin girl named Mary, but had no earthly father; therefore, He was called the Son of God. The Bible records that He lived a perfect life, never sinning, so that He Himself could become the payment for our sin. He suffered as no other man. He was mocked and spat upon. He was beaten and whipped until his flesh hung off His body in a bloody mess. He was nailed to a wooden cross as a common criminal, sacrificing His own life, and shedding His own blood to pay for my sins, your sins – the sins of the whole world.

"For God so loved the world, that he gave his only begotten Son, that whosoever believeth in him should not perish, but have everlasting life. For God sent not his Son into the world to condemn the world; but the world through him might be saved." **John 3:16-17**

"Behold the Lamb of God, which taketh away the sin of the world."
John 1:29

"Now we believe, not because of thy saying: for we have heard him ourselves, and know that this is indeed the Christ, the Saviour of the world."
John 4:42

"And he is the propitiation (atonement or satisfactory payment) for our sins: and not for our only, but also for the sins of the whole world." **1 John 2:2**

I learned that I did not have to die a second death because of my sin. Jesus taught that just as we are all born physically, we must be born spiritually. He said, *"Except a man be born again, he cannot see the kingdom of God."* **John 3:3**

"That which is born of the flesh is flesh; and that which is born of the Spirit is spirit. Marvel not that I said unto thee, Ye must be born again."
John 3:6-7

"Being born again, not of corruptible seed, but of incorruptible, by the word of God, which liveth and abideth for ever." **1 Peter 1:23**

In other words, if you are born once (physical birth only), you will die twice (physical and spiritual death). If you are born twice (physical and spiritual birth), you will only die once. How wonderful this is!

HE IS THE LIVING SAVIOUR

Jesus Christ told His disciples how He would be put to death but rise from the dead three days later — and HE DID. History records that the same tomb where He was buried was found empty and that He was seen by many witnesses and proven to be alive again by *"many infallible proofs"* (**Acts 1:3).** He then ascended to heaven but promised to come again. Jesus is not a dream, a myth, or a philosophy. He is not just a historical figure or the face on a statue — but a living Saviour.

HE IS A COMING SAVIOUR

He will come again! He will surely come soon!

"And when he had spoken these things, while they beheld, he was taken up; and a cloud received him out of their sight. And while they looked stedfastly

toward heaven as he went up, behold, two men stood by them in white apparel; Which also said, Ye men of Galilee, why stand ye gazing up into heaven? This same Jesus, which is taken up from you into heaven, shall so come in like manner as ye have seen him go into heaven." **Acts 1:9-12**

"Be ye also patient; stablish your hearts: for the coming of the Lord draweth nigh." **James 5:8**

HE IS THE ONLY SAVIOUR

Some think there are many different ways to peace with God and to gain eternal life. Again, the Bible is very clear:

"Neither is there salvation in any other: for there is none other name under heaven given among men whereby we must be saved." **Acts 4:12**

"For there is one God, and one mediator between God and men, the man Christ Jesus."

1 Timothy 2:5

"And this is the record, that God hath given to us eternal life, and this life is in his Son."

1 John 5:11

HE CAN BE YOUR SAVIOUR

As I continued reading my Bible, I saw that Jesus Christ could be my personal Saviour if I believed on Him with all my heart. The Bible says:

"But as many as received him, to them gave he power to become the sons of God, even to them that believe on his name." **John 1:12**

"That if thou shalt confess with thy mouth the Lord Jesus, and shalt believe in thine heart that God hath raised him from the dead, thou shalt be saved. For with the heart man believeth unto righteousness; and with the mouth confession is made unto salvation. For the scripture saith, Whosoever believeth on him shall not be ashamed." **Romans 10:9-11**

I saw that anyone could believe and be saved – even me!

"For whosoever shall call upon the name of the Lord shall be saved."
Romans 10:13

FINALLY, PEACE AND PURPOSE

I knelt by my bed and bowed my head. Believing what the Bibles says about me, my sin, and my future, I prayed from my heart and asked Jesus Christ to be my Saviour, to forgive my sin, to save my soul, to give me everlasting life in heaven.

I received this living Saviour into my heart. That day I turned from idols to a living God. In my true and living Saviour, I found peace and a new purpose for my life. My way, the Buddhist way, led me to confusion, fear, and doubt. A friend led me to the Word of God. God's Word led me to Jesus Christ. I spent my life seeking to become enlightened. But when I believed and received Jesus Christ as my Saviour, I learned that He is not only the way to true enlightenment. HE IS ENLIGHTENMENT. If you have Christ, you have light, peace, eternal life, and purpose for living.

The Apostle John said this: *"He that hath the Son hath life; and he that hath not the Son of God hath not life. These things have I written unto you that believe on the name of the Son of God: that ye may know that ye have eternal life…"*. **1 John 5:12-13a**

Would you like to know my Saviour?

Would you like to have a personal relationship with your Creator? Would you like to know that your sins are forgiven? Would you like to know that you have eternal life? Would you like to have peace in your heart? If you will believe and receive Jesus Christ as your own personal Saviour, right now, from your heart, pray as I did:

"Lord Jesus, I now believe that You love me. I know that I am a sinner and deserve God's judgment on my sin. But I believe that you, Lord Jesus, died to pay for my sins with your shed blood. I am trusting only in You to save me, and I ask You to forgive me of my sin and be my Saviour. Please give me the gift of eternal life and help me to learn how to follow You and live the Christian life. Thank You for saving me today. In Jesus name, I pray. Amen!

_____

Name

_____

Date